Management
In 4 Weeks
The Complete Guide to Success

Martin Manser,
Dr Norma Barry,
Nigel Cumberland and
Di Kamp

The *Teach Yourself* series has been trusted around the world for over 75 years. This new series of 'In 4 Weeks' business books is designed to help people at all levels and around the world to earn

Martin Manser's major management experience has been in managing people and projects, including leading a team of nearly 100 people to manage one of the few 20th-century study Bibles (*The Thematic Reference Bible*, Hodder and Stoughton, 1996) to be originated in the UK. He has also led teams to manage the award-winning *Collins Bible Companion* (Harper Collins, 2009) and the best-selling *Macmillan Student's Dictionary* (Macmillan, 2nd edition, 1996). He is a Language Trainer and Consultant with national and international companies and organizations, leading courses on project management and business skills and communications.

www.martinmanser.co.uk

Norma Barry has four decades of experience working in managerial roles within the public sector from executive to director level. She has worked in a wide variety of policy areas and spent 15 years of her career working with businesses, including major energy and telecommunication companies, and food and drinks processing companies of all sizes. This experience gave her valuable insight into the private sector. Norma has a Ph.D. in Leadership and Change Management and an MBA from Cardiff Business School. She is passionate about leadership and management and has been an active volunteer within the Chartered Management Institute as well as with local business schools. Norma currently runs her own company, helping organizations identify their problems and put things right, in particular supporting them on managing change.

For more information, go to www.IOOS.co.uk

I have always been particularly interested in people management, primarily because during my career I experienced poor and ineffective management. However, I learned from these, sometimes painful, experiences which strengthened my resolve to continually learn about the practice of management through on-the-job experiences and reflection, supplemented by study and other development opportunities. People managers have considerable power to make a difference to others and the business of organizations. I hope that this book will help you become a good and respected people manager.

Nigel Cumberland has spent more than 20 years working all over the world, with the past 10 years spent in the executive coaching and leadership training field. He had previously worked as a finance director with Coats plc, where he managed global multicultural teams, and he has also built up high-performing teams for some of the world's leading recruitment firms: Adecco SA, Hays plc and Harvey Nash plc. In addition, he created his own award-winning recruitment firm in Hong Kong and China, St George's, which was later sold to Hays plc.

Today Nigel runs a talent and leadership training and coaching consultancy called the Silk Road Partnership. He regularly consults, gives workshops, and lectures to organizations on how to optimally develop and grow leaders and talent. Because of his extensive worldwide experience, Nigel understands the global and cultural issues and challenges of creating, motivating and leading teams – in locations as diverse as Hong Kong, Budapest, Guatemala City, Kuala Lumpur, Shanghai and Dubai.

He was educated at Cambridge University, is a Founding Fellow of the Institute of Coaching Professional Association (ICPA), a Harvard Medical School affiliate and has Certified Practitioner status with the International Association of Coaching (USA). He is also a Fellow of the Institute of Leadership and Management (UK) and a Fellow of the Chartered Institute of Management Accountants (UK). Nigel currently lives in Dubai and Kuala Lumpur with his wife, Evelyn, son, Zeb, and stepdaughter, Yasmine.

Di Kamp is Chief Executive of Meta (UK) Ltd. The company specializes in helping organizations and individuals to develop excellence in management practice. Di has helped a number of organizations to enhance their performance development systems, and has trained both managers and their appraisees in how to use appraisals to enhance performance.

Management In 4 Weeks

The Complete Guide to Success

Martin Manser,
Dr Norma Barry,
Nigel Cumberland and
Di Kamp

IN 4 WEEKS

First published in Great Britain in 2015 by Hodder & Stoughton. A Hachette UK company.

First published in US in 2015 by The McGraw-Hill Companies, Inc.

This edition published 2015. Copyright © 2014 Martin Manser, Dr Norma Barry, Nigel Cumberland and Di Kamp

Based on original material from *Introducing Management, Successful People Management, Managing Teams, and Successful Appraisals (In A Week)*.

The rights of Martin Manser, Dr Norma Barry, Nigel Cumberland and Di Kamp to be identified as the Authors of the Work have been asserted by them in accordance with the Copyright, Designs and Patents Act 1988.

Database right Hodder & Stoughton (makers)

The *Teach Yourself* name is a registered trademark of Hachette UK.

British Library Cataloguing in Publication Data: a catalogue record for this title is available from the British Library.

Library of Congress Catalog Card Number: on file.

Typeset by Cenveo® Publisher Services.

Printed in Great Britain by in CPI Group (UK) Ltd., Croydon, CR0 4YY.

Paperback ISBN 978 1 473 605 268

eBook eISBN 978 1 473 605 275

1

The publisher has used its best endeavours to ensure that any website addresses referred to in this book are correct and active at the time of going to press. However, the publisher and the author have no responsibility for the websites and can make no guarantee that a site will remain live or that the content will remain relevant, decent or appropriate.

The publisher has made every effort to mark as such all words which it believes to be trademarks. The publisher should also like to make it clear that the presence of a word in the book, whether marked or unmarked, in no way affects its legal status as a trademark.

Every reasonable effort has been made by the publisher to trace the copyright holders of material in this book. Any errors or omissions should be notified in writing to the publisher, who will endeavour to rectify the situation for any reprints and future editions.

Hachette UK's policy is to use papers that are natural, renewable and recyclable products and made from wood grown in sustainable forests. The logging and manufacturing processes are expected to conform to the environmental regulations of the country of origin.

Hodder & Stoughton Ltd
338 Euston Road
London NW1 3BH
www.hodder.co.uk

Also available in ebook

Contents

WEEK 1

Introducing Management In A Week

Introduction

Congratulations! You've made it! Your bosses have seen your potential. They have noticed your hard work and the skills you have and have promoted you to a manager.

How do you feel? Excited? Thrilled at the prospect of showing your abilities and skills even more? Exhilarated at the opportunities that will open up for you to shine even further? Perhaps a little overawed at some of the responsibilities that will come your way? Concerned, even anxious, about some of the burdens that the management role will bring?

Week 1 will guide you through what can feel like the maze of tasks of a manager. Principles are clearly explained with case studies giving examples of how – and sometimes how not – to manage.

Where do you start? How do you see your way more clearly? Week 1 breaks down the art of management into easy steps:

Sunday Becoming a manager: what the changes will mean to you in your new role

Monday Managing people: recruiting, developing and motivating your staff

Tuesday Managing a team: encouraging members of your team to work well together

Wednesday Managing your work: setting goals, managing systems and procedures, solving problems and making decisions

Thursday Communicating effectively: keeping lines of communication clear through good listening skills, effective use of email and telephone and holding better meetings

Friday Managing a project: working out – and keeping to – aims, outputs, costs and schedules

Saturday Managing yourself: being aware of yourself, becoming organized and making good use of your time

Each day of the week covers a different key area and the material is structured by beginning with an introduction that gives a 'heads-up' as to what the day is about. Then comes the main material, which explains the key lessons to be learnt by clarifying important principles that are backed up by case studies and quotations. Each day concludes with a summary, next steps and multiple-choice questions, to reinforce the key learning points.

There are many other books on management available that will explain theories of management, but Week 1 is written to guide you reliably through the basics.

SUNDAY

Becoming a manager

Today we're going to look at:

- what managing is
- some challenges you will face
- the differences between managing and leading
- the qualities of a successful manager.

Dictionaries give different definitions of the verb 'manage'. Our main concern is with *organizing other workers and making decisions about how a business or department is run*. In practice this will mean that you usually *tell other people what to do rather than doing it yourself*. The italic text shows the crucial differences between what you have done up to now and what you will do now you are a manager. You will:

- organize other workers
- make decisions about how a business or department is run
- tell other people what to do rather than doing it yourself.

You are not uninformed, however. You will have had experience. In the past, you will have been organized by your boss who made decisions about how the business or department should be run. So you have thoughts about how well or badly that management was undertaken. Also, be assured that your bosses have identified potential in you that can be developed successfully.

What is managing?

We can usefully divide managing into separate tasks:

- **Plan**: know your goals and work out how to achieve them.
- **Organize**: do what is necessary to make the plan happen. Bring structure and make arrangements. Allocate the necessary resources to your team. Assign work to your team members; if necessary, recruit or train your team. Coordinate with others. Delegate work, responsibility and authority. Work efficiently, with minimal waste of time, money and other resources.
- **Lead**: motivate, encourage and, above all, communicate with members of your team to show them they are valued and get the best out of them so they work effectively.
- **Control**: not in the control-freak or manipulative sense, but being direct, making decisions about how to work most effectively to see that your goals are met. Monitor actual timings and costs against planned goals and take steps to ensure that the agreed outputs, standards and so on are met.

Looking at the four points above, think which of these come naturally to you and which you will need to work harder at to cultivate. Think about your new role and analyse it in terms of each of these task points.

What goals will you need to *plan*? How will you *organize* the necessary resources to achieve that plan? How will you *lead – motivate –* your team members to get the best out of them, *controlling* and giving direction to make decisions to see that your goals are met?

Challenges you face

Challenges you face as a manager may include:

● hiring the right staff
● making the most of scarce financial resources
● training your staff
● managing difficult members of your team
● motivating and encouraging your team
● communicating well with your team
● making better use of your time
● managing budgets
● managing projects
● managing yourself better.

We will deal with these, and more, in this text.

Becoming a manager

When Karen first became a manager, she was in charge of people who had previously been on the same level as her. She was once one of them but was now senior to them.

She had lots of ideas when she became team leader, such as introducing new daily briefings and performance targets. However, rather than implementing these changes gradually, she tried to introduce them all at once. Unfortunately, the team did not cope well with this and their attitude to her became negative. She decided to have one-to-one meetings with each colleague to find out their thoughts on the changes and hear their suggestions. These sessions proved to be opportunities for them to understand that the changes were for the good of the team, and gradually Karen was able to introduce all the changes successfully.

Managing and leading

What is the difference between managing and leading? Roughly speaking, managing is turning leadership into action.

Let's consider this in more detail. Leaders set a particular course: 'We're going to expand into the Chinese market.' Managers put that into action, for example: 'We're going to understand the culture, build a base, recruit staff there and implement a whole range of other activities to make the basic idea of "expanding into the Chinese market" a reality.'

So leaders set the overall direction and give vision; managers work out the detail in terms of organizing people, planning and budgeting. You will probably have agreed with this last sentence, but notice that it includes a crucial aspect: that of emotions. Leaders appeal to the emotions to set a course of change, wanting to inspire people to follow a vision. Managers, in contrast it seems, have the less exciting task of ensuring that the work, in all its detail, is completed.

In practice, however, the distinction between 'leader' and 'manager' may not be so clear-cut. Your role may be 'team leader' and your responsibilities will concentrate on the detailed tasks, systems and processes to ensure that the work is completed. You will also, however, need leadership skills to motivate the members of your team to achieve these goals.

Proving your capabilities

Louise first joined the help desk at the hospital's IT department via an agency. She'd always been interested in computers and was good at explaining things to other people in a pleasant and clear manner. She was quickly taken on to the permanent staff at the hospital.

Colleagues gradually noticed that she was quick to pick up knowledge and that she had good organizational skills – from arranging rotas to organizing the staff's Christmas meal. She also often deputized for the team leader when he was unavailable. She was promoted to acting team leader when the team leader was on sick leave. Louise proved her capabilities so well that when the team leader's job became vacant she applied and was offered this role. Her work skills, linked with her dedication, hard work and commitment to the role over a period of years meant that she was an ideal person to manage the team.

Qualities of a successful manager

What kind of a person makes a successful manager?

- Someone who is self-motivated – a good manager will have initiative and determination; he or she will not need external persuasion in order to work.
- Someone with good directional and organizational skills to organize people, processes and resources.
- Someone who is able to plan ahead and set clear goals.
- Someone who is focused on the important aims of achieving goals and increasing performance.
- Someone who has vision and is able to inspire others by their words and their example.
- Someone who is proactive in looking ahead, rather than reacting to changes as they happen.
- An effective communicator, able to communicate clearly in spoken and written forms (e.g. emails, reports).
- Someone who is able to think strategically, taking a view above the detailed.

- Someone who is good with finances, setting budgets and establishing systems that monitor and control expenditure.
- Someone who is good at analysing information, both in words and numbers, text and financial data, at home with both text documents and spreadsheets.
- Someone who is decisive, with the ability to take the initiative and make decisions. Sometimes even making the wrong decision can be better than making no decision at all!
- Someone with good interpersonal skills: open and approachable, trustworthy. Someone who respects others.
- Someone who is able to motivate others, coaching, supporting and facilitating their staff.
- Someone who is good at networking with others to develop trusted relationships.
- Someone who is able to delegate to members of their team.
- Someone who is able to work well under pressure.
- A good team player – one who works well, establishing clear roles and encouraging personal responsibility.
- Someone who is able to recruit (and retain!) good staff.
- Someone who is able to take control, building on previous successes to make things happen.
- Someone who is confident and optimistic – able to boost staff morale and encourage them to see challenges in a positive light.

- Someone who is effective at using time well, especially doing things right the first time.

- Someone who is committed and persistent in completing tasks reliably.
- Someone who is adaptable, able to deal with people well and solve problems creatively.
- Someone who is good at managing themselves, being aware of their own strengths and areas that need development.
- Someone with honesty and integrity, who deals with all staff fairly.

Tip

A few years ago I went to a day's course on leadership at which various skills (e.g. giving vision and direction, having courage, being able to inspire others) were stressed. The final comment of the day has stuck with me, however: 'Most importantly, if you had to choose between skills and integrity, choose integrity.'

The function which distinguishes the manager above all others is his educational one. The one contribution he is uniquely expected to make is to give others vision and ability to perform. It is vision and moral responsibility that, in the last analysis, define the manager.

Peter F. Drucker (1909–2005), US management expert

Back to the shop floor

As Managing Director, Joe felt he needed to 'get back to the shop floor' and find out what his staff really thought of his organization. So he sat alongside members of staff for several days, listening to their concerns. They didn't feel their work was valued, and communications from 'them' (senior management) were thought to be very poor. At the end of the week, Joe was able to take these valuable lessons back to his role as MD and begin to change the company's ethos and practices.

Summary

Today, we've begun to consider:

- what a manager is and does
- key aspects of being a manager
  - directing, planning and organizing work
  - giving instructions to workers
  - making decisions about aims and work
  - supervising and motivating staff
- the differences between being a manager and a leader
  - leaders set the overall direction and vision; managers turn that vision into action
  - in practice, the distinction between manager and leader may not be clear-cut
- the qualities that make a successful manager.

Next steps

1 Summarize your role in 10 to 15 words.
2 List the three main functions of your role.
3 Which of these three comes most easily to you?
4 Which of these three do you consider most difficult? Why? What will you do about it?
5 To what extent are you also a leader in your role as manager?
6 Consider which qualities of a successful manager you need to cultivate.

SUNDAY
MONDAY
TUESDAY
WEDNESDAY
THURSDAY
FRIDAY
SATURDAY

Fact-check (answers at the back)

1. A manager is:
a) a successful person ❑
b) someone who works hard ❑
c) someone who organizes work and gives instructions to colleagues ❑
d) someone who bosses others around. ❑

2. Managing is:
a) turning action into leadership ❑
b) setting a vision ❑
c) just about coping with difficulties ❑
d) turning leadership into action. ❑

3. As team leader, your role is:
a) to give orders to the team ❑
b) to manage the team ❑
c) to allow the team to do what they want ❑
d) to give days off to the team. ❑

4. A manager needs to be:
a) poorly motivated ❑
b) self-motivated and good at motivating others ❑
c) self-motivated ❑
d) good at motivating others. ❑

5. A manager needs to:
a) be good at organizing ❑
b) be poor at organizing ❑
c) not care about organizing. ❑
d) Sorry, what is organizing? ❑

6. A manager needs to:
a) be confused about the goals they want to achieve ❑
b) not care about the goals they want to achieve ❑
c) be clear about the goals they want to achieve ❑
d) change their mind about the goals they want to achieve. ❑

7. A manager needs to:
a) be totally absorbed by basic financial information ❑
b) be uninterested in basic financial information ❑
c) not care about basic financial information ❑
d) be able to understand basic financial information. ❑

8. A good manager should:
a) be proactive not reactive ❑
b) be reactive not proactive ❑
c) know the difference between proactive and reactive ❑
d) not understand the difference between proactive and reactive. ❑

9. A good manager should:
a) make decisions, but change the decision later ❑
b) never make any decisions at all ❑
c) be decisive, making clear decisions ❑
d) be hesitant, afraid to make decisions. ❑

10. In the final analysis, which is more important in a manager: skills or integrity?

a) both ☐
b) neither ☐
c) skills ☐
d) integrity. ☐

MONDAY

Managing people

So you're a new manager. Who will you manage? People are not things like machines, computers or processes – they are individuals, with different personalities. Some colleagues are keen to work, others lack motivation. Some colleagues are quick, others are slow; each has their own approach and style of working. How will you cope? How will you get the best out of them?

Today we look at:

- recruiting the right staff: the different steps you need to take
- motivating your staff: some useful hints, tips and techniques
- performance management, to evaluate colleagues' work
- developing your staff so that they gain new skills and abilities.

Each of these is vital: you want the best staff and you want them to reach their full potential. You need to build good relationships with them. This is about believing in your colleagues, having confidence in them.

Recruiting the right staff

It is difficult to find the colleagues you want. We joke, 'You can't get the staff these days', but it may be true. How do you find the best staff? Here's part of the secret: you need to know the kind of people you want.

Work out a timetable for the various different elements of the task, beginning at the end – in other words, the ideal date when you want the person to start. Working from where you are now, include time for: agreeing job description, person specification and method of application; advertising the post; receiving applications; dealing with references; shortlisting; interviewing; offering the job; applicant accepting offer; signing of contract.

Defining the job and the person

You need to start with a **job description**, which will state:

● what the purpose of the job is
● what the main responsibilities of the job are
● who the person will be responsible to.

Don't just use the standard job description that may be on your computer or filed in the Human Resources (HR) Department; now is a good time to review it and to refine the tasks and requirements of that position.

You will also need to define the skills, qualifications and experience the person will need. You will do this in a **person specification**. Some of these will be essential, others desirable. For example, to be a team leader at a Customer Services help desk, it is essential to have previous experience of working in Customer Services. Are you looking for a good team player or a lone ranger who is better at working by themselves? Are you looking for someone who can plan ahead? Someone who works well with spreadsheets?

Advertising the job

So, you've agreed and written up the job description and a person specification, now you need to move the recruitment process forward. Your Human Resources Department will help you with this. Advertise the post internally (e.g. on your organization's website) and externally. Advertise on the internet and intranet, in internal news bulletins and newspapers. If appropriate, go to an agency.

You will need to decide how to handle applications: whether candidates should fill in an application form (physically or online) or send a covering letter explaining why they think they are suitable for the job, accompanied by their CV.

You will also need to decide whether to ask for references and, if so, when (before or after the interview).

When you receive applications, you will then, with colleagues, shortlist possible candidates according to the objective criteria you decided in the job description and person specification. Note why you are not pursuing certain people and their applications in case this is queried later. Consider how many people you want to interview. Is ten too many?

Interviewing staff

The key point of interviews lies in the preparation. Be clear on the time and place of the interview, and give candidates sufficient advance notice (e.g. allow a week between shortlisting and the actual interview). On the day, allow enough time for the interviews themselves and time between interviews for the interviewers to make notes and confer before the next interview.

Think through what you want. Will candidates be required to give a presentation or take a test? If you want them to give a presentation, will a projector and laptop be available? And will they be required to bring some proof of identity or examination certificates?

Decide who will carry out the interviews. Do you require another person or possibly another two? Depending on how many candidates you are interviewing, is it better to do the interviews in a block, say over two days, so candidates are fresh in your mind. This may not always be possible, which is why it is vital to make notes.

Prepare the interview room, making sure it is clean and that water is available for candidates and pens and paper for interviewers.

Work hard at phrasing your questions. Apply the agreed criteria in the job description and the person specification in the interview process. It is important that each candidate is treated equally in the interviews: they should all be asked the same questions in the same order. Avoid closed questions that can be answered by a simple yes or no. Instead ask open questions. You could start with a general question such as, 'Tell us why you think you can fulfil this role'. Your aim is to enable the candidates to talk about themselves, their previous experience and how they could fill the job you are interviewing for. Check that you are clear on basic matters such as pay scales.

There are certain questions that you cannot ask, by law, such as a person's sexual orientation or their marital status. Your HR department will advise you on this.

Make sure you have discussed with the other interviewers when you will be able to let candidates know whether you are offering them the job.

A model interview

Harry welcomed the candidates to the day's interviews and tried to help them relax by making small talk. At the beginning of each interview, Harry started by explaining to each candidate the role and purpose of the job, the type of person the company was looking for and how the interview would proceed.

There were three interviewers on the panel and each asked the candidate the questions they had agreed in advance, with one or two supplementary questions to clarify their answers. They discussed the candidate's previous experience, what challenges they had faced in their previous job, their strengths and where they felt they could develop their performance. They allowed time for the candidate to ask questions and provide any other information they thought would be relevant. During the interview, each interviewer wrote many notes, which later formed the basis of their evaluation, discussion and decision on the best person for the job.

Evaluation

You will have all the information before you and you need to be as objective as possible in deciding to whom you should offer the job. Consider the facts as you have them from the candidates' applications, interviews and any references. Don't let yourself be persuaded by a person's attractive appearance or warm personality; you are interested in their ability to perform the job.

Offering the job and induction

Your HR department will guide you on your organization's practice regarding job offers/letters of appointment and contracts. You should also inform other candidates that they were not successful.

If the new colleague has come from outside the organization, then make sure you have a good induction programme to show them how your organization works, and to make them feel at home and integrated into their new workplace. It's not only about big ideas such as the ethos of your organization and its health and safety policy, but also about the small details of how to apply for holidays and who to contact if they are ill.

Staff Handbook

A typical Employees' Handbook (also called Employee Handbook, Employee Manual, Staff Handbook) contains sections on:

absence

appeal procedure

bullying

confidentiality

contract of employment

data protection

disciplinary procedure

equal opportunity and non-discrimination policies

expenses guidelines

flexible working procedures and conditions

grievance procedures

health, safety and fire

holiday entitlement

hours of work

maternity and paternity leave

notice to terminate employment

payments, including annual review

pension scheme arrangements

personal development

probationary period

redundancy policy

retirement age

sickness and sick pay procedures.

Motivating your staff

It's Thursday afternoon and members of your team have, it seems, stopped working and are discussing tonight's football match. You try to get them back to work, but fail. And it's like that all too often. How can you motivate your staff? Or you may be coming to the end of a long project. As Team Leader, you should be aware of the motivations and emotions of members of your team. Colleagues are probably tired and their levels of energy and enthusiasm may be beginning to wane. How do you encourage them?

Someone who is well motivated is positive, does their job well and enthusiastically and wants more responsibility. Such a person can boost the morale of colleagues and help them work well. On the other hand, someone who is poorly motivated will not seem to care about their work. They may turn up late and complain about small details. Such a person can have a negative effect on other colleagues.

Here are some tips to motivate staff:

- Show that you value them. Listen to them. Be available for them to bring their concerns to you. Understand them. Try to find out 'what makes them tick'. Talk *to* them, not *at* them. Find out what interests them outside work.
- Show that you value their work. Imagine a worker who produces a small part in a large machine without knowing what the large machine is for. He would feel more fulfilled if he knew the broader picture – and it will be the same with your team.
- Ensure their work is interesting and challenging. No one likes boring, repetitive tasks. Make sure your colleagues' work contains at least some interesting tasks that will stretch them.
- Communicate with them, both formally in meetings but also informally as you walk down the corridor for a coffee break. By 'communicating' I mean speaking, not emailing or texting! (See **Thursday** for more on communicating.)
- In group meetings, encourage team members, constantly affirming the team's commitment to reach the goal.

- Delegate more of your own work (see also **Tuesday**). Delegate whole tasks where possible. I once delegated three different aspects of the same task to three different people, and all felt frustrated and unfulfilled at the thirds they were given.
- Delegate work clearly (see also **Tuesday**). Do colleagues know exactly what is expected of them? Vague and unclear instructions not only demotivate colleagues but also waste time.
- Encourage uncooperative colleagues to try a new system if they are reluctant to follow it. Or even ask them if they could suggest new ways of solving a problem.
- Know colleagues' strengths and weaknesses. Try as far as possible to make sure they are 'round pegs in round holes' rather than 'square pegs in round holes'. This may be difficult, as there will always be aspects of work (perhaps unexciting administrative tasks) that it seems no one wants to do.
- Encourage your colleagues to focus on the goal and recognize their progress on the way. When I go on a long-haul flight, I keep an eye on our progress. For example, I work out on a 13-hour flight what percentage of the journey I have covered after, say, 45 minutes (6 per cent), 1.5 hours (12 per cent) and so on. Focusing on the end goal, dividing up the overall journey time and measuring progress in a concrete way helps me feel I am on my way to reaching that goal.
- Take one step at a time. Our proverbs tell us, 'Rome wasn't built in a day', 'The journey of 1,000 miles begins with a first step'. Sometimes the longest journey can be the first step.
- Focus on specific, measurable and realistic goals (see SMART goals below), not on vague ideas.
- Try to remain positive even when doing a structured task. That structured task is a significant part of a bigger picture.
- Offer coaching and opportunities for development to all colleagues in areas where they need further help (see below).
- Recognize colleagues' achievements. Even saying, 'Thank you, you did that well,' is an acknowledgement of gratitude.

Publicly affirm and recognize colleagues' achievements; praise their work in front of others. Bring in food or buy each of them little treats, such as chocolate. Issue certificates for achievements: it's amazing how competitive colleagues can be for a certificate.

- If you have come to the end of a project, celebrate that fact by all going out for a meal.
- Involve colleagues in decision making and setting budgets. If your company or organization is undergoing a period of change, then involve your colleagues at an earlier, rather than a later, stage. They will then feel valued.
- Encourage colleagues to make positive suggestions as to how to work more effectively.
- Ask a trusted colleague to come with you to a meeting of other managers. Let them accompany you for a few meetings and then gradually delegate some of the responsibilities to them.
- Recognize that on some days you will not feel motivated. You cannot feel fully inspired all the time. On days when I don't feel at all motivated, I really have to push myself to make an effort and often – but not always! – a sense of fulfilment comes.
- Overcome negative feelings – 'feel the fear and do it anyway'.

Performance management

Most organizations have certain procedures in place to consider colleagues' performance. Such procedures, usually included in your Employees' Handbook are commonly known as 'performance management', but other terms such as 'performance appraisal' and 'coaching development' are also used.

Appraisals

In an appraisal, a manager meets regularly (e.g. yearly or twice yearly) with a member of their team to discuss that colleague's work. In particular, the manager will consider the following:

● The colleague's performance since the last review. What has gone well? What evidence can you show to demonstrate this? Have the goals that were set then been fulfilled? If not, why not?
● Possible future development needs. In what areas would they benefit from training, or do they need support? What skills do they need to develop to enable them to progress in their career? You may gather information about their work from other individuals they work with, such as fellow team members, co-workers, subordinates, customers. When feedback is given from a range of people at different levels in the hierarchy it is known as 360-degree appraisal, indicating the all-round picture this will give of an individual.

The general tone of an appraisal is important. I was taught to follow the 'high-low-high' method – begin and end with praise and commendation and sandwich in between discussion of an area that has not gone well. A key aim is to get the appraisee to do most of the talking. Listen to your colleague's explanation of an area of their work where they are performing less well – there may be mitigating factors that have affected their work. Remain fair, positive and constructive and tackle weak performance by identifying causes and pursuing appropriate remedies. (Your company will have procedures in place for instances where required standards have not been met on a long-term basis.)

An appraisal should end by setting objectives. These objectives should be SMART:

S: Specific – defining the desired results
M: Measurable – quantifiable so that you know whether the objectives have been reached
A: Agreed by both the manager and the person being appraised
R: Realistic – objectives should be achievable but not too easy; should develop and challenge ('stretch') the colleague's resources and skills
T: Timed – giving a date for completion.

Making appraisals less difficult

Jack and his colleagues hated the yearly appraisal – the dreaded annual review – so they suggested that each member of staff should meet with their boss for an informal one-to-one chat every month.

The informal one-to-ones meant that difficult issues could be identified earlier and tackled more quickly, before they became serious. For example, Julie's boss saw that she was really struggling not only with her own workload but also that of a colleague who was on long-term sick leave, so her boss was able to bring in help more quickly. And Peter had been on a really helpful report-writing course, the results of which his boss asked him to pass on to others at their staff meeting. The introduction of one-to-ones meant that relations between colleagues and managers were better, managers were better informed about their staff and annual appraisals became far less of an ordeal.

Developing your staff

Your appraisals will show the development needs of your staff, and your next task is to work on these. People may have both immediate development needs (such as learning how to use new software or improving their time-management skills) and longer term needs (such as developing their leadership skills). Your goal should be to enable each person to achieve their full potential.

It is hoped that you will have finances set aside in your budget for training.

Training courses

As a manager you should consider the best ways to develop your staff. For example:

- **on-the-job training**: directly relevant to individuals – but you need to find an effective trainer
- **in-house training**: useful if your whole organization needs to develop certain knowledge or skills but may not be relevant to particular individuals
- **external training** led by a professional expert
- **personal coaching/mentoring**: see below.

On-the-job training

Rose was seconded one afternoon a week for several weeks to help Sarah, a new team member, learn how to use the new software. First, Rose demonstrated how to operate an aspect of the software, explaining as she did so. Sarah then had a go herself while Rose talked her through it. Finally, Sarah did the task and explained what she was doing to Rose, who was delighted with the results. Using a step-by-step showing and telling method, Sarah quickly learnt how to use the software.

In looking for courses, consider:

- the outcomes of the course: what will your colleagues be able to do as a result of attending a particular course?
- the background and credentials of the trainers.

After a training course, it is important to have some form of evaluation to ensure that some of the principles 'learnt' on the course have been digested and integrated into your colleague's work practices. Remember: 'use it or lose it' – apply what you have learnt or you will forget it.

Benefits of an outside facilitator

I was due to lead an in-house half-day training session on report-writing skills. I arrived early at the company's offices, as I like to, and was offered a cup of coffee by one of the people who was to attend the course. Another member of staff's immediate response to the offer was, 'Well, you never make me a cup of coffee!' I immediately sensed tension in the organization. The course went very well, and I was commended for having enabled two different groups who normally didn't talk to each other to work together successfully. Sometimes inviting an outside facilitator into a company can achieve significantly more than a colleague within the company.

Coaching and mentoring

Coaching and mentoring are more personal and direct ways of developing a colleague and their skills. The differences could be summed up as follows:

Coaching	Mentoring
More short term	Often more long term
More formal and structured	More informal
Is directed at specific issues or the development of specific skill areas	Considers the person as a whole and provides guidance in career development
Could be undertaken by your line manager or even a colleague on the same level as you but with more experience	Undertaken by an individual higher up in your organization (but not your boss) or from a different organization

A good coach or mentor will:

● be good at listening to what the person being coached is saying and not saying – they will be able to 'read (and hear) between the lines' and ask good questions
● not always respond with answers but will encourage the person being coached to actively come up with solutions to difficulties – they are more likely to take action if they have worked through the issues for themselves than if a coach has simply provided an answer
● bring a different way of thinking about an issue or a problem as they seek to understand it.

Discussing aspirations

Sarah met regularly with Janet, her mentor. Janet wasn't Sarah's line manager, so Sarah felt able to discuss her work freely and confidentially with Janet. In particular, Sarah was able to talk through her aspirations. The mentoring included discussion of Sarah's short- and mid-term training needs and, after the mentoring sessions, Sarah was able to approach her line manager to discuss these with her.

Summary

Today, we've looked at:

- recruiting the right staff
  - defining jobs and people
  - job descriptions and person specifications
  - advertising jobs
  - interviewing staff
- a range of ways to motivate your staff equally so that they feel valued and appreciated

- performance management
  - appraisals (formal)
  - one-to-ones (informal)
- developing your staff
  - training
  - coaching and mentoring.

Next steps

1 Look at your job description and the job descriptions and person specifications of members of your team. In what ways do they need refining to reflect what you all actually do?

2 Think of members of your team who are well motivated. What can you do to motivate them even more?

SUNDAY

MONDAY

TUESDAY

WEDNESDAY

THURSDAY

FRIDAY

SATURDAY

3 Think of members of your team who are poorly motivated. What can you do to motivate them more?

4 Read any sections of your Employees' Handbook with which you are unfamiliar.

5 Check that the development needs identified in your appraisals link in with your organization's training and development needs.

6 Consider whether you need a personal coach or mentor and, if so, what you will do next.

Fact-check (answers at the back)

1. When drawing up a job description:
   a) rush it through, knowing it will change quickly anyway ❏
   b) spend so much time revising the existing one that you miss the deadline you have set yourself ❏
   c) use the existing one, without checking whether it is still valid ❏
   d) prepare it carefully so that it reflects the job's main purpose and responsibilities. ❏

2. Preparation for an interview is:
   a) a nice-to-have if you have the time ❏
   b) a luxury ❏
   c) essential ❏
   d) unimportant. ❏

3. When motivating staff you should show them:
   a) that you don't care about them ❏
   b) that they are valued ❏
   c) that you are the boss ❏
   d) the door. ❏

4. Appraisals should always be:
   a) only positive ❏
   b) constructive ❏
   c) negative ❏
   d) unfair. ❏

5. In an appraisal it is important to:
   a) let the person being appraised talk ❏
   b) keep the person being appraised silent ❏
   c) not tackle difficult issues ❏
   d) talk only about difficult issues. ❏

6. When setting objectives, they should be SMART. S stands for:
   a) strange ❏
   b) slippery ❏
   c) specific ❏
   d) silly. ❏

7. Regular, informal one-to-ones are a good way of:
   a) replacing yearly appraisals ❏
   b) allowing difficulties to be discussed openly at an early stage, before they become serious ❏
   c) avoiding difficult issues ❏
   d) getting to know your boss. ❏

8. After a training course, evaluation is:
   a) a waste of time ❏
   b) essential ❏
   c) a nice-to-have ❏
   d) a luxury. ❏

9. In a business sense, a coach is:
   a) an experienced person from outside your organization who will guide you informally in the long term ❏
   b) a colleague who will deal with a short-term issue that you have ❏
   c) a long-distance bus ❏
   d) your manager. ❏

10. A good coach or mentor will:
   a) only listen and nod wisely ❏
   b) be no help at all to you ❏
   c) talk and advise you a lot ❏
   d) listen and encourage you to work out answers. ❏

TUESDAY

Managing a team

We're used to thinking about sports teams such as football teams, with forwards whose main responsibility is to score goals, midfielders who set up attacks, and defence and the goalkeeper to stop their opponents from scoring.

I once played the clarinet (fairly badly, and I'm not being modest) in a youth band. We gave a series of public concerts. There was nothing like it – my huffing and puffing as a second clarinettist somehow contributed to a gloriously energetic whole ensemble.

So what is a team? It's a group of different people working together towards a common goal. Let's break this definition down into its parts:

- 'A group of different people'. You will have a diverse range of people in your team with different skill sets, personalities and styles of working. This is the team's strength, not a weakness. What would life be like if we were all exactly the same?
- 'Working together towards a common goal'. It is hoped that your team is not just sitting round talking about nothing in particular but is focused on achieving a definite goal or goals.

Today we will look at:

- the diversity of your team members
- developing strong teamwork
- delegating work to your team.

The diversity of team members

The key factor here is that team members bring a valuable and wide range of different roles that complement one another: one person's weakness is balanced out by another person's strengths.

So what are the different roles?

A widely known set of different roles was developed by Dr Meredith Belbin as he looked at how members of teams behaved. He distinguishes nine different team roles:

- **Plant:** creative, good at coming up with fresh ideas and solving difficult problems in unconventional ways.
- **Resource investigator:** outgoing, good at communicating with outside agencies
- **Coordinator:** good as chairperson, focusing team members on the goals; a good delegator.
- **Shaper:** dynamic action person who can drive a project forward through difficulties.
- **Monitor/evaluator:** able to stand back and bring objective discernment.
- **Team worker:** bringing harmony and diplomacy for good team spirit.
- **Implementer:** dependable, efficient, practical organizer.
- **Completer/finisher:** able meticulously to follow through on details to complete a project.
- **Specialist:** giving expert technical knowledge.

For further details and information on how to identify colleagues' different roles, see www.belbin.com.

I led an away day for a group I'm connected with. As we began to work together as a team, I ended up (re-)discovering that I had skills in coordinating and chairing, so I was formally asked to chair meetings. Of course, some people offer more than one role. For example, our resource instigator, who is good at communicating with many outside contacts, is also an excellent team worker who brings tact and good spirit to team meetings.

This analysis is useful since it can reveal that there may be gaps; your team may be lacking certain skills, which you can then seek to cover. For example, the discussion above revealed that we had no monitor/evaluator who could stand back and objectively assess ideas. Identifying someone with those skills was therefore one of our aims.

As well as the different roles that people play, team members should be just that: team members, willing to work alongside others. The word 'synergy' has come to the fore in recent years. It is often defined as 2 + 2 = 5, i.e. when two groups of two people work together, the result is greater than the sum of their individual skills. Something extra happens: the combined effect is greater.

Settling into a new role

Andrew had worked in a remote part of the country. He was used to facilitating the development of projects by email and in a few face-to-face meetings. When he later got a job working as a member of a team, he found it difficult to settle into the role. He was not flexible enough and was used to getting his own way, and would tend only to work with others if he was leading a project rather than working on projects led by others. He had to learn to work with others.

Developing strong teamwork

As team leader, you are responsible for encouraging your team. What we discuss here builds on motivating your staff, which we considered on **Monday**. Here we are concerned with encouraging members of your team to work together successfully. To do that, you need to:

- Communicate a vision. Where is the team going? What is its purpose? You need to present a strong and inspiring vision of your goals.
- Set your team goals clearly. There is nothing like an abstract statement that is not earthed in reality to turn people off. It is hardly surprising that colleagues come out of a team meeting feeling cynical when a vision has been outlined but no practical implications have been drawn from that vision. A vision must be turned into practical steps.
- Ensure that your values as a team are agreed. Do team members trust and respect one another? Do individuals feel important and part of something bigger than themselves? Encourage team members to remain positive, to believe in the strength and unity of the team.
- Clarify the responsibilities of each member of the team so that each individual knows their own responsibilities and those of the other members of the team. Different members of the team will bring different skills – so play to colleagues' strengths. Don't give the responsibility of chairing a meeting to someone who is unclear or indecisive.
- Ensure that lines of authority and responsibility are clear. Be clear about whether individual team members have authority to spend sums of money up to a certain amount, or whether they should direct all requests for purchases through you, as team leader.
- Be flexible about what is negotiable and try to accommodate different styles of working. Listen to suggestions from colleagues. Be prepared to 'think outside the box' to creatively challenge existing patterns of thinking and working and find solutions to difficulties.

- Be fair and treat all your colleagues equally, even though you may like some more than others.
- Make sure that team members all work as hard as each other and 'pull their weight'. You cannot afford to carry 'passengers' – those team members who work significantly less than others.
- Show enthusiasm in your work. Enthusiasm is infectious, and so is the lack of it. If you are half-hearted it will show in your tone of voice and body language, and colleagues will be aware that you may be saying all the right words but not believing them yourself.
- Encourage openness. As far as you can, involve members of the team in making decisions. Bring out those who are shy and use your skills of diplomacy to quieten those who talk too much.
- Encourage team members to use their initiative. They do not always need to come back to you to solve small difficulties but can be enterprising and resolve issues themselves.

The four stages of team building

A project team was appointed to develop a change-management strategy for a project. When the project team first met, everyone was friendly and there was a sense of excitement as the leader explained the project's aims and they began to get to know one another and work out their roles (known as 'forming'). Fairly quickly, however, issues began to surface as different colleagues had diverging ideas and conflicts began to emerge ('storming'). Fortunately, the team leader stepped in and acted as mediator.

Gradually, team members worked through these challenges and, although discussions still became heated at times, they began to trust one another and were able to reach broad agreement on the way ahead ('norming'). They realized that getting the project completed was more important than protecting their own positions. They

> were then able to work well together to formulate and eventually implement the strategy ('performing').
>
> The names of the four stages were first proposed by American psychologist Bruce Tuckman in 1965.

- Encourage colleagues to look out for one another so that, for example, when one colleague is struggling, a fellow team member can step in and help.
- Challenge the team to work even more effectively. Don't encourage them to sit back but be constantly on the lookout for better ways of doing things that save time or money. For example, are team members entering the same data into two different spreadsheets? Combine them into one, so that the task is not duplicated.
- Set in place effective monitoring controls to track what you are doing (see also **Wednesday**) and then evaluate your progress regularly. For example, if you find that staff expenses claims are not being properly checked, then you must act on this promptly.
- Celebrate success. Recognize the success of individuals. In some cultures colleagues are shy or embarrassed about doing this, but it is an important part of valuing and appreciating people. Celebrate team success. If you have completed a project, go out and mark the occasion by doing something different, such as having a special lunch or an evening meal. Such times help develop a sense of belonging to a team.
- Give feedback. As team leader you should give informal feedback to team members on whether they are doing well ... or not so well. Be specific (e.g. 'I thought the tone of your email in response to the complaint was excellent.'); encourage accountability and deal with difficulties sooner rather than later so they do not become serious.
- Provide opportunities for members of your team to approach you if they need help. You should not be aloof.
- Encourage fun. Hold team-building days where you deliberately mix people up into different groups from those they are normally in. Set tasks in which the groups compete

against one another. The resulting banter will produce laughter and relax people, and you will see sides of people that you have not seen before.

Good team meetings

Nabila was a good team leader. The meetings she led were particularly good. She kept close to the agenda, which had been circulated in advance, and she followed up the action points from the previous meeting. She gave out general information about how the company was performing and led fruitful discussions on how her unit could improve their efficiency even further. She was particularly good at encouraging everyone to participate and express themselves. She always summarized the discussions and came to a clear decision about the next step. She made sure minutes were circulated promptly after meetings so that colleagues were all clear about what they should do. The result was that colleagues in her team all felt inspired and well motivated.

Delegating well

There are lots of reasons why managers don't delegate: you think you can do it better yourself, members of the team are too busy, the task is too urgent, your colleagues aren't quite ready to take on such demanding work. Most of these reasons are essentially about the fact that you don't trust members of your team to carry out the tasks. But when will they be fully ready? When will they have enough time?

You need to adopt three approaches:

● **Plan ahead as much as you can.** Spend time doing this. You know when key tasks (e.g. the annual budget) are required. Build sufficient planning time into your diary (paper, electronic, digital, in the cloud, wherever – but make sure you have some means of planning!).

- **Delegate work to those who are nearly ready to do it.** No one is ever fully ready. Were you? The delegated tasks will stretch those who are nearly ready for them, but that's what you want, isn't it?
- **Delegate more rather than less.** There are a few matters you cannot delegate (e.g. managing the overall team, allocating financial resources, dealing with confidential matters of performance management and promotion), but you can and should delegate many of your actual work tasks and some routine admin activities.

How to delegate

So, you've decided to delegate tasks. How do you go about doing this? Here are some steps:

- Know your team. Who would be the best person to carry out the tasks you want to delegate? Remember the suggestion above: choose colleagues who are nearly ready. If no one is at that level, then provide training so that at least some of them are. Share the load wherever possible. But don't delegate too much work to your best colleague.
- Be clear about the tasks you want to delegate. This is the most important part of delegating. Don't give vague instructions (e.g.

'Could you just write a short report on failings in security?'); be specific. Explain yourself well: 'I'd like a ten-page report giving examples of major security breaches together with possible reasons behind them and recommendations on how to avoid them in future.' Allow plenty of time to explain the task and give your colleague the opportunity to ask questions to clarify what you want them to do.

● Check that the person has understood the task you want them to undertake. Do not just ask, 'Have you understood what I want you to do?' Ask, for example, 'Could you summarize what you will be doing?' Their response will show how much they have understood.

● Give background details, so that the person knows why they are doing the task and where it fits into the overall scheme of things, but without giving an exhaustive account of all the details.

● Where possible, follow up any spoken instructions in writing with a full brief, outlining the work.

● Break down the task into its parts. Write clear briefing instructions, giving concrete examples of what needs to be done.

● State the date and time by which you want your colleagues to complete the work. Remember that what may take you (with all your experience) only half a day will probably take them much longer – perhaps two days.

● Agree how often you want the person to report back to you, particularly (but not only) when they have completed certain agreed targets.

● If a colleague is slow at doing their work, ask them to give you a progress update at the end of each day.

● Be clear about the authority and responsibility you are giving the person. After all, you remain ultimately responsible as manager even though you have delegated the work.

● Supervise their work properly: provide the necessary equipment and other resources they need.

● Let the person decide the details of how they will undertake the work. Allow them to do the work in their own style.

● Where problems or difficulties arise, encourage the person to come to you with them but also to bring their thoughts on possible solutions, together with figures on financial costings for such solutions and the time they would take. This makes better use of your time: they are closer to the details of the task than you are. Your task is then to make a decision based on their suggestions.

- Provide sufficient additional coaching or training to enable the person to undertake and complete the task.
- When they have completed the task, thank the person to whom you delegated the work, expressing your appreciation. Recognize them and their achievement.

A growing confidence

Steve joined a charity as a volunteer some years ago. He showed interest in going further and was given some simple administrative tasks to do, which he completed well. Eventually he started to help in finance and after a few years became a Finance Assistant. With the Finance Director being on leave for a month, the charity had to complete the figures for September within five working days of the month end. Steve took control for the first time and actually calculated the figures in four days, allowing the other directors to sign them off on the fifth day. Steve was a real asset to the charity and he went on to study for a professional accountancy qualification. This all happened because his bosses saw his potential and gave him the opportunity to grow and so his confidence increased.

Summary

Today, we've looked at:

- the diversity of your team members
- appreciating the different roles people play
  - filling gaps for missing roles
- developing strong teamwork
- motivating your team to work together as a unit, with each member playing to their strengths
- establishing a strong vision and clear goals
- ensuring each member of the team knows what their responsibilities are
- delegating well
  - planning ahead
- giving clear instructions on the task you are delegating, especially on what the end result is (e.g. a report of one or ten pages?) and when you want the work
  - trusting colleagues to whom you are delegating work.

Next steps

1 Using the Belbin analysis (see also www.belbin.com), consider what role you play.
2 Again using the Belbin analysis, consider what roles are played by others in your team.

SUNDAY
MONDAY
TUESDAY
WEDNESDAY
THURSDAY
FRIDAY
SATURDAY

3 What practical steps can you as team leader take to develop even stronger teamwork among your team?

4 Does each member of your team understand clearly what their individual responsibilities are? Does each team member know the others' responsibilities?

5 Think about what work you can delegate. Plan ahead.

6 Are you clear when you explain the tasks you need to delegate? Do you trust members of your team to undertake the work you have given them?

Fact-check (answers at the back)

1. A team is:
a) a group of individuals ❑
b) a group of individuals who work well together ❑
c) a group of individuals who work well together towards a common goal ❑
d) a group of individuals who work badly together. ❑

2. When looking at people's roles, it is important that:
a) everyone has the same role ❑
b) there should be a healthy mix of different roles ❑
c) no one knows their role ❑
d) no one should have more than one role. ❑

3. When encouraging effective teamwork, focus on:
a) the strengths of the team ❑
b) your favourites in the team ❑
c) past failures of the team ❑
d) weaknesses in the team. ❑

4. Effective team members:
a) criticize one another publicly ❑
b) don't care at all about other team members ❑
c) form cliques in the team ❑
d) remain positive, believing in the strength of the team. ❑

5. When giving feedback to a colleague whose work is consistently below standard:
a) avoid discussing it for fear of giving offence ❑
b) discuss it with them sooner rather than later ❑
c) talk about it at a team meeting ❑
d) talk about it every time you see them. ❑

6. When a team member approaches you with an idea:
a) ignore them ❑
b) listen to them and consider it ❑
c) listen to them but forget it immediately ❑
d) think you know better than they do. ❑

7. When delegating work:
a) don't worry about explaining a task as the team member will pick up what is needed ❑
b) explain quickly so you can get on to more important tasks ❑
c) explain the task clearly. ❑
d) Sorry, what is delegating? ❑

8. When delegating work:
a) check occasionally, giving your colleagues the freedom to make mistakes ❑
b) check constantly to make sure they know you're the boss ❑
c) never monitor their work ❑
d) forget you ever gave them work in the first place. ❑

9. When a team member brings a problem to you, encourage them also to bring:
a) a pizza ❑
b) ten different ideas as to how you might solve it ❑
c) a further problem while they are talking to you ❑
d) thought through solution. ❑

10. When a task has been completed well by a colleague you should:
a) praise them because you like them personally ❑
b) forget all about it ❑
c) recognize their achievement ❑
d) ignore them because you mustn't show favouritism. ❑

WEDNESDAY

Managing your work

Your work as a manager is primarily about managing people and teams. However, to enable you to work efficiently and effectively in those areas, you will also need to learn how to deal with the systems that make up a significant part of your work as a manager.

So today we're concerned with:

- thinking strategically and setting goals
- setting and managing budgets
- developing other systems
- solving problems and making decisions
- dealing with change.

Some of these procedures may seem dry and boring, but learning these skills will provide a firm support for your work. Without them, you would not know where you were, where you were going, nor what the costs were, and you would sink under a weight of problems. With these systems in place you will know your aims and goals and what your costs are, and will be able to work well, solve problems and make good decisions.

Thinking strategically

What is the hardest task in the world?
To think.

Ralph Waldo Emerson, US poet, essayist and philosopher

You need to stop and think about what you want to achieve.
Double your profits? Open ten new shops in the next two
years? Have a new office on every continent? Whatever your
aims, you need to think strategically and focus your thoughts.
Here are some questions to help you do this:

● What is your destination? Where are you trying to take
your organization? What results (outcomes) do you want to
achieve? For example, using the tool of change management
(see below), you might want to change your organization and
move it on to embrace fresh ideas and manufacture a new
range of products.

● What steps (goals) can you set that will be important stages
on your journey to that destination? Remember that the
goals should be SMART (specific, measurable, agreed,
realistic, timed – see **Monday**) so that you know if and when
you have achieved them.
● Who else will you involve in this planning process? Your
plan should not simply be the result of your own thinking;

it will be the joint effort of your senior managers and other colleagues in your team.

- What assumptions does the plan make? For example, does it assume a certain figure for customer demand for a product that is based on a particular rate of growth in the overall economy? What will happen if that growth figure is not met?
- Have you fully considered the basic resources of time, finance and personnel? How long will your project take? How much will it cost? Do you have the staff to undertake it? If not, where will you find them?
- Have you broken down your plan into manageable parts? Add further details and information on the key issues regarding the basic time, finances and personnel.
- What contingency factors are you building into your budget? Ten per cent is a figure widely quoted to cover unforeseen costs.
- Is the quality of your work and its outputs a priority? Don't accept second best. Make sure you get things right first time.

A SWOT analysis

A SWOT analysis examines your:

- Strengths: what is your company or organization good at? What do you do better than your competitors? What is your unique selling point (USP)?
- Weaknesses: what is your company or organization weak at? What do you have a poor reputation for?
- Opportunities: what directions and trends are there that you could profitably follow up?
- Threats: what problems does your company or organization face at the moment, e.g. increased competition from other companies or constraints on your company's income?

Thinking about these issues will enable you to make good use of the strengths and opportunities and minimize the weaknesses and threats. Undertaking a SWOT analysis is not an end in itself; you need to progress and deal with the issues raised.

Putting goals into action

So you've set out a grand strategic plan and identified certain goals at stages on the way to fulfilling that plan. What are the next steps? You need to clarify the roles of your colleagues. You don't want two people each doing the same work, while neglecting other work that needs to be done.

As we saw on **Tuesday**, an important part of managing teams is to clarify the roles of the different members. Not only should each person know their own role and responsibilities, but also the different roles and responsibilities of the other team members, so that everyone knows what is required of them and where they fit into the overall strategy.

When you give targets and goals to colleagues, they know what to aim at and that is likely to increase their motivation as well as stretching their abilities.

Setting specific goals

As the manager of a café, Teresa was wise – she knew that the goals she set her team members had to be few in number ('less is more'). She also knew that they had to be specific – not simply, 'Be more customer focused' but, 'Take customers' orders for drinks within two minutes of their sitting down at their table.' And by looking at the numbers of customers who came into the café at different times during the day, she recruited sufficient staff for the peak periods to help meet her targets.

Setting and managing budgets

As a manager you will need some financial skills. Some of these may be more technical, others are relatively easy to grasp.

Setting the budget

The basis for a future budget will be the budget for the current year, and you will need several different kinds of accurate information to enable you to make good decisions. Such information will include:

- data so far this financial year
  - income
  - expenditure
  - significant points of variance between actual and budgeted income and expenditure, and reasons for such variances
  - profit or loss and, if the latter, a consideration of the reasons
- aims for next year
- trends for next year that your organization wants to pursue
- increases in pay
- inflation
- improvements in productivity
- plans or projects your organization wants to implement
- contingency.

Putting together a budget for the future is not simply a matter of typing numbers into a spreadsheet. You also need to consider:

- whether the assumptions made are realistic, e.g. will the prices of raw materials remain stable over the next 12 months? Will your company really grow and capture your target of, say, 10 per cent more of the market next year?
- staff costs
- overheads (general business expenses). Do they accurately reflect actual costs?

Managing your budget

One of your responsibilities as a manager may be to manage your team's budget. Again, accurate information is vital. Ensure that your financial software produces regular reports on income and expenditure analysed into 'cost centres', to which particular items of expenditure are allocated. You can then monitor and review income and expenditure and act accordingly.

If you are exceeding your budget, here are some tips to reduce your spending:

- Only spend money on essentials – what you definitely need – not on 'nice-to-have' items. You may be able to postpone buying certain services or products.
- Think of ways in which you can work more effectively and efficiently:
  - Are all your meetings necessary? The agendas at most of the meetings at one company I came across were about the meetings themselves, not about the actual work!
  - Are there some aspects of your work that you could stop doing completely?

- Reduce expenses where possible. Change from first class to standard class travel. Can staff travel at cheaper periods of the day?
- Reduce working hours by stopping overtime or extending the period in which the office is closed for the Christmas and New Year break.
- Freeze posts when colleagues have left. However, this will mean that the remaining members of the team have to take on additional roles and responsibilities, which may not be popular.

	BUDGET 2011/12	Actual	Difference
	£	£	£
PERSONNEL			
Salaries	88,700	89,000	(300)
Expenses	2,500	1,572	928
OFFICE			
Telephone	2,000	1,612	388
Insurance	2,100	2,000	100
Water rates	500	389	111
Heat & light	6,400	7,003	(603)
Photocopier, post & stationery	7,500	9,000	(1,500)
Website maintenance	300	352	(52)
Office furniture/equipment	200	210	(10)
Miscellaneous	500	179	321
MAINTENANCE			
General maintenance	9,000	8,790	210
First aid	1,800	1,840	(40)
Security alarm service	320	600	(280)
Heating service contract	600	750	(150)
Refurbishment	0	0	0
Supplies (kitchen)	1,000	753	247
Miscellaneous	500	310	190
IT EQUIPMENT			
IT Equipment	2,700	2,900	(200)
MISCELLANEOUS			
Conferences	200	0	200
Bank charges	350	358	(8)
Acccountancy fees	1,500	1,652	(152)
CONTINGENCY	12,000		12,000
TOTAL	140,670	129,270	11,400

Comparing budget with actual figures

61

Notes

- In the 'Difference' column, figures indicate where the actual is less than the budget; figures in brackets show where the actual is more than the budget.
- The figures show that although some expenditure – notably salaries, heat and light, security alarm, IT equipment, heating service contract, accountancy fees and particularly photocopier, post and stationery – were higher than budgeted, because there was a substantial figure for contingency, there was an overall balance of £11,400.

Developing other systems

I remember it well; it was just about the time when we were all getting computers. Every day for a month I reflected on the fact that I was repeating the same tasks every month. I needed systems and procedures – or at least forms to fill in – so I didn't have to 'reinvent the wheel' every month. So I developed some procedures and systems – spent time to save time – so that I could concentrate on the real work, the content of the procedures, rather than on the procedures themselves.

There will be a whole range of procedures that you need to complete regularly, such as:

- filling in/checking time sheets
- checking the photocopier usage
- ensuring that holiday procedures are being followed
- preparing for annual goal setting
- ensuring that your policies on Health and Safety and Data Protection are being complied with
- preparing for the annual budget
- managing your budget.

You need 'operational controls'. You can introduce all sorts of wonderful procedures, but experience shows that they all fall by the wayside if no one is checking up on the processes. Anything you say you are going to do on a regular ongoing basis, or any statements that you make about what senior management needs, must be checked.

Management reporting

You will need to put in place processes, linked with your accounting systems, to provide clear and consistent information to your senior managers on such key issues as cost, quality, outputs and growth. These will be in the form of key performance indicators (KPIs), which give an objective measurement of how well or how badly the strategy of your company or organization is being implemented.

Your goal is to enable senior managers to make informed decisions not only so they can analyse performance against targets but also so they can plan strategically for the future.

Solving problems and making decisions

Much of your time as a manager will be taken up with the two processes of solving problems and making decisions.

Solving problems

Here are some guidelines:

● Ask whether it is your problem. Is it your responsibility to respond to it, or is it someone else's? Or is it just one of those things you have to live with? If the problem is yours:
  – How important is it? Will solving it have a significant effect on your work? Apply the Pareto principle (named after the Italian economist and sociologist, Vilfredo Frederico Pareto (1848–1923) and also known as the 80:20 rule). For example, 80 per cent of problems may come from three major issues and 20 per cent from 20 minor issues. It's better to concentrate on the 80 per cent caused by the few major issues than become preoccupied with the 20 per cent caused by many issues.
  – How urgent is it? If the problem will become more serious if you do nothing about it, then act sooner rather than later.
● Occasionally, however, some problems can turn into positive opportunities, so don't always think you have to solve them all.

- Get to the root of the problem. Think; discuss with other colleagues; analyse the problem by separating it into its parts to help you define it more closely and understand it more fully.
  - In particular, concentrate on the causes – not the symptoms or effects – of the problem. So if someone's work is below standard, don't keep on moaning about it by giving examples. Instead, try to find out why and ask whether they need training, or consider whether they would be more suitable for different kinds of work.
  - Keep on asking questions, especially the question 'Why?', so you gain a complete understanding of the real issue. Often it's more about asking the right questions than giving the right answers.
- Gather information about the extent of the problem. If the quality of products is falling, does this affect 1 in 1,000 products or 900 in 1,000?
- Concentrate on the big issues. Don't get bogged down in detail. ('He's always late, because the number 101 bus is always late. Here's the times it's turned up over the last month: 8.12, 8.31, ...'.)
- Use your experience. As you progress as a manager, you will develop that sense of 'I've been here before. How did I solve the problem last time?'
- Consider different responses. Here are some techniques you could use to respond creatively to problems:
  - Brainstorm: take a flipchart. Ask one person to state the problem and then get them to write down ideas thinking about the problem from different angles, e.g. your customers' and your competitors'. Encourage participants to build on one another's ideas; don't criticize or evaluate them. At the end, participants agree how to take the best ideas to the next stage.
  - Draw up a flow chart that shows the different stages that led to a problem, how the problem is expressed (i.e. its symptoms) and the connections between the problem's causes and effects.
  - Think 'outside the box'. Is the problem difficult to put into words? Then draw it or work out if you are better explaining it using a painting, a piece of music or by role play.

- Draw a pattern diagram (see **Thursday**).
- Conduct a SWOT analysis (see earlier today).

Making decisions

Here are some guidelines:

- **Act, don't over-analyse.** By temperament, I'm an analyser. Fortunately my wife is an action person – that's why we make a good team. Ultimately, you need to stop analysing and make a decision.
- **Review the possible solutions.** We don't live in a perfect world, so it's unlikely that every decision you make will be a perfect one. You may have to make a decision now, with the full knowledge that you may need to return to the issue in two years' time.
- **Discuss the matter with other colleagues.** If necessary, consult an expert. They may shed light on issues, risks or alternatives that you have not thought of. Try to reach a collective decision: at least if the decision is wrong, blame will come to the whole group and not just one person. If necessary, discuss a delicate issue with a colleague in private rather than in a group, as 'political' matters may come into play in the wider group.

Dealing with change

One key aspect of your role as a manager may be change management: you may need to make significant changes to your operating procedures to reduce costs. What you need to do is move colleagues on from the 'We've always done it this way' way of thinking, which may be firmly embedded in their culture.

Responses to change

- **People don't like change.** 'We've always done it this way' is the mantra they may repeat. 'Things worked as they did – why do we need to change?'

- **People are uncomfortable with change.** Many people like routine, and their patterns of life will be disrupted if changes are brought in.
- **People feel threatened by change.** Change can create fear of the unknown. Changes may affect a colleague's sense of identity.

Leading change

Here are some of the keys to leading change.

Understand your organization

What is the organization's general atmosphere? Is there a climate for change? Is the prevailing mood one of positive confidence, a 'can-do' supportive mentality, or are attitudes negative and cynical with a lot of back-biting and in-fighting? Be aware not only of what is going on at the centre of your organization but also at its edges, and what is not (or no longer) going on. Talk to your colleagues, and even more importantly, listen to them (see also **Thursday**).

Emphasize the vision, the goal

Don't get sidetracked by minor issues. Your organization's mission statement may be concerned with serving the community, but that focus may have got lost. Refocus your team members' vision on that goal so that they understand it. In managing change, you will constantly need to explain why you are doing what you are doing.

Convince colleagues that there must be change

When you are trying to introduce change in an organization, it is vital that this is not seen as only one person's favourite subject. Senior managers must be committed to change and the results of the changes must be shown to have a direct relationship with one of your organization's key goals. It is vital to have a good strategy in place that will move from your vision and goal through your values to help earth your plans in reality. You need to explain clearly to team members why changes are needed (e.g. because of falling productivity or decreasing profits as companies are choosing your competitors) and the benefits changes will bring.

Develop fresh values

Turn your vision and goal into values that determine the emphasis and ethos of your organization. Make them as practical and simple as possible. (I led a writing course for a group of leading police officers and kept on asking them to simplify their values in ordinary words. It took two hours, at the end of which the boss said, 'Martin, you've changed my writing style in two hours!') You may be able to develop the former values of your organization or you may need to rework them totally.

Involve your colleagues

In the early days of change management, involve the colleagues who will be part of the changes. Don't leave them in the dark: involve them in setting the vision and strategy and in making decisions. Get influential colleagues on your side. Enthuse as many people as you can.

Communicate well

As we will see on **Thursday**, good communication is essential in a company or organization, and this is even more essential when you want to move an organization through change. Rumours about possible changes to people's jobs, roles and location of jobs can all too easily arise, and these can lower morale and lead to poor motivation. Clear, well-thought-out, planned communications are vital in order to bring your colleagues with you. Formal, public communications are significant, but the informal, passing-in-the-corridor type conversations are also important. One long-standing friend of mine deliberately allows extra time on a visit to the farthest end of his organization's workplace so that he can stop and talk to people on the way.

Recognize positive achievements and efforts, celebrate milestones. One club I'm involved with in my spare time celebrated the initial decision to change with a meal for the committee in a restaurant.

Stay focused on the goal but be willing to negotiate on the way to reach it

Keep stating your goal and why changes are necessary, but be flexible on the detail and style of the ways in which colleagues can reach that goal, so they feel fully involved. Try not to be deflected from your main goals by colleagues who want to make small unimportant changes.

Go for quick wins

Find an aspect of change that can be implemented fairly quickly and relatively easily and will produce the results you want, to demonstrate to the wider audience that change is happening and to bring about a positive response.

Introducing changes gradually

Martha was promoted to team leader and had many good ideas about changes she wanted to bring in (e.g. team statistics, rotas, new personal targets). However, her colleagues reacted badly to the speed of changes and her mentor had a quiet word with her ('Go for "Evolution" not "Revolution".'). So Martha slowed down and introduced the changes at a more measured pace. The result was that her colleagues' self-confidence increased as they successfully navigated the changes.

Summary

Today has been concerned with managing your work:

- standing back, thinking strategically and setting goals that can then be translated into action
- setting and managing budgets
- developing other systems
- solving problems and making decisions
- dealing with change.

Next steps

1 Do you know the strategic goals of your company or organization?
2 What assumptions do they make? Do you think they are valid?
3 Is your strategic plan well translated into clear goals and targets?
4 How much do you understand the budget and finances of your company or organization? What steps can you take to increase your understanding?
5 What regular activities do you undertake that you can work on more efficiently?
6 What methods can you use to solve the problems you are facing?
7 How can you be more effective in bringing about change in your company or organization?

Fact-check (answers at the back)

1. When translating your strategic plan into goals, the goals and targets should be:
   a) non-existent ❏
   b) many and clear ❏
   c) few and clear ❏
   d) many and vague. ❏

2. In a SWOT analysis, SWOT stands for:
   a) storms, welcome, offices, trouble ❏
   b) study, wheels, origins, time ❏
   c) steps, wisdom, output, thinking ❏
   d) strengths, weaknesses, opportunities, threats. ❏

3. Putting an amount for contingency in a budget is:
   a) a nice-to-have ❏
   b) a luxury ❏
   c) essential. ❏
   d) What is contingency? ❏

4. KPIs are:
   a) Kentucky pink improvements ❏
   b) key performance indicators ❏
   c) kangaroo performance indicators ❏
   d) key performance isolators. ❏

5. When trying to solve a problem:
   a) keep asking 'Why?' until you get to the root of the problem ❏
   b) be satisfied with superficial causes ❏
   c) look at the symptoms of the problem ❏
   d) look at the effects of the problem. ❏

6. When trying to solve a problem:
   a) save money above all ❏
   b) draw diagrams of the car park ❏
   c) gather all the details together ❏
   d) concentrate on the big issues. ❏

7. At work, you sometimes have to spend time to save time.
   a) This is irrelevant. ❏
   b) I haven't got time to consider this. ❏
   c) True ❏
   d) False ❏

8. When introducing change:
   a) criticize colleagues for their poor performance ❏
   b) constantly state why you are making the changes ❏
   c) be silent once you are making the changes ❏
   d) be silent about why you are making the changes. ❏

9. In leading an organization through change, good communication and leadership are:
   a) essential ❏
   b) unimportant ❏
   c) nice to have ❏
   d) a luxury. ❏

10. A quick win is:

a) part of a change that
you hope will fail ❏

b) an aspect of change
you can quickly
implement and will
produce good results ❏

c) the winning scorer
in a football match ❏

d) a celebration of victory. ❏

THURSDAY

Communicating
effectively

'I never knew that was happening.' 'No one told me about that.' 'That's the first I've heard about it.' Do these sound familiar?

Communicating well is a significant part of your role as a manager. Roles and responsibilities cross over each other and you can spend a lot of time sorting out who should be doing what, when it would have been better if all that had been clarified earlier.

So today we stand back and consider different ways in which you should communicate as a manager, through listening, emailing, using the phone, writing reports, giving presentations, negotiating and resolving conflict.

We will also look particularly at meetings – their purpose, preparing for them, chairing them, participating in them and following them up – and ways to improve your reading techniques. All these are core skills that you should try to cultivate to become an even more effective manager.

SUNDAY

MONDAY

TUESDAY

WEDNESDAY

THURSDAY

FRIDAY

SATURDAY

Listening

Listening may seem a strange place to start, but as is often stated, 'God gave us two ears and one mouth', so before we're tempted to speak it is wise to listen.

- Listening focuses on the other person. Often when someone else is talking, we're focusing on what we are going to say in reply. Don't be tempted to interrupt the other person while they are talking. Stop and really listen to what they are saying. Make eye contact with them. Rephrase what they've said in your own way to help clarify the meaning in your own mind (e.g. 'So what you're really saying is that the whole process needs to be looked at again'), a process called 'reflective listening'.
- It values the person you are listening to as an individual in their own right, so that you understand 'where they're coming from', why they are working or speaking as they are.
- Listening encourages you to ask the right questions. As you focus on the other person (not yourself), you will want to know more. We can distinguish:
  - closed questions. These can be answered by a straight 'Yes' or 'No': 'Was the project late?' 'Yes.' 'Will you be able to give me the figures by 5.00 p.m.?' 'No.'
  - open questions. These get people talking, using 'why', 'how', 'who', 'when', 'where', 'what': 'Why do you think the project is running late?' 'Because we didn't plan for the extra work the customer now wants.' Most of the questions you should ask as a manager should be open questions.
- Listening attentively enables you to perceive your colleague's response to what you are saying by being sensitive to their body language and tone of voice, as well as hearing the words they're saying.
- It allows you to 'listen between the lines', to become aware of any underlying messages – your response could be, for example, 'So I guess what you're saying is that you need someone else to help you complete this task on time'.

- It allows you to distinguish between facts and opinions. You will hear both, and you can discern what is objective information and what are subjective thoughts on this information.
- Listening builds trust between people: you show that you are genuinely interested in them. This forms a basis to help you work well with them.

Susie was angry

Susie was angry. She worked late every evening to complete her tasks on the project but she felt her work was not appreciated or valued. It was only when a new colleague, Jan, started to work alongside her that something happened. Jan was concerned less about herself and her own work (which she did well) and more about her colleague – she cared enough to stop and listen to Susie. Susie was in tears as she poured out her heart to Jan, and at the end of their conversation Susie told Jan, 'Thanks for listening. You're the first person I've been able to talk to about these things.'

The basics of communication

In the seminars I lead on communication, I discuss the basics under the headings A I R:

- **Audience**: we adapt what to communicate according to our audience. So, for example, an email to a colleague at the next desk to us will be written in a different tone from one to the company's Managing Director or an external consultant.
- **Intention**: what exactly are you trying to communicate? What is your message? If you are not clear about it, the readers of your email or report won't be clear either.
- **Response**: what are you expecting your colleague to do as a result of your communication? Have you made clear what you want your colleague to do next? You don't want them to say, 'Yes, I get that, but so what?'

Email

Emails are great. We can communicate with colleagues all round the world instantly. But emails also have their disadvantages. For example, we can receive too many unwanted ones that stop us dealing with the tasks we are supposed to be dealing with.

Here are a few tips:

- Put a clear subject in the subject line; this will help your reader know what the email is about.
- Use 'cc' ('carbon copy', from the days of paper) and 'bcc' ('blind carbon copy') sparingly. Only send copies to those who really need to see the email. To explain 'cc' and 'bcc': if I am emailing Colin and cc Derek and bcc Ed, then Colin will see that I have copied the email to Derek but Colin will not see that I have copied the email to Ed. 'bcc' can also be useful for bulk emails when you don't want individuals to know who else is on your emailing list.
- Unless you are writing to a close colleague, include some form of opening and closing greetings. Your organization's policy and your own personality will guide you about what

is acceptable (e.g. I find 'Hi Martin' difficult to accept from someone I don't know at all).

● In a long email, put the key information at the beginning, so that it will be clear as your reader opens the email. Spend some time laying out your email. Plan in advance what you want to say. Group sentences in paragraphs concerned with one subject. Remember that if your message isn't clear to you, then it certainly won't be clear to your readers!

● Keep your sentences to 15–20 words. On one of the courses I teach on clear writing, a participant's key message was buried in brackets at the end of a 67-word sentence!

● Pay attention to the tone of your email. Could what you say be misinterpreted? 'I look forward to receiving your report soon' could be interpreted as 'Why are you late with it?' Add a suitable, sincere closing greeting.

● Make sure the spelling, grammar and punctuation are correct.

● Use abbreviations that are generally known, not obscure ones.

● Avoid capitals, which indicate shouting.

● Include other contact information at the end of your email, including your job title, phone numbers (landline, mobile) and postal address. Your reader might want to phone you to clarify a point.

● As with all forms of communication, check that what you are saying is accurate before you send it. We've all received emails inviting us to a meeting on Tuesday 14 September, only to discover that 14 September is a Wednesday. The result is that many colleagues spend precious time emailing requests for clarification and then having to respond a second time once they have the exact date. It would have been better if the person who originally sent the message had checked the details first.

Reading emails

Try to discipline yourself to opening and responding to emails at fewer points during the day. During periods that require concentrated work, switch your email off. The time taken to open an email and then think, 'I'll just reply to this now I've opened it', adds up and can have a significant effect on your overall work.

Don't forget the phone

To discuss something complex, communicating by telephone is often better than email. Before you make the call, jot down the points you want to discuss.

The phone also remains a useful tool to build and develop professional relationships, since you can react immediately and check whether someone has understood what you are trying to communicate and, if not, you can explain it again differently.

Meetings

Sometimes it seems as if life consists of going from one meeting to another without actually achieving anything. How can we make sure the meetings we attend count? We can consider:

- the purpose of meetings
- preparing for meetings
- chairing meetings
- participating in meetings
- following up from meetings.

The purpose of meetings

Meetings are useful to:

- inform colleagues, e.g. to introduce new goals or give an update on progress
- discuss with colleagues, e.g. plan together the way ahead or evaluate a solution to a problem
- reach a decision and agree the next steps to be taken.

Team meetings are also particularly useful in order to develop a sense of team identity as members interact with one another. As team leader you can use team meetings to motivate your team (look back at **Monday** and **Tuesday**).

Preparing for meetings

The key to a successful meeting lies in the preparation. It is essential that you:

- **Know the purpose of the meeting.** Many of our meetings have no clear purpose and could easily be shortened or even cancelled. You need to be crystal clear about what you are trying to achieve.
- **Plan a venue and time (start, finish) in advance.** I've been to some meetings at the stated venue but arrived there to find the meeting is in a different place
- **Invite the key people to participate in advance.** If you want a boss with a busy diary to be present, then it is no good inviting them the day before; you need to have invited them well in advance. It is also useful if you can discuss in advance, in private with key people, any agenda items that could be controversial.
- **Circulate an agenda in advance.** This means you will have thought about the structure and purpose of the meeting beforehand. Also, circulate important papers with the agenda rather than at the meeting itself. Ideally, such papers should be no more than one page each.
- **Prepare the meeting room.** Plan the seating: chairs around a table invite discussion; a chairperson at the end of a long table with ten seats either side, less so. If a PowerPoint presentation is being given, ensure that a projector and connecting lead are set up. Check that the heating or air conditioning works.
- **Read reports in advance.** If reports have been circulated before a meeting, then read them. I have been in too many meetings where we have sat during the meeting reading material which should have been read in advance.
- **Ensure that you come up with accurate information.** For example, if the meeting is one to monitor progress, take all your latest data on progress with you.

Chairing meetings

The chairperson is the person who sets the tone for the meeting and guides the participants through the discussion. Their tasks include:

- keeping to the agenda so the meeting starts and finishes on time

- introducing and welcoming newcomers, or asking participants to introduce themselves
- reviewing progress on action points from previous meetings
- bringing in key individuals to contribute at appropriate points
- stating key aims and objectives
- summarizing progress of the points being discussed
- drawing together the points discussed, to reach conclusions, to make decisions; if a point has been controversial, the chairperson can express exactly what is to be minuted, to avoid possible misinterpretation later
- ensuring action points are clear, particularly who is responsible for following up particular points. The action points should be SMART (specific, measurable, agreed, realistic, timed – see **Monday**).

A good chairperson is a diplomatic and organized leader, someone people trust and who values, motivates and involves others. Ideally, they will be able to quieten down those who talk too much and draw out those who talk too little but who can still make valuable contributions. A good chairperson will also sense when the time is right to bring a discussion to an end and will be able to come to clear decisions.

Participating in meetings

Everyone has a part to play in a successful meeting. I have never understood how people can come out of a meeting asking, 'What was the point of that?' when they themselves have not contributed anything. Each of us has a role to play by:

- listening well and concentrating: switch off your phone, avoid sending text messages, don't interrupt when someone else is talking
- asking for clarification if we are unsure about a point that has been made: it is highly likely that other colleagues will also want clarification but have been afraid to ask, e.g. for fear of looking ignorant
- being constructive: even if we disagree with what has been said, there are positive ways of expressing a difference of opinion by challenging an idea without angrily criticizing a person expressing an idea or publicly blaming an individual for a wrong action
- confronting issues: focus on the real issues – don't get sidetracked; too many of our meetings avoid discussing 'the elephant in the room', the subject everyone is aware of but is not discussed because it is too uncomfortable
- being willing to change your mind: if you are listening and persuasive arguments have been offered, then allow yourself to be convinced by them and change your opinion about an issue.

Videoconferencing

Videoconferencing means that you can link up with colleagues via the internet and avoid spending time and money travelling. Here are some tips to help you plan a videoconference session:

- Make sure the room in which the meeting takes place has good acoustics and is tidy.
- Agree and circulate the agenda in advance to all participants. Appoint a chairperson who can introduce the participants. Email any special presentations (e.g. PowerPoint) in advance.
- Identify individuals by having cards in front of them with their name on.
- Remind participants to look at the camera while they are talking. Ask participants to listen while other people are speaking.

Follow-up to meetings

A meeting where decisions are made but no one acts on these decisions is a waste of time. If colleagues have action points to pursue, they should follow them up.

The minutes of a meeting are a record of what happened in the meeting, including its action points. The person taking the minutes does not need to write down everything that goes on, but significant decisions, especially the action points concerning dates, schedules and financial matters must be noted specifically.

The sooner the minutes of a meeting are circulated to those who were present and other key colleagues, the more likely it is that people will follow up the action points asked of them.

A good chairperson will also follow through on progress of the key action items; they will not leave it to the next meeting only to discover that action has not been taken and valuable time has been lost.

Writing reports

- As with any other form of communication, think about what you want to say. One good way of helping you to start thinking about a report is to draw a pattern diagram (also known as a Mind Map). Take a blank piece of A4 paper. Arrange it in landscape position and write the subject matter of the report in the middle. (Write a word or a few words, but not a whole sentence.) You may find it helpful to work in pencil, so you can rub out what you write if necessary.
- Now write around your central word(s) the different key aspects that come to your mind. You do not need to list ideas in order of importance; simply write them down. To begin with, you do not need to join up the ideas with lines.
- If you get stuck at any point, ask yourself the question words 'why', 'how', 'what', 'who', 'when', 'where' and 'how much'. These may set you thinking.
- When I do this, I am often amazed at: (1) how easy the task is; it doesn't feel like work! The ideas and concepts seem to flow naturally and spontaneously. (2) How valuable that piece

of paper is. I have captured all (or at least some or many) of the key points. I don't want to lose that piece of paper!

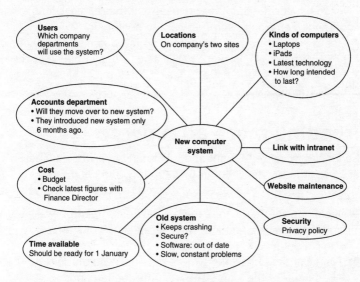

An example of a pattern diagram for a report on buying new computer systems

- Be clear about your audience, intention and response (see earlier today). This will determine, for example, how much information you should include in your reports. If in doubt, discuss with colleagues. In other words, don't agonize over writing ten pages when senior management only want one page.
- Use a report template that your company or organization has already established to give a structure to your report.
- Make sure your message is well planned and well structured.
- Write clearly and, if possible, simply, using only those abbreviations and technical expressions with which the readers of your report are familiar.
- Draft as much as you can to give yourself a psychological boost that you have actually written something. Then go back over your material, editing it.

- Be as concise as possible. You may have heard of the quotation, 'I have written you a long letter because I didn't have time to write you a short one.' Writing concisely is an art to be learnt – but it is very useful. If the report is long, present a one-page summary at the beginning.
- Use correct grammar and proper punctuation. Shortage of time is no excuse for using careless or sloppy English or the forms or abbreviations (textspeak, SMS language) you use to close friends.

Reading more effectively

So far today, we've thought about listening and writing. There are two other forms of communication: reading and speaking. Here are some guidelines to help you read more effectively:

- Decide on your aims in reading a particular text. Do you want simply to check a fact, gain an overall sense of a text, or grasp a detailed knowledge of a subject?
- If you want to undertake a more detailed read of the text:
  - Look out for the signposts: the introduction and conclusions; the words 'firstly', 'secondly'; the beginning of paragraphs; such expressions as 'on the one hand' and 'on the other hand' which guide you through the structure of the text, which can be helpful to your understanding.
  - Reword the main points in your mind, on computer or on paper. Express the author's key points in your own way.
  - Think about the author's argument: do you agree with them? Does the text make assumptions that you disagree with? Ask questions of the text and see if they are answered. Engage your mind.
  - At the end, see if you can recall the main points, or even better, see if you can explain the main points to someone else.

Reading statistics

Here are some guidelines on reading and understanding numbers presented in tables:

- Check the basics: the dates covered; the sources used; the scale used; the context of the figures, e.g. if the figures represent a sample, how large is that sample? Are the assumptions reasonable? Are certain figures omitted? Why? Check the definitions of terms used. Are they sound? If percentages are shown, percentages of what?
- Take one row or column and think through its content and implications to understand the data.
- Compare figures in columns and consider any trends. Do the numbers show a consistent pattern that increases or decreases? For example, is actual expenditure consistently higher than budgeted?
- Consider averages. Calculate the average for a particular row or column and see what variations and exceptions there are. Try to work out reasons for such differences, e.g. variations because of higher or lower income or differing levels of employment.
- Read the text that accompanies the data and check you agree with it; be particularly wary of phrases such as 'significant', 'these figures of course show'.
- Be careful about putting too much confidence in extrapolations of data that assume a trend will continue.

Giving presentations

As a manager, you will be called on at times to give a presentation. Here are some guidelines:

- Prepare by planning well. Know your audience. Senior managers? Colleagues?
- Work out your key messages. Be crystal clear on what you are trying to say. Express it in a maximum of 15 words on paper. Keep your 'headlines' simple. Don't try to cram too much in – 'less is more'.
  - Break down your key points into subpoints. Work on your words. Use short, everyday words rather than longer ones. So, use 'try' rather than 'endeavour'; 'need', not 'necessitate'; 'stop' or 'end' rather than 'terminate'; 'harmful' rather than 'detrimental'.

- Vary the way in which you communicate. Ask questions. Give a case study to back up the point you are making. Be creative. Find a picture that will illustrate your talk (but beware of any copyright issues).
- Work on the different parts of your presentation. Work especially hard on the beginning, so as to capture your audience's attention with your introduction ('Did you know ...?' 'I was reading in today's newspaper ...'), and the end ('So the next step is ...') to draw together and reinforce application of your key points.
- Structure your main points in a logical sequence. If you can structure them by making them all start with the same letter of the alphabet, or with 'ABC' (e.g. one of the talks I give on writing encourages the audience to be accurate, brief, concise), then your points will be more memorable.

- Think what the response of your audience is likely to be. Interested? Bored? In need of persuasion? Sceptical? Anticipate likely reactions by dealing with them in your preparation or in preparing answers to their questions.
- Know how long you will speak for. Fifteen minutes? An hour? People will be grateful if you finish early (but not too early!) but will not appreciate it if you go on too long.
- Prepare any handouts of your presentation. How many will you need? When will you give them out – before or after your presentation?
- Think of the practicalities. What is the layout of the seating? At one workshop I led with 45 delegates I complained that the suggested seating looked too much like that of an exam room, so we adjusted it. Don't forget the heating, lighting and air conditioning.
- Write down your presentation. Either write down (1) every word you plan to say or (2) notes that you can follow. If you do (1), then don't read it out word for word from your paper. Hopefully, your thoughts will have become part of your way of thinking. As you gain more experience, you will probably find you can work from notes.
- Be enthusiastic; be positive. You've a message to declare. Go for it! Be natural; be yourself. It took me years to discover and work out my own style for giving presentations. I was

amazed when a colleague contacted me after a space of five years to ask me to lead a workshop at his company. He said, 'I remember your style'.

● Factor in a break. If your presentation is going to last longer than 45 minutes, then schedule a break so that your audience can relax for a few minutes.

If you are using a PowerPoint presentation:

● Allow plenty of time to prepare the presentation, particularly if you are not familiar with the presentation software.
● Don't try to put too much information on the slides. Keep to your headings, not the complete outline of your talk.
● Keep to one main font. Use a large font, ideally at least 28 pt. Aim to have no more than six lines per slide (do you remember peering over people's heads trying to read tiny print on a slide?). A sans serif font is easier to read than a serif one. Headings arranged left (not centred) are easier to read; capitals and lower case letters are also easier to read than text in all capitals.
● Work out which colours work well, e.g. red on grey, yellow on blue.
● Use tables and charts to support your message. Bar charts, pie charts, flow charts giving the key information all work well.

- Use illustrations that support your message, not ones that show off your (lack of!) design or animation skills.
- Don't put the key information at the bottom of slides; colleagues far away from the screen may not be able to see over other people's heads.
- Rehearse the presentation with your notes/text in advance.
- Check whether you or a colleague will supply the projector and leads to connect the projector to your laptop and a screen. Arrive early to set everything up.
- Put your presentation on a memory stick (saved in earlier versions of PowerPoint for good measure) in case your laptop fails and you have to view it from someone else's laptop.
- Make sure that when you give your presentation, your eye contact is with your audience, not with your laptop or the screen.

Negotiating: win-win situations

In negotiating, we are aiming for a win-win situation. (This is different from normal behaviour where one person wins at the expense of another's loss.) For example, my son Ben has just moved to Asia and he wanted to sell his camera. His friend Rob wanted a camera to take photographs on his travels. Ben sold Rob his camera. Both won: both gained what they wanted – Ben money, Rob a camera.

In his book *The 7 Habits of Highly Effective People*, Stephen Covey points out that the key to a win-win situation is our character.

If you're high on courage and low on consideration, how will you think? Win-Lose. You'll be strong and ego-bound. You'll have the courage of your convictions, but you won't be very considerate of others. ...

If you're high on consideration and low on courage, you'll think Lose-Win. You'll be so

*considerate of others' feelings that you won't
have the courage to express your own. ...*

**High courage and consideration are both
essential to Win-Win. It's the balance of
the two that is the mark of real maturity.
If you have it, you can listen and you can
empathically understand, but you can also
courageously confront.**

The 7 Habits of Highly Effective People Personal Handbook,
Stephen Covey (Simon & Schuster, 2003), p. 91.

Colleagues who negotiate win-wins:

- communicate clearly, honestly and positively
- treat the opinions of others with respect, listening well
- respond constructively to possible areas of improvement.

Based on *The 7 Habits of Highly Effective People Personal Handbook*,
Stephen Covey (Simon & Schuster, 2003), p. 93–4.

A good negotiator

Danielle was respected as a good negotiator in contracts.
The secret of her success lay in good planning. She spent a
long time thinking through different business models and
pricing levels so that when it came to the negotiations,
she knew exactly what approach to take. After both sides
had presented their initial case, she was sometimes able
to detect the weak points in the arguments of the other
side and exploit them according to her own personality.
When they came to the final bargaining she had clarified
the critical issue (the price) in her mind and knew the
less significant matters she could be flexible on – she
didn't mind bringing delivery of the products earlier by
six weeks. She was assertive and firm on what was non-
negotiable, however: the price. So she was able to settle
and close deals well and arrange the next steps in business
relationships between the two sides.

Resolving conflict

At times you are bound to meet conflict. Trust breaks down. Personalities clash. Departments each want a bigger slice of the budget or want to avoid the most cutbacks.

Deal with conflict quickly; tackle the issues. Don't be cautious and fearful about speaking directly and clearly about difficulties.

You may find the books *Difficult conversations: how to discuss what matters most* (by Douglas Stone, Bruce Patton, Sheila Heen), Michael Joseph, 1999, and *The Peacemaker: a biblical guide to resolving personal conflict* (by Ken Sande), Baker, 1991, very useful. The following is based on what those authors helpfully suggest:

- Distinguish the incident – what is happening/happened – from feelings about the incident. Consider separately:
  - The incident – someone said something; someone is to blame. Try to focus on the real issue. Listen closely. Ask open questions. Understand other people's interests as well as your own.
  - Feelings about the incident, e.g. anger, hurt.
  - The identity of the person. Sometimes, a person's identity, including their self-worth, will feel threatened. Calmly affirm your respect for them.
- Do what you can to resolve the issue and maintain the relationship if possible; prepare and evaluate possible solutions to agree on the way forward.

Under pressure

Elaine was under pressure. She was actually doing two jobs, each taking up three days a week. She was getting very stressed and knew she could not continue doing such work indefinitely. At both informal one-to-ones and the formal half-yearly appraisal she expressed frustration with her manager Ron. Ron said he would act to resolve the difficulty, but unfortunately, over a period of several months, nothing happened. He awkwardly avoided eye contact with her whenever they passed in the corridor.

Things turned out better, however, when Ron moved on and was replaced by Sheila. Her motto was 'under-promise and over-deliver' so, for example, when she said she would check the financial data for the previous month by the end of week 3 in the following month, invariably she had completed it by the end of week 2. So within a few weeks of Sheila taking on Ron's role, she had sorted out Elaine's work patterns to everyone's satisfaction. Soon Elaine began to enjoy her work again.

Summary

Today has been concerned with communicating effectively:

- listening well
- asking the right kinds of questions
- communicating in different ways, e.g. email, phone, writing
- running better meetings
- writing better reports
- reading more effectively
- giving good presentations
- negotiating well and resolving conflict.

Next steps

What practical steps do you need to take to improve the following? Choose three areas you particularly need to focus on:

1 your listening skills
2 your questioning skills
3 your planning of emails
4 your writing skills
5 your reading skills
6 your planning of meetings
7 the effectiveness of your meetings
8 your presentation skills
9 your negotiation skills
10 your ability to resolve conflict

Fact-check (answers at the back)

1. Reflective listening is:
   a) thinking about listening ❏
   b) rephrasing what someone has said to you ❏
   c) listening to yourself while looking in a mirror ❏
   d) meditating on life. ❏

2. When sending emails:
   a) cc everyone who could be interested ❏
   b) use cc sparingly, only to those who really need to see the email ❏
   c) keep cc on all the time ❏
   d) I don't know what cc stands for. ❏

3. When reading emails:
   a) answer them all immediately ❏
   b) delay answering them until Friday afternoon ❏
   c) look at them at particular times, so you can concentrate on your work ❏
   d) never answer them at all. ❏

4. When attending a meeting:
   a) arrive late ❏
   b) fiddle with a pen ❏
   c) arrive promptly, having read the agenda and reports ❏
   d) arrive promptly, not having read the agenda and reports. ❏

5. During meetings:
   a) be indecisive ❏
   b) never reach a decision ❏
   c) come to decisions but don't record them ❏
   d) come to decisions and ensure they are properly recorded and reviewed. ❏

6. At the end of a meeting:
   a) stay behind to clear up ❏
   b) forget the action points ❏
   c) act on the points that it was agreed you would follow up ❏
   d) complain that it was a waste of time. ❏

7. When writing reports:
   a) show off everything you have learnt ❏
   b) be selective about what you have learnt ❏
   c) use long words to try to impress your boss ❏
   d) don't worry about wrong grammar, spelling or punctuation. ❏

8. When preparing a presentation:
   a) put a maximum of six lines on one slide ❏
   b) put all your points and subpoints on one slide ❏
   c) put all of your talk on the various slides ❏
   d) try to impress colleagues with your animation skills. ❏

9. In resolving conflict:
   a) ignore people's feelings ❏
   b) don't listen to what happened ❏
   c) only listen to people's feelings and ignore the real issues ❏
   d) distinguish the real issue from colleagues' emotional responses to the issue. ❏

10. Preparing for negotiations is:
    a) a waste of time ❏
    b) essential ❏
    c) a luxury ❏
    d) sometimes worthwhile. ❏

FRIDAY

Managing
a project

As part of your work as a manager, you've been asked to manage a project. You feel excited but also rather overwhelmed at the prospect. The challenge seems great. Where do you begin?

- Lay firm foundations as you clarify your project and plan carefully.
- Gather together the key personnel involved in the project and clearly communicate to them the project's aims, outputs and schedule.
- Break down the project into smaller parts.
- Cost your project well as you draw up a budget. Make sure you have rigorous controls in place to monitor costs and quality as you implement the project.
- Implement your project successfully. After preparing well, you can now put the project into practice.
- Complete the project's final stages and evaluate your project. What lessons can you learn for next time? What went well ... and what did not go so well?

Planning your project

When I begin a project, I use a pattern diagram (see **Thursday**) to help me in my initial thinking. If you do the same, all sorts of thoughts will come to you.

For a start, discuss with your end users their precise requirements. What do they want – and what do they not want? Consider the project's context. What needs is it intended to satisfy? How has the present situation developed? How does the project align with the overall strategy of your company or organization?

You can then:

- Work out the best way to deliver the required outputs. What precisely does the customer want to be delivered?
- Consider the size of the team of people you will need in order to meet those requirements.
- Prepare a schedule for the project. When are the final outputs needed? For example, if the project is to complete the manufacture of toys for Christmas, they need to be available for delivery in, say, September not December. Work backwards, including the key stages as you now see them, to where you are now.
- Work out costs and prepare a budget. Make a business case and gain approval for the project from senior management.
- Ensure you have the agreement of senior management for your aims, outcomes and the resources needed. This may involve carrying out a feasibility study to make sure the project is sound.
- Develop monitoring procedures to help you control the agreed costs.
- Assess possible risks you may face. For example: is the authority of the project leader clear? Is the schedule realistic? Have sufficient financial resources been made available?

Assemble a project team

At an early stage in your planning, gather colleagues into a project team to ensure that the preparation is undertaken well.

The people or organizations with a strong interest in the outcome of a project are called its stakeholders. Circulate a list of stakeholders, showing their names, job titles, contact details (phone, mobile, email, fax).

The stakeholders would typically be:

- **Project sponsor:** a senior member of staff, e.g. a director, who can prove that the project's costs and benefits are worthwhile. They will also need to convince other colleagues that the project is important enough to pursue given certain resources. They will have the authority to reach decisions and approve the spending of the required money and other resources.
- **Project manager** (probably you): the person who reports to the project sponsor and is responsible for implementing the project. The project sponsor should give the project manager the responsibility and authority to carry out the project.
- **Team members**: the project manager, in liaison with the project sponsor, can delegate tasks to members of the team. If team members are less experienced, then as project manager you will need to train, monitor and supervise your colleagues more.
- **The users** (or customers): the people who will use the end result of the project. It is important not merely to consult such people but to understand their needs and involve them at every stage of the project so that they 'own' it and feel a valued part of the decision-making process.
- **The suppliers**: the people who carry out tasks or provide services to assist in the completion of the project. They

may be within or outside your organization. Examples are colleagues working in departments dealing with sales, accounts or computers. Suppliers will ensure that the requirements of the project are met within the agreed timescale and financial resources.

Updating a website

Jones & Co wanted to update their website to make it more usable by its customers and to enable customers to order goods online. As manager, Sally called together colleagues from sales, IT and marketing departments to discuss how to tackle the project. Because Sally involved colleagues from the different departments, she made sure the project was planned well. At the meeting, they discussed a range of ideas, divided the work into three different stages and allocated someone responsible for each stage, with definite dates given for the completion of each stage. After the meeting, Sally circulated the minutes to each participant. The result was a well-planned basis for the project.

Defining a scope of work

Having undertaken your initial planning, you can now add further detail to the thinking to produce a 'scope of work', a statement of the project's objectives and outcomes. This builds on the information that you have already obtained.

A statement of the scope of work is important for two reasons:

● It may form part of the legal contract between you and outside suppliers. If disagreements arise, the different sides will turn to the contract (scope of work) to read what is stated there about the disputed matter.
● It also provides a definite standard against which progress can be measured.

The scope of work will include statements of:

● the project's objectives, background, scope and limits (i.e. what the project is and is not going to do)

- the customers' expectations – this should specify in detail what the project will deliver (e.g. the exact type and number of products)
- the budget, showing the financial resources needed
- a list of other physical resources (e.g. new offices, computers)
- criteria for acceptance (e.g. if I am writing a book, the publisher will make a payment to me only when they consider the work I deliver is of an acceptable standard)
- a list of the main colleagues on the project team
- delivery dates for the products
- assumptions made about the project; risks that could have an effect on the implementation of the project.

A contract will include a scope of work and will specify payments and payment dates (e.g. linked to the delivery of certain products) and other relevant facts, such as patents on products and rights of ownership.

Dividing up the work

Chris felt overwhelmed by the sheer enormity of the project to begin with, but it seemed less daunting when he broke up the work into separate manageable parts. He did this in a work breakdown structure, which showed the project's various tasks. Although his aim was to list all the significant tasks, he knew he would not achieve that immediately, so he discussed the tasks with more experienced colleagues, developing successively more exact definitions of what he wanted to achieve, until he gradually reached the goal of a full specification. He also compiled a spreadsheet showing the tasks, roles and times needed for the different tasks. He had been advised by his senior manager to make allowances in the schedule for project start-up, administration and holidays and also for staff illness and other possible contingencies that could affect the schedule. He was then in a position to allocate members of his team to the various activities, considering how long each activity would take.

Costing your project
Work out the cost of your project

From the work breakdown structure, you can now begin to assign costs.

- Decide who will undertake the work: you, colleagues in your department, colleagues in other departments, or will you outsource some of the work to an outside supplier? For each one of these, you need to know the hourly (or day) rate of the people concerned. Also check to what extent company overheads are included if your project is charged for colleagues from another department in your organization.
- Decide how much work to outsource to outside suppliers, for example if they have greater expertise than your own staff. You will need to give them a precise brief as to the work required, including schedule, work required and payment. Remember to build into your budget time to brief a range of possible suppliers, evaluate their bids and reach a decision on who to choose, brief the supplier at the outset of the work, administer and keep track of their work.
- Decide an approximate level of contingency to handle risks and other uncertain events that will arise.

Working out your hourly rate

Suppose you earn £20,000 per year. If we divide this figure by the number of days you work productively, i.e. omitting holidays and allowing for illness, this could give 46 weeks per year: £20,000 ÷ 46 = £434.78 per week or £86.96 per day, assuming 5 days per week. If we divide that figure by the time per day you spend working productively, say two-thirds of seven hours (= 4.66 hours), that comes to £18.66 per hour. This is the amount you are paid per hour gross, i.e. before tax and other deductions.

That is only half the story, however. Your actual cost to your organization is about twice that figure, allowing for the overheads, taxes it pays as an employer, rent of office building, heating, power, water, etc. So the cost to your company or organization is £18.66 × 2 = £37.32 per hour.

This means that if a business meeting lasts seven hours and is attended by six colleagues, then the cost of that meeting to the organization is 7 × 6 × £37.32 = £1567.44. This is probably significantly more than you thought!

Return on investment

Return on investment is the percentage return you make over a certain time as a result of undertaking the project. It is calculated according to the formula:

ROI = (profits [or benefits] ÷ investment [your costs]) × 100

One way of considering return on investment is to work out the payback period, the time taken for the profits or benefits to cover the cost of your investment.

For example, a project to train all your staff in report-writing skills might cost £50,000, including fee for tutor, materials and administration. Its benefits could be measured in terms of savings of work time and productivity increases of £60,000 over one year, so the return on investment is (60,000 ÷ 50,000) × 100 = 120%.

Finalize the project budget

Ensure that you have included the cost of:

- colleagues: the time spent by your colleagues, colleagues in other departments, people in outside companies or organizations, including start-up and administration time
- equipment or facilities needed for the project, such as computers or offices
- other human-resource costs such as recruitment and training
- other departments' costs such as IT and marketing.

Your budget should also include:

- cash-flow predictions during the whole of your project
- any income forecasts that are part of the project
- the cost centres to which particular items of expenditure will be allocated during the implementation of the project
- contingency: a figure of about 10 per cent of your total costs is often suggested.

Example of extract of a budget for a conference	
Costs	£
Speaker	4,000
Venue	6,000
Marketing	3,000
Administration	3,000
Office	2,000
Contingency	2,000
	20,000
Income	
Delegates' fees	22,000
Net profit	2,000

You can work out the break-even point (the point at which the money you receive covers your costs). For example, if delegates' fees are £400 each, you will need 50 delegates (50 × £400 = £20,000) to cover costs. So the break-even point is £20,000. If you have more than 50 delegates (e.g. in the example shown the income is £22,000, i.e. 55 delegates at £400 each), a profit is made. If you have fewer than 50 delegates, you will make a loss.

Implementing your project

As you put the project into practice:

- Confirm commitments of the key personnel involved and the financial resources available. Check that they can all start on a certain date or as soon as possible afterwards.
- Continue communicating with the other stakeholders to keep them in the picture about the status of the project.
- Make sure you have defined the activities each person needs to undertake. Look at your work breakdown structure and make sure that it specifies:
  - the work to be undertaken
  - the start and end dates
  - key milestones: when certain proportions of the work are completed; when a certain level of income has been achieved; or when a certain output has been delivered and accepted by the customer/user.
- Keep your work breakdown structure as accurate and up to date as possible.
- Control the project's costs by ensuring you have mechanisms in place to record actual expenditure, assigning costs to particular cost centres.
- Prepare monthly summary statements of actual costs and income against those in the project budget, keeping the budget and cash flow as accurate as possible.
- Plan for change, whether on a significant scale in a major disaster (e.g. an act of terrorism or a prolonged period of severe adverse weather), internal project changes or small changes.
- Keep going, remaining focused, positive and determined.

Rescuing a failing project

Imran was called in to trouble-shoot a failing project. The existing project manager was not coping with the responsibilities of the project. Fortunately, Imran had a good working relationship with him. Imran quickly noticed that basic points were missing: meetings were poorly structured with the barest agenda. During the meetings, discussions rambled on without decisions being made. Even when key action points were agreed, they were not noted, followed through or even reviewed at the next meeting. It was hardly surprising that the project was in a mess! As Imran had good relationships with all his colleagues, he was quickly able to put in place well-structured meetings, good chairmanship, minute-taking, action points and reviews at the next meeting.

He also paid particular attention to making sure there were regular progress reports, showing: a summary of the project's progress; the stages completed in the previous month; the actual hours spent on the various stages; actual costs incurred; variations from expected figures in costs and output, together with reasons for those variations; and finally a forecast of the new final completion date and costs.

With good people-management abilities and detailed task-orientated skills, Imran got the project back on track successfully.

Completing a project

You will have agreed a list of the items you need to complete as clearly defined signs that the project has come to an end. These could include:

- ensuring the output of a certain number of products
- ensuring that the quality of what you deliver reaches the agreed criteria, e.g. verifying that a computer software system fulfils the required specifications

- testing new equipment to make sure it functions to the required standard
- training end users, e.g. by preparing manuals or running courses for those who will use the computer equipment you have installed
- completing final administrative tasks, e.g. final progress reports, especially those concerned with financial resources.

Evaluating your project

The project is complete! You're celebrating and are enjoying the feeling of a job well done. Is there more to be done? Yes: you need to conduct a post-project evaluation. This brings together the project's key points so you can see what went well, what did not go so well and also, significantly, what lessons you can learn for the future.

Acknowledge failures

The critical aspect here is to learn from your mistakes – neither to ignore them and pretend they did not happen nor make them so widely known that blame is attached to an individual for the rest of their working life. If your organization has good relationships, then trust and respect will have developed.

Don't be content with the superficial lesson. Look for the deeper reasons, such as why a project was delayed:

- Were adequate monitoring controls in place?
- Were communications good between colleagues, or were key colleagues not informed about significant decisions?

However, ensure that the evaluation is professional: your purpose is not to attach blame on individuals but to be positive and to outline a few realistic lessons that can be learnt and applied in future projects. For example, don't say: 'Chris forgot to order the spare parts on time', but: 'Checks need to be made in advance that orders for spare parts are submitted two weeks before they are needed.' Any constructive criticism of individuals' contributions should be undertaken privately, not in a wider forum.

A project well delivered

I was recently in charge of a project to deliver 5,000 books to an exhibition in the UK in March. We delivered the text to the printers on schedule in October, but were delayed by packaging difficulties which meant that, with shipping time, the books would not reach the UK until April. We therefore had to send the books by airfreight to meet the March deadline. The result was a satisfied customer: we delivered what we said we would. We focused on fulfilling the customer's expectations, even though we incurred higher costs of airfreight.

We later held an evaluation meeting for this project, at which all the key personnel were present. The decision to send 5,000 copies by airfreight was commended – the books were well received and sold out at the exhibition. Minor suggestions were made to improve the design. Costs were reviewed, which were slightly over budget.

The response to the initial set of books was so good that we agreed to produce a further set for next year. Schedule and costs were agreed. Finally, a suggestion was made to tighten up on our internal communications between team members to make them even more effective. Minutes of the meeting have been circulated to record the lessons learnt.

Recognize success

As well as acknowledging failures, mistakes and where you could have undertaken the work better, also recognize those areas that have gone well.

Identify what you have delivered. For example:

- the desired output in terms of the products, services, etc. delivered
- outputs measured according to the agreed quality standards
- actual expenditure compared with the original budget
- a good return on investment – compare the benefits that your organization has received against the costs incurred

- the actual time taken compared with the original schedule
- robust control procedures in place to track and monitor costs and schedules
- efficient organization so that roles and responsibilities were clearly defined
- good communication between members of the team
- the satisfaction of your customers/users and other stakeholders with the outcomes of your project.

Check the financial figures to see how actual expenditure compared with the planned expenditure in your original budget.

Acknowledge your team's work. Affirm key individuals as you thank them for their work. Celebrate your team's success in a way that is appropriate to your company or organization, inviting your project sponsor, your customers/users and other stakeholders. You could, for example, pay for a meal out for all the staff concerned and their partners.

Document lessons learnt. Identify what worked well ... and what did not go so well, and consider what measures should be taken to avoid making the same mistakes again. Such documented identification will help you on future projects. Produce a final end-of-project review and report for your project sponsor, summarizing the progress of the project, the lessons learnt and any recommendations. Ensure that these are written up. Keep your record, especially of good practice and measures to be taken to avoid making the same mistakes again.

Summary

Today, we've looked at managing a project and its various stages:

● preparing for and planning your project well, laying firm foundations as you clarify the aims and parameters and begin to assemble a project team
● working hard at costing your project in a budget, including a contingency figure to cover unexpected events
● making sure you have rigorous controls in place that monitor costs and quality as you implement the project
● putting the project into practice and completing its final stages
● evaluating your project so that you can learn lessons for next time.

Next steps

For a project you are to undertake:

1 Define its aims in 15 words.
2 Begin to work on a budget.
3 What monitoring and reporting controls do you have in place to track costs, quality and schedules?
4 Work out the hourly rate that you cost your company or organization.

Fact-check (answers at the back)

1. Defining project aims is:
a) a waste of time ❏
b) important if you can
   spare the time ❏
c) nice to have ❏
d) essential. ❏

2. A project needs:
a) spontaneity ❏
b) careful planning ❏
c) no planning ❏
d) poor motivation. ❏

3. Stakeholders are:
a) only the users of the project ❏
b) the team members
   of a project ❏
c) all the key people
   involved in a project ❏
d) the directors at lunch. ❏

4. A work breakdown structure is:
a) a plan for when the
   project breaks down ❏
b) a plan of the benefits
   of a project ❏
c) a plan of the different
   activities in a project ❏
d) a plan of the people
   needed in a project. ❏

5. When compiling a schedule,
   include the following:
a) time for lunch ❏
b) time for holidays ❏
c) money spent on office
   equipment ❏
d) staff salaries. ❏

6. Contingencies refer to:
a) unplanned events
   that could significantly
   delay the project ❏
b) planned events that could
   significantly delay the project ❏
c) bad weather ❏
d) good weather. ❏

7. Your project budget should be:
a) as cool as possible ❏
b) as futuristic as possible ❏
c) as flexible as possible ❏
d) as exact as possible. ❏

8. A cost centre is:
a) a unit to which items of
   expenditure are allocated
   in a project ❏
b) a supermarket that
   sells good quality food ❏
c) a unit of profit ❏
d) a measure of the
   company's overheads. ❏

9. Tracking changes involves:
a) monitoring and reporting
   changes to control them ❏
b) correcting your text ❏
c) reporting only positive
   changes to the project board ❏
d) only monitoring changes
   and doing nothing with
   your results. ❏

10. When dealing with lessons you have learnt:

a) discuss them, but don't write them down ❏

b) discuss them and write them down but do nothing about them ❏

c) note them and act on them in future ❏

d) ignore them, so that you make the same mistakes again. ❏

SATURDAY

Managing
yourself

So, we're coming to the end of our week. How have you been getting on? We've looked at managing people and teams, managing work procedures, communication and projects. Perhaps the greatest challenge – even more difficult than some of those just listed – is learning to manage yourself. So in a sense, managing yourself is the key to unlocking your potential so that you can be a successful manager.

Today we will consider:

- being aware of yourself
- getting organized
- making good use of your time
- managing your boss
- coping with stress.

Each of these is important as you develop as a manager. If you don't give them any attention then you will probably still function as a manager but there will be severe limitations on your effectiveness. With them sorted, you will fulfil your potential and be successful.

Being aware of yourself

What kind of person are you? Quiet or assertive? Decisive or unsure? Confident or timid? Good at analysing words and figures or better with people? Excellent at details; not so good at the big picture – or the other way round? Highly emotional or more controlled? Good or poor at motivating others?

Ask trusted friends, but remember that you can change. My normal personality is to be quiet, retiring even, but over a period of time I made myself talk to people in social situations to the point where I am now much more confident and relaxed about meeting new people. You can change. If necessary, undertake training in areas where you need to develop: seek professional help, including a coach or mentor, for deeper guidance.

Getting organized

As a manager, you need to be organized:

- Tidy your desk. Remove clutter of paperclips, elastic bands and boxes of staples (which you probably rarely use). Put them away in a place where you can find them. Giving yourself space for your essential papers, monitor and keyboard or laptop, will give you room to think.
- If you have an in-tray and out-tray, make use of them. Sort out the papers that have stayed at the bottom of your in-tray for some time.

- Make sure your chair is well adjusted and has a foot rest.
- Arrange your computer screen at a safe and comfortable height, with the top of the screen just below eye level and at least 63 cm (about 25 inches) from your eyes.

Managing your time

Here are some tips on good time management.

Know what time of day you work best. Are you a morning person or an afternoon person? Jealously guard the time at which you work best: make sure that you use that period of time for completing tasks that require high levels of energy and creative thinking, not for doing routine administrative jobs. Don't be tempted to say, 'I'll just get these little things out of the way' at this time; instead, undertake the most challenging piece of work.

Have some form of diary: paper, electronic, digital, in the cloud – the medium doesn't matter, but the principle is vital. You need to write down (or its electronic equivalent) your tasks and appointments, what you have to do, where you have to be, who you have to email or phone.

Work out a system that functions well for you. I personally write down all my tasks (large projects, meetings, minor routine admin) on the relevant day in my A4 week-to-view diary. At the end of a day, I prepare the next day's to-do list. This used to be a straightforward list, but I now turn my A4 page to landscape orientation and list major tasks/meetings/appointments on the left-hand side, phone calls and emails in the centre, and minor routine tasks on the right-hand side. Look at your to-do list during the day and cross off the tasks as you complete them. Work not completed one day goes onto the next day's to-do list.

Distinguish the urgent and important from the less important. Some tasks are urgent – others can wait. Plan in all important tasks. Begin now with the important and urgent. Plan ahead. I plan major projects on a weekly basis on a wall planner and also on the Friday before the following week. (So on Friday afternoons I plan the work for both the next week and also the following Monday.)

Be proactive; set priorities – focus on the big picture, but also don't forget to see your priorities work out practically.

Start with undertaking the tasks you don't want to do, or the largest or most difficult part of a task. As noted above, don't say to yourself, 'I'll just get these little jobs done and then I'll go on to the longer task' – that could mean you delay getting started. And if you've got only 35 minutes available for a task (before a meeting, for example) challenge yourself to fit in 45 minutes' worth of work – rather than saying to yourself, 'It's only just over half an hour – how can I manage to do much in that time?'

Put regular items in the diary. I have a major monthly planning time on a Thursday afternoon in week three of every month (Thursday, as I know I complete my creative work Monday to Wednesday; afternoon, as I complete my major thinking tasks in the morning; week three, as I have accurate figures from reconciled bank account data by that time in the month).

File clearly, whether on hard copy or digitally. Think where you are going to be able to retrieve that document from most easily. File under such directories as 'accounts', 'sales', 'invoices'. File in alphabetical or date order.

Write notes to yourself. Perhaps you think you will be able to recall a particular point, but why tax your brain with trying to remember information, particularly if it's detailed? I know I've got to proofread a book in a month's time, so I've already built up a file containing points I want to check.

Work efficiently. Group all your outgoing phone calls and respond to emails only at certain times of the day.

Deal with papers only once. Read a document then act on it or bin it. Don't keep returning to the same piece of paper: be decisive. Only file documents that are important and that you need to keep.

Get things right first time. Going over a piece of work and having to undo what went wrong earlier is a bad use of time. Not only is your work affected, but that of other colleagues and probably the perception of your customers too. Quality in your work now is vital.

Delegate work more: See **Tuesday.**

Make the most of 'slack' time, e.g. when you are waiting for the computer or printer or in a few odd minutes before a meeting. Catch up on non-urgent reading or compose a routine email during such times.

Use your computer as a computer, not just as a typewriter. One key feature I often use is 'autocorrect'. So I've stored on my computer many of the basic English words we constantly use (e.g. the, that, was, were, because, and) and have reduced them to a smaller number of keystrokes: e.g. 't' for the, 'th' for that, 'w1' for was, 'w2' for were, 'bec' for because, 'a1' for and). I did this (and with hundreds of other words too) in preparation for an 8,000,000-word book I edited over a period of six years, and I reckon it saved me two weeks' work. So if the name of your company or organization has, say, 20 keystrokes, you can type an abbreviated form. For how to use autocorrect, press F1 in Word and follow the links, or type 'autocorrect' into the Word help menu on a Mac.

Managing your boss

It may seem odd to include a section on managing your boss in a book *Introducing Management*, but you need to remember that you need to communicate not only with those who report to you but you also with your boss to whom you report.

● Find out about your boss's aims, values, challenges and style. Adapt to their style. For example, my boss prefers contact by phone rather than email, so I'm alert to that and adapt accordingly. He dislikes detail and wants the bottom line, so although I love detail, I have to follow his way.

- Communicate at the right level, usually giving more information rather than less. Keep your boss as informed as they want to be. If you can see a problem looming ahead, alert your boss as soon as possible, so that they are aware of it and can act accordingly before the matter becomes serious.
- When presenting your boss with a problem, offer a solution at the same time. This shows you have thought about it.
- Support your manager in meetings. Be loyal to them.
- Discuss priorities with your boss and make decisions with them. Discuss what they want you to do, especially if they continue to give you task after task. Agree on your goals and then, when your boss gives you an additional task, discuss with them whether that achieves the agreed goal or not. If necessary, give them the responsibility of making the decision: 'Actually, I'm working on [this project] now. What do you want me to do?' Learn to say no when necessary.

Management styles

At his interview, Carl was asked about which management style he adopted. Wisely he responded that he had several, to suit different occasions, the people he is managing and the tasks they are doing, rather than having a 'one-size-fits-all' approach.

So he said that at times his style is democratic, involving the whole team in the decision-making process. He uses this especially in change-management situations when he wants the team to be committed to change. At other times, particularly when dealing with very urgent matters, he is directional and simply has to tell people what to do ('The customer has changed his mind and wants new figures by 3.00 p.m. today'). That wasn't his preferred style, however, he added, wanting to give responsibility to his team members, together with training, support and clear instructions and trusting them to get on with the tasks using their own good judgment.

Coping with stress

We're coming to the end of our week on *Introducing Management* and you may be feeling a little overwhelmed: managing people, teams, policies and procedures, projects ... good communication is vital, as is the ability to manage yourself. How can you avoid getting stressed out by it all?

Acknowledge that stress will come. In fact, a little stress may

be good for you, but if it gets out of control it can become a problem. You may know the particular ways in which stress may affect you personally. Plan for it, even though you won't know when it may strike:

- Build in regular times off. Don't overfill every moment of your 24 hours. For example, if you're busy for two weeks, make sure in week 3 you have some slack 'me' time.
- Build in regular patterns of exercise and breaks. Join a gym; play sport. During the first few years of my working life I pushed myself too hard and had to learn to relax. So now I make myself take regular walks. However brief, physical exercise helps. I find the occasional walk in a nearby park at lunch helps particularly.
- Eat and drink sensibly. You know the rules – apply them! You can't remain healthy in the long term on a diet of junk food, and drinking and smoking excessively.

- Have a life outside work – yes, really! Spend time with your partner, family, friends. Join a club. Take up a hobby. Take holidays without feeling guilty … and without all your electronic gadgets! Take up other activities and be reminded what it is to be human.

If it all gets too much:

- Visit your GP.
- Switch off the TV or computer earlier and get more sleep.
- Discuss matters with your boss. Can you be relieved of some areas of work? Can some activities be delayed? Delegate more!
- Focus on what you can do – a little is better than nothing.
- Learn relaxation techniques for your body – even simple deep-breathing techniques can work wonders. Focus on the positive in your mind.

Saying no

Bob felt flattered to be asked to join a committee to look at succession planning, but he wasn't sure about it. He felt he was already fully stretched and that a further commitment might just be too much. Bob had lunch with Mike, the chairman, who told him about the responsibilities, but Bob said no at that time. Bob added that he thought it likely his other commitments would lessen six months later when he was due to have an assistant who could cover some of his responsibilities. Sure enough, six months later, Mike asked Bob again and then, with some fresh capacity because he had the assistant, Bob accepted the offer.

Summary

I wish you well with your role as manager. You will have successes ... and probably a few failures. (Remember, 'the person who never made mistakes never made anything'.) The main thing is that you will learn about how to get the best out of other people – how to motivate them, how to inspire them – and how to get the best out of yourself.

Soon you will have mastered everything in Week 1 and be ready for further promotion as your career progresses. Remember, go for quality: it's all very well dreaming about the future, but do a good job with the task in hand now.

Next steps

1 What are your strengths and weaknesses? What can you change?

2 What is the next step in your company or organization? What do you want to talk over with your coach or mentor?

3 What courses could you go on for training in specific areas (e.g. new software, time management) and wider areas like leadership?

4 How could you be better organized?

5 Think of three ways in which you can make better use of your time. Plan them into your diary for next week now.

6 Work on changing your lifestyle and work patterns to help you cope with stress.

Fact-check (answers at the back)

1. Being organized as a manager is:
   a) a nice-to-have ❏
   b) unimportant ❏
   c) essential ❏
   d) I'm too laid back to answer. ❏

2. As a manager, having a diary or some form of recording work and appointments is:
   a) essential ❏
   b) nice to have ❏
   c) unimportant ❏
   d) I haven't got the time to answer. ❏

3. Always complete the important tasks before the tasks that are urgent.
   a) True ❏
   b) I'm not sure. ❏
   c) I don't care. ❏
   d) False ❏

4. Complete all the small tasks before tackling the major ones.
   a) False ❏
   b) True ❏
   c) I'm not sure. ❏
   d) I don't care. ❏

5. Forward planning is:
   a) a luxury ❏
   b) I haven't got the time to answer. ❏
   c) a waste of time ❏
   d) essential ❏

6. Spending time thinking how and where to file documents is:
   a) I haven't got the time to answer. ❏
   b) essential ❏
   c) a nice-to-have ❏
   d) a waste of time ❏

7. When I present my boss with a problem:
   a) I leave them to come up with a solution. ❏
   b) I don't trust them to solve it. ❏
   c) I also come up with a solution. ❏
   d) I never see my boss. ❏

8. I know what days of the week and what time of day I work best and so:
   a) I treat that time like any other period of time. ❏
   b) I do my best to guard and reserve that time for quality work. ❏
   c) I fill that time with small routine tasks. ❏
   d) I go home at such times. ❏

9. When I'm asked to take on another task:
   a) I never say 'No'. ❏
   b) I always say 'No'. ❏
   c) I always say 'Yes'. ❏
   d) I sometimes say 'No', asking if it is part of my job. ❏

10. When seeking to avoid stress:

a) I never get stressed. ❏

b) I'm always stressed
anyway. ❏

c) I plan my lifestyle
to cope with it. ❏

d) I hope I don't get stressed. ❏

WEEK 2

Successful People Management In A Week

Introduction

Week 2 focuses on people management and is primarily for new or aspiring managers. It is also a useful reference tool for junior and middle managers who are looking to develop their skills and are, possibly, seeking progression in their careers. Week 2 aims to give readers a sound understanding of the concept of people management; the role of people managers; people motivational theories; the various people management styles and their appropriateness; the tools available to people managers to help them do their jobs effectively; techniques for managing performance; and an insight into how people managers can develop their teams. It concludes with advice on how to survive as a people manager in tough times.

Each of the following chapters provides concise accounts of various aspects of people management for every day of the week. The reader is expected to spend between one and two hours each day studying the daily topic and checking his or her understanding against the specified learning goal.

At the end of Week 2, readers should have gained a full appreciation of:

The meaning of people management

The functions of a people manager at various levels in an organization

How to apply motivational theories to people management

The managerial tools that are available and the situations in which they can be used

The various people management styles and their benefits and drawbacks

Advice and tools for the development of teams

Management, along with leadership, is one of the most studied topics on organizations. There is a wealth of literature covering the subject and there are many views on what makes a good manager and their roles together with how effective teams are managed and developed. Many hold the view that management is best learned through doing. Nevertheless, Week 2 provides practising, junior and aspiring managers with a fundamental understanding of the principles and challenges of managing people together with guidance on how to be an effective people manager. It should help them underpin their practice with sound, simply presented summaries of various theories and techniques.

What is people management?

Managers get things done through people, whether they are concerned with developing and selling services, or making and selling manufactured products. People managers work in all functions of a business and, apart from manufacturing products or providing services for customers, they can be involved with delivering services internally for other parts of the business. For example, the human resources and finance functions often provide services for other parts of the business or organization, and sometimes charge for these services. Finance, HR, communications, IT, sales, marketing and operational managers all use people to develop, make and sell services or products.

Managers in various functions have to manage people in order to deliver and meet work objectives. These people may work in the unit or team for which the people manager is responsible or be others within or outside the organization, such as contractors.

Effective people management is vital to the success of any business and the efficient functioning of organizations. There are many views on what makes a good people manager so we will be summarizing these and looking at what makes a poor people manager.

Today we will develop an understanding of:

The concept of people management

How people management relates to leadership

The debate around whether management is an art, science or profession

What makes a good people manager

The concept of people management

There are numerous views on what constitutes people management. It is difficult to define because there is no general agreement as to what people managers do. Fundamentally, people management is about organizing human and other resources to achieve efficient performance in meeting an organization's objectives. It is about making sure that employees are able to deliver the services or products of a company or organization within required timescales and to a satisfactorily high standard. It has been defined as the process of controlling and monitoring people through leading, motivating and inspiring individuals within teams, which may vary in size. In addition, people management is about ensuring that staff have the necessary knowledge, skills, experience, aptitudes and attitudes to perform in their allocated jobs. People managers also have a responsibility to look after the health and welfare of those they manage, and to provide developmental support.

It is accepted that people are the biggest asset of any enterprise and that success is very much dependent on the quality of employees. People management is not an easy task. Those in the role are expected to lead, motivate, inspire and encourage people who will in all probability have differing abilities, attitudes and behaviours. The people manager needs to know and understand individual members of his or her team in order to get the best out of them. He or she is also likely to be involved in recruiting, appraising, disciplining and dismissing staff.

The role of a people manager can vary considerably according to the size and the nature of the business. For example, those working in small businesses may need to be more adaptable and flexible in their roles due to the limited staff resources available, while those in larger organizations will have more clearly defined roles and may be expected to work in hierarchical structures and according to bureaucratic processes, as in public sector organizations. We will be covering the work of people managers in more detail on Monday.

Service-related business-to-customer businesses demand people managers who are highly skilled in client relationships and who have excellent negotiation and conflict resolution skills. Business-to-business manufacturing and service delivery companies require people managers who are able to understand the clients' business challenges, are good at negotiation and able to manage the relationships effectively. In creative and new media companies, normally there are less formal organizational structures so people managers need to know how to ensure that the culture and climate of the enterprise enables innovation and inspiration to flourish. This means creating the space and the right environment to allow creative ideas to emerge for commercial exploitation.

A well-known writer on organizations, Henry Mintzberg, identified ten distinct roles for managers and categorized these into decision-making, interpersonal and information processing. Each of these involves engaging with people in order to make the right decisions, maintaining effective working relationships and gaining the information necessary to carry out the job. However, people managers generally have more loosely defined jobs than those they manage and are in a position to make choices about the style and content of their jobs. They have more responsibility to make judgements, balance arguments and take decisions.

There is an ongoing debate about the differences between the leadership and management of people. A number of people claim that there are distinctive differences between management and leadership. They maintain that management has the following features.

- It is process-driven and about compliance.
- It involves controlling people, their work and time.
- It is about doing things properly and accomplishing things.
- It involves information-processing for decision-making.
- It is characterized by predictability and order.
- Communication is key, particularly informal communication through meetings, telephone calls and email.
- It is concerned with troubleshooting, solving ad hoc problems and resolving conflict.

- It is people-orientated and requires an understanding of the unique abilities and characteristics of those with whom a manager interacts in order to manage relationships for the good of the business.

Others believe that leadership is different from management because it involves:

- directing and guiding an organization or function
- scanning the external environment
- setting and articulating the organizational vision and strategy
- mobilizing employees through tapping into their emotions
- empowerment of the workforce
- influencing staff and stakeholders
- making sound judgements
- driving change and organizational transformation.

Regardless of the debate about whether someone is a leader or manager, there is evidence to show that people cannot be neatly categorized into the role of leader or manager. All management and leadership involve people, and most leaders manage and most managers lead. The extent to which people managers lead or manage is often dependent on how the individual concerned decides to carry out the role and the particular situation. Generally, less senior people managers are focused on operational issues, while those higher up in an organization tend to be more concerned with directing, influencing and guiding.

There has also been an ongoing debate about whether people management is an art, science or profession. However, what is clear is that management is about getting things done within businesses and organizations, even though it may apply science and use art to provide insights and vision. It cannot be properly defined as a profession because it cannot be learned formally in the same way as other professions such as the law, accountancy and engineering. Management involves people whose behaviours and actions cannot be predicted and situations which cannot be foreseen. People management is, therefore, a practice that is learned and developed through experience within particular contexts or environments. It is an intuitive process that involves taking action, reflecting and continual learning. The 'people manager' often subconsciously absorbs various signals and experiences to inform his or her decision-making and future practice.

The features of people management

People management takes place at all levels of an organization and in all functions, as organizations cannot deliver without people. Managers are found at first-line supervisory levels, where they are mainly concerned with ensuring that a small team is delivering its tasks to time and to a satisfactory quality. These roles are often relatively well-defined, but nevertheless provide plenty of scope for deciding how to manage individual team members and the team as a whole. There is also scope for first-line managers to contribute to the wider aims of companies and organizations as they are closest to the customer and in a position to obtain first-hand information about customer needs and how services can be improved. Junior managers are often protected from the politics of organizations and wider business stresses. They are frequently expected just to ensure that workers deliver services or products efficiently and effectively.

Generally, middle-line managers are those that are responsible for managing a few teams or, within a relatively small enterprise, a function. Their roles are more challenging as they are often expected to contribute to the wider objectives of the organization and are answerable to senior management and directors for the performance of their teams or the business function. They relate upwards to senior managers and directors and downwards to their teams within their operational or functional areas as well as maintaining relationships with managers in other related areas of the business and clients and customers.

Senior managers or directors tend to be regarded as the leaders of enterprises. They are the ones that create the vision and strategy for the organization and carry out top-level communication with key stakeholders, including those that may have a financial interest in the business. Middle managers usually report to them on the performance of functional and service areas. Senior and director post holders are expected to take the key decisions for a business's survival and growth.

The qualities of a people manager

Successful people managers possess a range of qualities, many of which are vital to the role. For example, a people manager who does not possess excellent interpersonal skills and have empathy with people is unlikely to be effective in motivating staff to give of their best in delivering business objectives. Furthermore, a people manager whose behaviour is inconsistent and displays moodiness will inevitably fail to achieve first-rate performance from staff. Good personality, social skills, understanding and emotional stability are therefore fundamental to the role of a people manager.

A people manager needs to be personable and accessible to staff at all times. He or she should take time to know the staff and be understanding and sympathetic to any personal issues that may impact on attendance and performance. However, clear boundaries need to be maintained between the people manager and team members, as people managers have the tough task of continually having to balance the needs of the work with those of individuals. There is no easy solution to this challenge as it is individual and situation dependent. However, the people manager needs to be fair, open and consistent in the way all staff are treated.

It is important not to try too hard to be popular by pleasing staff members. People managers should exercise tough love. While it is good to be liked, for a people manager it is more important to be respected. Respect does not come as a result of your position as a people manager, it has to be earned. Treating all staff with respect and fairness will help in establishing your reputation as a good people manager.

Continual communication is key to successful people management. Communication needs to be clear and concise, and delivered in an open and transparent way. People quickly pick up on insincerity and dishonesty, so any people manager who fails to be honest and sincere will quickly lose respect and it will be very difficult to regain this.

People need to be trusted to do their jobs and will react badly to being micro-managed. Successful people managers delegate effectively and stretch staff to perform to the best of their abilities and capabilities. They give regular praise for a job well done and constructive feedback when improvements are needed. They should also be open to receiving feedback on their own performance and acting on that feedback. People will respect you even more if you are prepared to acknowledge your own mistakes and put them right.

While a certain level of intelligence is important in any managerial role, this on its own does not make a good people manager. A people manager needs to know how to use intelligence and apply this with common sense. He or she needs to be knowledgeable about the business and the team's work, and continually imparting this knowledge to the team in an open and transparent way. The only situation where this should not happen is when the people manager may be aware of sensitive or confidential information that would be harmful to the business or its people if leaked out. The people manager should protect the team by also managing upwards and protecting his or her team from problems that more senior managers may be grappling with.

Poor people managers are uncommunicative, vague, lack good social skills, are distrustful of staff and delegate work ineffectively. They frequently change their minds. People respond negatively to such behaviours and will therefore not perform to their maximum competence. There are numerous features of successful and unsuccessful people management. Examples of such features are listed below.

Successful people managers	Unsuccessful people managers
Energize and motivate teams	Adopt a narrow interpretation of their role
Encourage excellence and initiate change	Focus on outputs at the expense of people
Inspire trust	Are excessively controlling
Resolve conflicts amicably	Avoid dealing with conflict
Align values and behaviours to corporate goals	Display unethical values
Adapt their management styles to situations	Adopt one management style for all situations

Delegate with support according to capacity and ability	Fail to delegate key tasks and micro-manage
Develop and coach people	Are reluctant to share their knowledge and skills
Seek feedback and act on it	Avoid asking for feedback
Communicate clearly and effectively	Are vague communicators
Develop responsive interpersonal relationships	Frequently 'divide and rule', thereby fostering internal competition among team members
Are visible and available	Are inaccessible and disengaged from the team
Lead by example	Display unacceptable behaviours
Openly praise staff and give credit for achievements	Rarely provide positive feedback and take personal credit for team's achievements
Are even-handed in their treatment of people	Treat people differently
Surround themselves with able people	Select mediocre staff who are unthreatening
Are accountable upwards and downwards	Are focused mainly on impressing senior management

Summary

Today has been about understanding the basic concept of people management, the role of the people manager and the importance of people management to the success or failure of organizations. We have discussed the differences between leadership and management. The debate around whether people management is an art, science or profession has also been explored and we have concluded that it is primarily a practice.

We have also looked at the differences in managerial responsibilities at various levels within organizations and undertaken a comparison of the features of successful and poor people managers.

You have now been provided with a fundamental understanding of what people management is about and a broad appreciation of how it relates to leadership. Tomorrow we will explore what people managers do in more depth.

SUNDAY

MONDAY

TUESDAY

WEDNESDAY

THURSDAY

FRIDAY

SATURDAY

Fact-check (answers at the back)

1. People management is about:
   a) Selling ❏
   b) Designing ❏
   c) Organizing and controlling ❏
   d) Public relations ❏

2. The success of a business is primarily dependent on:
   a) The product/services ❏
   b) Sales ❏
   c) Finance ❏
   d) People ❏

3. Mintzberg's ten roles of people managers are *not* categorized into:
   a) Directing ❏
   b) Decision-making ❏
   c) Information-processing ❏
   d) Interpersonal ❏

4. The people manager's job is:
   a) Loosely defined ❏
   b) Clearly defined ❏
   c) Undefined ❏
   d) Prescriptive ❏

5. A feature of management is:
   a) Environment scanning ❏
   b) Initiating change ❏
   c) Controlling people ❏
   d) Developing strategy ❏

6. A feature of leadership is:
   a) Information processing ❏
   b) Constant and organized ❏
   c) Directing and empowerment ❏
   d) Informal communication ❏

7. People management is:
   a) An art ❏
   b) A science ❏
   c) A profession ❏
   d) A practice ❏

8. People managers are found at:
   a) First-line supervisory level ❏
   b) Middle management level ❏
   c) Director level ❏
   d) All levels ❏

9. People managers at supervisory level:
   a) Develop strategy ❏
   b) Take key business decisions ❏
   c) Motivate teams ❏
   d) Manage several teams ❏

10. Successful people managers:
    a) Have high intellects ❏
    b) Manage detail ❏
    c) Are concerned about process ❏
    d) Have excellent social skills ❏

SUNDAY

MONDAY

TUESDAY

WEDNESDAY

THURSDAY

FRIDAY

SATURDAY

MONDAY

What do people managers do?

Today, we will explore in detail the role of people managers and the challenges they face. The key functions of team selection, directing and focusing staff, dealing with problems and issues, monitoring and controlling performance, developing the team and liaising with middle management will be covered.

As stated in the Sunday chapter, people management is not easy. There is no prescription or guide book that can teach you the practice adequately because all individuals are unique. They bring to the workplace their particular experiences and behaviours in the same way as you, their current or prospective manager. Furthermore, every management situation is different. You rarely get the same situation arising more than once so you continually have to apply your knowledge, skills, experience and intuition to each particular situation.

People managers recruit and manage staff often with the help of a human resources department. They also motivate and direct teams to deliver the organization's objectives efficiently and effectively. As part of their role they are expected to build and develop teams to perform to the best of their abilities and deal with problems, issues and conflicts.

Today, we are going to look in more detail at:

The various tasks of people managers

What people management actually involves

SUNDAY

MONDAY

TUESDAY

WEDNESDAY

THURSDAY

FRIDAY

SATURDAY

The role of a people manager

People managers are in positions of power. They have power, authority and influence over the daily working life of their team members. The use or abuse of this power can have either positive or negative impacts on people and therefore the business.

As a people manager, you have a responsibility to reflect on your behaviour to ensure that it is continually making staff feel that they are making a useful contribution and that you are always there for them in times of difficulty. You have the challenge of maintaining your team's enthusiasm and commitment, regardless of the pressures you or they may be under. This is not an easy task. While you can control yourself, many of the problems among the people you manage are outside your control. These problems can be many and varied. They frequently relate to people's lives outside the office. For example, the pressures of the arrival of a new baby, sickness in the family, money problems, relationship worries or health issues can all impact on a person's performance at work. These problems cannot be resolved by you, but you may be able to contain them using your power and influence to make it easier for the individuals concerned to deal with their problems.

There may also be relationship or motivational problems within the team that you will need to deal with on a day-to-day basis. Good communication, listening, mediation and influencing skills together with a fair and open approach to issues are vital in such situations. Staff will always respect a people manager who has taken the time to understand the issue, hear both sides and take tough and fair decisions. Effective use of your power and influence can have a positive impact on individuals and their particular problems, and improve the overall functioning of the team.

The role and functions of people managers can vary considerably depending on the sector they work in or their specialism. However, there are tasks which are common to nearly all people managers, such as:

- selecting the right team, where there is scope to do so
- directing and focusing the team on their individual and the team's goals and objectives

- monitoring and controlling performance
- dealing with any problems or issues that may arise
- managing conflict
- coaching and developing the team, while understanding an individual's particular learning style
- liaising with middle management.

We are going to cover how these activities should be approached, together with the challenges people managers are likely to face in carrying out these functions.

Selecting the right team

Sometimes, people managers have little choice over the recruitment of staff. They may inherit a team that has already been formed, be given employees from elsewhere in the organization, or offered members of staff who have been recruited by the HR department. Therefore, you may not have much scope to recruit and select your own team. You could inherit a fully staffed team that has been in existence for some time, a team that is subject to some change in which there are vacancies or a team that needs to be built from scratch. Regardless, you are likely to be involved in the recruitment and selection of staff at some point. When recruiting and selecting staff it is important to work closely with the organization's HR department or professionals in order to ensure the appropriate recruitment processes are followed and that you stick to the company's employment policies.

If you inherit a team that has been in existence for some time, it is probable that they will have well-established roles and ways of working. You will need to take time to understand the way people work and interact with each other before identifying and introducing any changes. If you decide to make changes it will be important to communicate to everyone the reasons and take account of their views before making any final decisions. In cases where you propose to go ahead with changes, you should justify why and reassure staff that any comments they have made have been fully taken into account.

In the case of vacancies within a team, you may recruit for these either through internal or external advertising. Whichever method of advertising you use, you will need to draw up a job and person specification in consultation with the HR function. The former will need to cover the tasks required, while the latter will set out the particular knowledge, skills, experience and behaviours needed for the post. Examples are presented below.

Job description

Job title: Marketing Manager

Location: Sales and Marketing Team, Headquarters, Oldtown

Reporting arrangements: Position reports to the Sales and Marketing Manager.

Job purpose: To implement the marketing plan and manage the marketing budget.

Key responsibilities and accountabilities:

Management of two marketing executives and one administrator.

Management of financial budget.

Draw up and implement a marketing plan for the business.

Advise senior management on marketing and PR in relation to key strategic objectives.

Organize marketing campaigns.

Approve press notices and media features.

Develop, implement and monitor an internal communications strategy.

Undertake market research.

Draft tenders, select and manage advertising and PR agencies.

Prepare and implement a social marketing strategy.

Monitor and evaluate marketing activities.

Dated:

Person specification	
Qualities, skills and experience	**How criteria will be assessed**
Minimum of two years' managerial function within a marketing department (E)	Application and interview
Strong, effective communicator (E)	Presentation and interview
Good team-working skills (E)	Interview
Ability to see the big picture and contribute to marketing of company top-level strategic aims (E)	Interview
Excellent written skills (E)	Application and written test
Experience of external public relations activities (D)	Application, written test and interview
Experience of internal communications (D)	Application, written test and interview
Knowledge of monitoring and evaluation techniques (E)	Interview
Experience in social marketing and website development (E)	Application and interview
Competent in market research methodologies (E)	Interview
Management experience of marketing campaigns (E)	Application and interview
Experience of managing external PR and advertising agencies (D)	Application and interview
Personal characteristics and attitude	Application, interview and references
Pleasant, sociable and enthusiastic	
Displays commitment, flexibility and adaptability	
Clean driving licence and willing to be away from home overnight	
Educational requirements	Application and certificates
Degree in relevant discipline (E)	
Masters degree in marketing or business (D)	

(E) essential; (D) desirable

The selection process provides an opportunity for you to explore and identify whether the applicant has the necessary requisites for the job and to assess their suitability for the particular position. The aim is to find the best matched person for the post. Applications should be measured objectively against the requirements set out in the job and person specifications in order to select candidates for testing (if needed) and interviewing. Following sifting of applications, interviews should be held to assess applicants' suitability for the job and how well they would fit into the team and culture of the organization. The same process would be followed for establishing an entirely new team. However, in such cases you should consider carefully the mix of skills, personal qualities and characteristics necessary to establish a well-functioning team, in particular the diversity of team members. It is customary to seek written references for candidates but these can be unreliable for a number of reasons so it is often worthwhile speaking informally to previous employers and character referees to gain a more accurate picture of the individual's performance and behaviour in the workplace and socially.

Job descriptions and accompanying person specifications are useful documents for people managers. They can serve many purposes, such as:

● giving job applicants a clear description of the role
● setting out what is expected of team members
● providing a basis for measuring performance
● providing a useful document for settling any disputes between the people manager and a particular team member
● identifying areas for training and development
● providing an essential reference document for dealing with disciplinary issues
● providing an objective basis for performance reviews and appraisals.

All new recruits should be given an induction which covers basics rules and guidance on subjects such as:

● working times, holiday and sick leave allowances
● coffee breaks and lunch arrangements
● the dress code

- location of the toilets
- the organization's vision, mission, goals and values
- HR policies, health and safety, diversity and environmental policies and practices
- the job expectations.

An induction training plan should be given to the new staff member either before or immediately they start work. Taking new entrants into the business through an induction programme will help settle them in quickly so they become productive in a relatively short time as well as contributing to their retention and reducing dependence on you as a people manager. As part of the induction process, new staff members should also have a full briefing on the job they are expected to do, the processes to be followed and timescales for delivery of overall expectations. We touch upon this point in more depth in the following section on directing and focusing the team.

Directing and focusing the team

Each individual within the team should have a job description, which sets out the tasks required of them. They should be clear about what is expected of them and how their roles relate to individual, team and organizational goals and performance targets. These targets can be many and varied, according to the particular function of the team and/or individual. They could relate to the number of products manufactured or processed, the number of products or services sold, the number of marketing opportunities exploited, the number of internal customers helped with problems and so on. Targets should relate to the overall business plan/strategy for the organization or functional area. At an individual level, targets should be included in annual performance management plans (see the Friday chapter).

As a people manager, it is your job to make sure that all teams' members meet or exceed their targets in terms of numbers, required quality and timescales. It is, therefore, vital that all your team members have a clear understanding of the expectations of them and the team as a whole. Poor communication is the cause of many of the problems that arise in teams. Staff need to be fully aware of:

● the scope of their responsibilities and how they are accountable for them

- the organizational values and culture
- the level of knowledge and skills expected for the role
- the actions to be undertaken
- the expected attitudes and behaviours
- the performance levels expected in terms of both quality and quantity.

Apart from ensuring that staff are aware of the above points, people managers need to deploy a range of skills to encourage, influence and motivate team members to deliver what is required of them. Later in the week, we will look in more detail at some aspects of the skills and behaviours of successful people managers such as appropriate management styles and motivational theories.

Neither people nor work situations are stable and predictable. Consequently, the people manager's role is ever- and fast-changing, and challenging. It is vital, therefore, that you, as a manager of people, reflect continually on the dynamics of various situations, in particular your own reactions and behaviours, and take action in response to this reflective practice. This is necessary for maintaining the harmony and output of the team, in addition to continuing with your own personal development in order to refine your qualities and skills to become an excellent and even more successful people manager.

Dealing with problems and issues

Day-to-day problems and issues will arise continually. It will often be your responsibility to resolve these. The nature and sources of these can vary considerably. Involving your team in sorting out problems is a smart move as they will feel you value their capabilities and opinions. This is the case in relation to both those problems you can solve and those that you may find difficult. You can do this by:

- seeking views on the problem or issue
- exploring with staff the options for dealing with the problem
- asking for recommendations.

Another advantage for you, as a people manager, in involving your staff in resolving problems and addressing issues is that they are also more likely to come to you with suggestions for improving the business, which will help build your credibility with senior management. Furthermore, staff retention is likely to remain at a relatively high level if people are feeling appreciated for their contributions to problem-solving.

Managing conflict

As a people manager, it is inevitable that you will have to deal with conflict as part of your day-to-day work. Conflict may arise between you and team members or between you and senior management. There may also be conflict between team members that you will need to resolve. On average you could find yourself spending about a day a week or more on managing conflict and trying to find resolutions. Conflict affects team morale, productivity, profit and customer relationships. If unresolved it can lead to legal proceedings, which are costly in terms of time, money and the organization's reputation. It is therefore worthwhile for the people manager to learn about the many causes of conflict and the best way to manage it.

For example, conflict can arise if:

- someone feels they are being treated unfairly
- they are asked to do something that does not suit them for one reason or another
- there is a clash of values and/or beliefs
- there is competition for limited resources.

The source of conflict may not necessarily relate to the work of the organization, as personal issues can also sometimes lead to conflict in the workplace.

Conflict can either be healthy or unhealthy for a business. Healthy conflict is when there is disagreement about a decision or course of action which necessitates the parties involved having to set out the arguments and explore each perspective in order to reach a reasoned decision or agreement. The process is useful for discussing all options, the risks involved and the benefits and drawbacks. The parties agree without acrimony and action is taken to move matters forward. Unhealthy conflict, however, can be very damaging for businesses. It needs to be managed and resolved quickly in order to minimize adverse impacts.

Conflict resolution is about dealing with the source of the conflict and agreeing action to eliminate or reduce it. As a people manager, you can deal with conflict through negotiation, dominance, compromise, influence, bargaining, mediation, arbitration or avoidance. If the last strategy is employed, unless one or other party leaves the business, the likelihood is that the conflict situation will worsen and be even more damaging for the organization. Furthermore, it is unlikely that dominance would lead to a resolution that would make people feel valued and good about themselves. Negotiation, compromise and influence are the most effective strategies. If these are unsuccessful, you would need to resort to mediation or arbitration.

The first stage, if possible, is to identify whether there are any signs of conflict within the team or between individual team members. The indications may be a noticeable falling off of support for new work, poor response to discussions and limited input into meetings. Other signs include a fall in productivity, higher than normal sickness leave and negative behaviours. If you suspect that there is a problem the important thing is to address it before the conflict escalates. If not addressed early, the likelihood is that there will be some obvious signs of conflict such as unresolved arguments, lack of cooperation or goodwill, or refusals to support other team members. Once you realize that conflict is present within the team and you are aware of the parties concerned, which could involve you, the next stage is to identify its root cause.

The causes of conflict are many and varied. They include:

- weak management
- unfair or unequal treatment
- lack of clarity in job roles
- inadequate guidance or training
- poor working conditions

- bullying behaviour and harassment by management or a team member
- unrealistic expectations.

This may not necessarily be easy, but it is important that you acknowledge the symptoms as quickly as possible and take further action.

Once the cause of conflict has been identified, you will need to find a resolution that is satisfactory to all parties involved. Your organization may well have an established policy or procedure for handling conflict, which you should follow in such circumstances. Often the issue can be sorted out quickly and amicably on an informal basis without having to resort to formal procedures. If unsuccessful at the informal stage, you will need to follow formal processes in close consultation with your HR department in order to avoid an employment tribunal claim or industrial action.

When conflict is first recognized it may be sufficient to simply monitor the situation as the parties concerned often resolve the matter themselves or move on. However, if a minor disagreement or personality clash persists or escalates you will need to intervene by having a quiet word with both sides, making each aware of the situation and how they can achieve their own goals without clashing with others. Use of your negotiation and influencing skills will be key and you may possibly need to find a compromise solution. If, as the people manager, you fail to sort out the conflict, you could consider asking for the advice or intervention of your senior manager. In cases where conflict problems appear to be developing into a major issue, it is beneficial to consider bringing in an independent mediator before going through formal processes which could be costly and damaging for the business.

Monitoring and controlling performance

As a people manager, you will carry responsibility for setting the team's and individual member's targets. Targets need to relate to wider business objectives and cover both quantity and quality of work produced. Deciding performance targets is not an easy task as they can have a considerable effect on team and individual motivation. If targets are too demanding and almost impossible to achieve, this will be demoralizing for staff. They will feel that no matter how hard they work, they will never be able to achieve what is expected of them. If targets are set too low, individuals and the team will not be stretched, and their sense of achievement will be diminished. It is, therefore, important for staff satisfaction and business success that you determine targets that stretch the team and are demanding, while ensuring that staff will be motivated to achieve them. Targets need to be achievable and measurable, in line with the SMART concept:

S – Specific
M – Measurable
A – Attainable
R – Relevant
T – Time-bound

Involving your team in setting and agreeing targets is a worthwhile exercise as they will feel that they are having some influence over the process and have ownership of the targets. You may need to negotiate these targets with higher management. If so, involvement of the team in this process should help you with providing senior management with the case and evidence for setting targets at particular levels.

Targets can be set daily, weekly, monthly or annually. There are often numerous internal or external factors that may impact on their achievement. For example, targets can be impacted through a new contract won or a contract lost, a supplier going out of business, supply problems, the absence of critical staff or a change in business direction due to external factors. Targets, therefore, need to be kept under review and, if necessary and appropriate, revised at regular intervals.

In order to control the achievement of targets, continual monitoring has to take place at regular, appropriate intervals. The timescales for monitoring targets will vary according to the nature of the work and the business. Monitoring can be done by a variety of methods, such as email communication, use of spreadsheets, reporting formats or through meetings. If progress is satisfactory and there is no need for any enquiry into failure to meet targets, the process can probably be effectively executed through email or paper communication. However, if there is significant over- or under-achievement of targets it may be necessary to hold a meeting with staff and possibly other representatives of the business to review the reasons, agree actions and amend the targets as necessary. Regular communication with the team is important in respect of any of the above monitoring methods. People need to know how well they are doing and whether they need to improve in any areas in order to meet or exceed targets.

At an individual level, people are usually given targets as part of their annual performance plan, which should be reviewed by their managers at least twice a year. These targets link with work objectives and personal objectives that relate to how the person concerned should increase their knowledge, skills level and experience to perform in the job at a higher level. We will cover this process in more detail on Friday when we will talk about how to manage performance.

Developing the team

A people manager will inherit staff members from a variety of backgrounds, each of whom will have their own unique life experiences, behaviours, intelligence levels and aptitudes. Individuals will inevitably have varying levels of skills, knowledge and work experience as well as differing learning styles. We will be dealing with the topic of coaching and developing the team in more detail on Saturday. At this point, we will simply note the importance of a people manager developing coaching and mentoring skills in order to develop staff and improve their overall performance.

Liaising with middle management

No people manager operates in isolation of managers elsewhere in the business. There is usually someone to whom the people manager is accountable. This could be a middle level line manager or a senior manager or director. Usually, the performance targets for the team together with budget allocations are agreed with the supervising manager or director to whom the people manager reports regularly. A close working relationship should be developed with this individual in order for the team manager to appreciate and understand the pressures on the business. The opportunity should also be taken to suggest ways in which changes could be introduced to help overall business performance. These communications may be formal, such as regular meetings and reporting, or informal email communications, telephone conversations and face-to-face discussions. Keeping each other up to date and aware of any issues is vital to business survival and development.

As well as managing downwards, the people manager also needs to consider the need to manage upwards. Sometimes, senior managers can place unrealistic or unworkable demands on the people manager's teams and may interfere in the management process. In such situations, the people manager has an obligation to communicate effectively with senior management about what can be achieved or what is workable, providing evidence wherever possible, as part of a realistic case. It is important to look for solutions and answers to help the senior manager concerned achieve a satisfactory response to the issue before him or her. If there is a case of senior management interference in your management you should take steps to reaffirm your role and responsibilities diplomatically.

Summary

We have covered the power, authority and influence of people managers, and what they actually do in practice.

We have emphasized the importance of people managers exercising their power and influence effectively to help those in their teams deal with personal or work-related issues, as well as the importance of being open to listening and being prepared to take tough but fair decisions. The importance and cost effectiveness of a well-planned and delivered induction training programme for new recruits has also been covered.

The role of a people manager has been categorized into that of recruiter, director, problem-solver, conflict manager, target-setter, controller, performance manager, team developer and acting as the link between the team and more senior management.

Tomorrow we will look at the subject of motivation, which is a key challenge for people managers.

SUNDAY

MONDAY

TUESDAY

WEDNESDAY

THURSDAY

FRIDAY

SATURDAY

Fact-check (answers at the back)

1. Job and person specifications are written by:
   a) The HR department ❏
   b) The job-holder ❏
   c) The people manager ❏
   d) The team ❏

2. Targets will be defined in a:
   a) Job description ❏
   b) Person specification ❏
   c) Performance plan ❏
   d) Job advertisement ❏

3. In dealing with problems the people manager should:
   a) Seek help from staff ❏
   b) Refer to his or her manager ❏
   c) Resolve the issue ❏
   d) Leave it to others ❏

4. Targets need to be...? Complete the words.
   a) S...... ❏
   b) M...... ❏
   c) A...... ❏
   d) R...... ❏
   e) T...... ❏

5. Targets should be agreed with:
   a) The people manager ❏
   b) The team ❏
   c) Senior management ❏
   d) The organization ❏

6. Targets should be:
   a) Reviewed monthly ❏
   b) Reviewed weekly ❏
   c) Reviewed annually ❏
   d) Reviewed according to their nature and level ❏

7. Causes of conflict include:
   a) Strong management ❏
   b) Equality ❏
   c) Favouritism ❏
   d) Social events ❏

8. Effective ways of dealing with conflict are:
   a) Unilateral decisions ❏
   b) Dominant style ❏
   c) Leaving the parties to sort things out ❏
   d) Listening and negotiating ❏

9. Individual performance targets should be:
   a) Reviewed weekly ❏
   b) Reviewed monthly ❏
   c) Reviewed annually ❏
   d) Reviewed every six months ❏

10. A people manager is:
    a) Only responsible for the team ❏
    b) Responsible for managing his/her manager ❏
    c) Responsible for managing upwards and downwards ❏
    d) Responsible for managing across the organization ❏

SUNDAY

MONDAY

TUESDAY

WEDNESDAY

THURSDAY

FRIDAY

SATURDAY

TUESDAY

Motivating people in the workplace

The topic of motivation of staff is of prime interest to people managers. A number of well-known theories on the motivation of people have been developed in the past half-century or so, and they remain relevant in to-day's work situations. Today we are going to learn about the work of the prominent writers on the subject and touch upon more recent motivational work, which tends to be based on the original theories.

First, we will cover the work of Abraham Maslow, who developed a hierarchy of motivational needs. His work was developed further by Frederick Herzberg's motivation hygiene theory and David McClelland's motivational needs theory, which will also be discussed. The work of Douglas McGregor will be touched upon because it is relatively controversial. He has maintained that in respect of motivation, people are divided into those who are not interested in work and those who are keen to work. He classifies these as types X and Y respectively, which gave rise to the theory's name.

Today you will learn about:

The key motivational theories in relation to people in the workplace

The importance of understanding these theories in order to manage people effectively

How people's motivational drivers can differ according to a number of factors

How you can use motivational knowledge to tap into the individual's motivational needs in order to get them to achieve work objectives

The importance of understanding motivational theories

Motivation within the workplace can be explained as the extent to which individuals want to engage in certain behaviours and actions that meet their personal needs in relation to work. All people have different needs and goals. They behave and act in a way that leads to meeting these needs and goals. The most successful organizations tend to have highly motivated workers. This is shown in terms of high productivity, high quality work with little wastage, quick responses to issues and employees being encouraged, and even required, to give feedback and make improvement suggestions.

Motivating the people you manage is a challenging task but fundamental to your effectiveness as a people manager. In order to motivate people, you need to have an understanding of the basic motivational theories, the personal motivations of various individuals for whom you have management responsibility, and techniques for applying the theories in order to help staff maximize their performance.

There are several well-known motivational theories. Although these were developed decades ago, they remain very relevant in today's workplace. Maslow's hierarchy of needs is one that is frequently referred to, as is Herzberg's motivation hygiene theory and McClelland's motivational needs theory. Another renowned theory, about which there is some debate, is Douglas McGregor's X and Y theory.

There is a view that people managers perform best when they focus on employee engagement to understand them as individuals, their particular motivations and recognize their achievements. Therefore, people managers need a basic understanding of motivational theories and to learn how to apply them in the right circumstances in order to maintain and increase the motivation of their staff.

Maslow's hierarchy of needs

Abraham Maslow developed his hierarchy of needs model during the 1940s and 1950s. It is based on the idea that it is the responsibility of employers to provide a workplace environment that encourages and enables staff members to fulfil their potential, which is referred to as self-actualization. He developed a hierarchy of needs based on five motivational stages, which are frequently presented as a pyramid diagram.

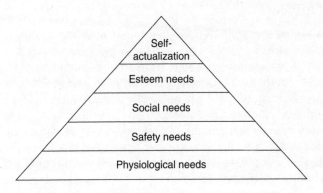

Maslow recognized that we are all motivated by needs, the most basic of which deals with our survival needs and is termed in the model as physiological (or biological) needs. He maintained that people's needs have to be satisfied according to the order given in the model. Maslow was of the view that only when the lower order needs are satisfied do we move on to the higher order needs.

In order to meet our physiological needs we seek the basic living requirements of food, water, air, shelter and sleep. Once this first need has been satisfied, people move on to satisfy their higher safety needs of keeping themselves and their families protected, secure and stable. The next stage in the hierarchy is social needs, which relate to belongingness and love within the family, other relationships and from the workplace. Once these needs are met we move on to meet our esteem needs, which are about our achievements, status, responsibilities and reputations. Finally, we seek self-actualization through personal growth and fulfilment.

The criticisms of Maslow's theory are that:

- individuals' behaviours respond to more than one need
- people may employ different behaviours in response to the same need
- it is not easy to decide when a need has been satisfied
- people's behaviours are far more complex than this model allows for and are affected by life experiences and events, and their frame of mind in certain situations.

A failure of someone to have their needs satisfied usually leads to stress and a decline in their work performance. As a people manager you need to have an understanding of this model together with knowledge about your staff in order to appreciate why someone is not performing as well as they could and failing to fulfil their potential. For example, if a team member is earning enough to meet his or her physiological needs but is in debt and his or her home is at risk (safety needs), it will not be possible to motivate them through feeling part of the work team (belongingness and love needs) and giving them further responsibilities (esteem needs). As a manager you will need to find ways within your power to help that individual meet his or her safety needs. This could be done through the offer of overtime, an interest-free company loan or debt counselling.

Herzberg's motivation hygiene theory

Frederick Herzberg's motivation hygiene theory claims that the factors which motivate people at work are different from and not simply polar opposites of the factors which cause dissatisfaction. Job satisfiers are about the factors involved in doing the job, while the job 'dis-satisfiers' are the factors which define the job context. There are similarities between Herzberg's and Maslow's theories as Herzberg argued that people's hygiene needs need to be satisfied before they can be motivated to perform well in the workplace. Examples of Herzberg's hygiene needs and how they relate to Maslow's hierarchy of needs are:

Herzberg's hygiene factors	Maslow's hierarchy of needs
Organizational policy	Safety needs
Work conditions	Safety needs
Relationship with manager	Belongingness and love needs
Salary	Physiological and safety needs
Benefits	Safety needs
Status	Esteem needs
Security	Safety needs
Relationships with colleagues	Belongingness and love needs
Personal life	Physiological, safety, belongingness and love needs

Herzberg's view was that the satisfaction of the hygiene factors was a prerequisite to motivating people through what he termed the true motivators:

● achievement
● recognition
● the work itself
● responsibility
● advancement.

Although similar to Maslow's model, Herzberg maintained that only the higher level needs of Maslow's hierarchy act as motivators, while the lower order needs are what he has termed as satisfiers, i.e. the hygiene factors. Management must, therefore, meet the hygiene factors in order to avoid employee dissatisfaction and the effects of this on the business. To motivate staff, Herzberg considered that job enhancement or enrichment factors should be introduced to tap into the intrinsic motivational drivers within individuals.

As a people manager you have some, but not complete, control or influence over the satisfiers. You are able to develop relationships with staff and foster good relationships between team members and others in the organization. You may also be able to influence salary and benefits, and possibly contribute to improvements in working conditions and organizational policies in a way that will help satisfy the needs of staff.

However, you will have little or no influence on the hygiene factors of job security and people's personal lives.

However, generally a people manager is able to use Herzberg's true motivators. For example, we discussed in Monday's chapter the importance of setting targets which relate to a person's achievements. These targets should be demanding, but not too hard so that individuals will feel that they have failed if they are not met. If targets are too easy, individuals will not feel stretched, which through lack of achievement could lead to feelings of unworthiness or not feeling valued. People need to be praised for their achievements and contributions at regular intervals and exceptional successes should be celebrated. This should be a regular feature of the people manager's role.

Another example is recognition, which is about being appreciated for your contribution to the team and the business. This may frequently relate to achievement of work objectives or contributions to the team or organization, which can come in many forms, such as:

- coming up with innovative ideas to improve organizational functioning
- supporting a colleague who may be struggling in carrying out a task
- arranging a social event
- volunteering to represent the business in your spare time
- going that extra mile for an internal or external customer.

It is important to show members of your team that you care and appreciate it when they do something well or outside their normal duties. It is also worthwhile letting others in the organization know about how well individuals are performing and when they are delivering over and above expectations.

As regards the work itself, people generally want interesting and challenging work in order to feel engaged and interested and to have a sense of achievement. Depending on the nature of your business, you may have limited scope to create interesting work. However, there are ways in which you can redesign jobs to make them less routine and you can share out the more mundane tasks among team members, including yourself. If staff see that you are also bearing a share of the routine work, their respect for you will increase and they will be more inclined to support you in times of crisis.

Responsibility is a positive motivator because if you assign responsibility to someone it implies you value and trust them. However, you need to be confident that the person to whom you are assigning responsibility has the competence, confidence and capacity to carry out the additional responsibilities. You also need to be sure that the action will not make other members of the team feel disgruntled.

Advancement usually refers to promotion, salary increase and improved job prospects. In order to achieve advancement people need to show they have the capability to take on increased responsibilities, have acquired new skills, have developed their competencies and can make a contribution to the business at a higher level. The people manager has a responsibility to provide individual team members with job experience, skills development and learning opportunities that will help them advance their careers. We will be discussing people development on Saturday, but it should be noted that not everyone is interested in or has the capability for career advancement so the people manager needs to be sensitive to the motivational needs of these individuals and find other ways to motivate them in the job.

McClelland's motivational needs theory

David McClelland's motivational needs theory is closely related to the theories of Herzberg. McClelland was of the opinion that there are the following three types of motivational needs:

- achievement
- authority/power
- affiliation.

He maintained that all employees of organizations have these needs to varying degrees. He further argued that the extent to which they are inherent in an individual determines a person's or manager's style and behaviour in respect of their personal motivation and how they motivate others.

173

For example, the achievement-dominated individual is driven towards the accomplishment of challenging goals and career advancement. They need to carry out difficult but attainable tasks at a high level. These individuals need success and to be praised and recognized for their efforts and outcomes. Financial rewards, security and status are not prime motivators. Achievement-motivated people seek personal responsibility and can make good leaders, although they can be too results-driven and demand a lot from staff.

Those that seek power and authority are driven to be influential and to be viewed as leaders who have an impact, and tend to dominate with their ideas. They have a need to control others and like to be in charge so that they can direct and influence others to achieve organizational goals. Power- and authority-driven people enjoy status and competition. They tend to be demanding of others, articulate and ambitious for leadership positions. However, their quest for prestige can impact adversely on their actual performance in their jobs.

The affiliation-motivated person has a need for people interaction and to develop friendly relationships. They want to be liked and popular. These individuals make good team players as they want to be accepted and are inclined to conform to group norms. Affiliation-motivated people have a preference for cooperation over competition, and are good in customer service roles and jobs that involve client interaction. As a people manager you need to be aware that because of the dominant need to be popular, these types can undermine objectivity and your decision-making capability.

McClelland claimed that most people have and demonstrate a combination of the above characteristics, but a number exhibit a strong bias to one particular motivational need, which inevitably affects their workplace behaviours and management styles. There is a fair level of support for McClelland's theory. The challenge for people managers is in determining the levels of individual needs and subsequently matching these to a job situation.

McGregor's X and Y theory

Douglas McGregor proposed that there are just two fundamental approaches to people management and that people and their managers can, therefore, be categorized into two types.

- Those with a leaning toward type X, which is based on the assumption that on average people dislike and will avoid work if they can; they prefer to be directed; avoid responsibility; are relatively unambitious; and want security first and foremost. McGregor claimed that these people call for an authoritarian management style whereby the manager dictates what is required and uses the threat of punishment in order to get them to work towards organizational objectives. This particular management style rarely gets good results from people and can be the cause of discontent and absenteeism.
- Type Y people, are said to find that effort in work is natural and easy. They are self-controlled and self-directed in pursuit of organizational objectives. They seek and accept responsibility. They do not need to be controlled or to have the threat of punishment hanging over them. Type Y people have the capacity to apply innovation, creativity and imagination in solving an organization's problems. As managers they are participative and bring out the best in people.

We will be exploring management styles on Wednesday and this will include the features of both autocratic and participative managers.

It is claimed that type X workers are best motivated through rewards, while type Y people are believed to be motivated by being allowed to create environments in which staff can develop and flourish. Critics of McGregor's theory take the view that it is outdated in the light of the trend for self-managed teams and that it represents two behaviour extremes.

The challenge of motivating people

One of your principal tasks as a manager is to motivate your people. Knowledge of the theories above will help you identify the individual needs and characteristics of your staff and adopt the most appropriate motivator in order to get the best out of them at work. Depending on the individual and situation, you will need to apply a variety of people management styles, which we will cover on Wednesday. One particular style is unlikely to be effective in motivating a team of people, each with different personal characteristics and motivational drivers. There are numerous techniques you can apply, such as giving praise and constructive criticism, helping to build an individual's skills, giving more responsibility, providing learning and development opportunities, redesigning jobs to make them more interesting and monetary rewards, if this is within your power.

The people manager needs to be aware of the benefits and drawbacks of the dominant motivational characteristics in the staff he or she manages in order to place people in the roles that best suit them and best meet their motivational needs. As a people manager you need to be continually assessing the motivational needs of team members and managing them in a way that meets these needs so that they perform to the best of their abilities and are content in their jobs. It is also important for you to be aware of your particular motivational needs and to reflect on and adapt your behaviours and actions accordingly.

It is vitally important to:

- communicate clearly and regularly with your staff
- ask their views on how to improve the working situation
- arrange social events occasionally
- know your staff in order to gain insights into their personal lives
- be flexible with small gestures
- say thank you so people feel appreciated and not overlooked.

Summary

In order to build an appreciation and understanding of people's motivational needs, we have studied the main, well-known motivational theories of Maslow, Herzberg, McClelland and McGregor.

You have been given an example of how Maslow's hierarchy of needs theory could be applied in today's organizational settings, and shown how Herzberg's motivation hygiene theory is similar to Maslow's theory, along with McClelland's motivational needs theory. McGregor's X and Y theory takes a different approach by categorizing people into those who do not want to work (type X) and those who do and are keen to achieve (type Y). McGregor's theory is linked to differing management styles, which we are going to explore tomorrow.

SUNDAY

MONDAY

TUESDAY

WEDNESDAY

THURSDAY

FRIDAY

SATURDAY

Fact-check (answers at the back)

1. Physiological needs relate to:
   a) Job security ❏
   b) Team work ❏
   c) Status ❏
   d) Survival ❏

2. Self-actualization needs relate to:
   a) Praise ❏
   b) Social acceptance ❏
   c) Personal growth ❏
   d) Status ❏

3. X and Y theory was developed by:
   a) Herzberg ❏
   b) Maslow ❏
   c) McGregor ❏
   d) McClelland ❏

4. Hygiene factors include:
   a) Security ❏
   b) Responsibility ❏
   c) Achievement ❏
   d) Work content ❏

5. Herzberg's true motivators include:
   a) Advancement ❏
   b) Salary ❏
   c) Status ❏
   d) Work relationships ❏

6. Which of the following is *not* included in McClelland's theory?
   a) Affiliation ❏
   b) Authority/power ❏
   c) Recognition ❏
   d) Achievement ❏

7. Type X people:
   a) Seek work ❏
   b) Are ambitious ❏
   c) Avoid responsibility ❏
   d) Are self-motivated ❏

8. Type Y people:
   a) Like to be directed ❏
   b) Seek security ❏
   c) Need to be controlled ❏
   d) Innovate ❏

9. McClelland's theory is:
   a) Motivation hygiene ❏
   b) Motivational needs ❏
   c) Hierarchy of needs ❏
   d) X and Y theory ❏

10. Herzberg's hygiene factor of relationships with colleagues links with Maslow's:
    a) Safety needs ❏
    b) Physiological needs ❏
    c) Esteem needs ❏
    d) Belongingness and love needs ❏

WEDNESDAY

People management styles

In the Tuesday chapter, we referred to the choice of people management styles when considering how to motivate staff. A management style reflects a people manager's preferred way of making decisions and controlling and relating to the work group.

People tend to have a dominant management style, although they can adopt differing styles for different situations. There are a number of accepted management styles, such as autocratic, democratic, paternalistic, bureaucratic etc. We are going to discuss the features of each of the most well-known styles today, together with their advantages and disadvantages. We will also be linking the motivational theories discussed on Tuesday to certain management styles and outlining situations in which particular styles would be appropriate.

At the end of today you should have an appreciation of:

different management styles

the pros and cons of using them in certain situations

People management styles

As shown on Monday, the work of people managers is multi-faceted. They have many roles to play in organizations and have to rely on people in order to complete tasks and deliver business objectives. How people managers carry out their roles and handle various situations depends on their management style, which can be constructive and positive, destructive and negative, or neutral and ineffectual in particular settings.

Today we are going to explore various management styles and their appropriateness for certain situations. As mentioned on Tuesday there are close links between people managers' particular management styles and their responsibilities for motivating staff.

Management styles relate to the characteristic ways in which people managers make decisions and relate to their staff. People tend to adopt a certain style according to their personal characteristics, life experiences and motivations. However, management style should be dependent on the particular circumstances of a situation. Good people managers will deploy a range of styles according to the people and work situations they are dealing with.

The most widely accepted forms of management styles are classed as:

- autocratic
- democratic
- bureaucratic
- consultative
- persuasive
- laissez-faire
- MBWA (management by walking about)
- paternalistic.

We are going to discuss the features of each of these and their advantages and disadvantages. We are also going to learn about the situations in which it may be appropriate to use them.

Autocratic

A people manager who is autocratic is inclined to take decisions without consulting those who may be affected or those who may hold an interest in the particular issue. Autocratic managers tend to make decisions and then expect staff to do exactly as they have been told. Little consideration is given to the impact of their decisions on others. There are two types of autocratic managers.

- A directive autocrat, who takes decisions unilaterally and expects staff to carry them out without argument and under close supervision.
- A permissive autocrat, who makes unilateral decisions but gives staff the freedom to decide how to carry out his or her instructions.

The decisions of either type will inevitably reflect the views and personality of the people manager concerned. On the positive side, an autocratic manager can be viewed as being confident and competent in managing the business. On the other hand, if those managed are strong and competent and fall into McGregor's Y category of people, they may well resent this approach and be resistant to accepting the decisions. This could lead to conflict within the group. Furthermore, this style tends to foster dependence on the manager.

There are occasions when this type of people management style may be appropriate, such as in times of crisis or when staff are inexperienced and do not have the capacity to contribute effectively to the decision-making process.

Democratic

The democratic people manager is at the opposite end of the spectrum to an autocratic manager. Democratic management is about full employee involvement and feedback. This type of manager involves everyone in the decision-making process and decisions are made on the basis of majority agreement. It involves extensive communication with those concerned. There are two types of democratic people managers: permissive and directive.

183

The former allows staff to carry out the decisions as they see fit, while the latter will be very involved with staff in carrying out decisions.

The advantages of a democratic style of manager are that staff will feel involved and valued, and the decisions made are likely to be acceptable to most of the team or work group. A democratic people management style can improve job satisfaction and the quality of work as well as generating enthusiastic ideas from staff. The disadvantages are that a considerable amount of time and effort is spent on decision-making which could possibly be used more profitably elsewhere in the business, and that there is no guarantee that the decisions will be in the best interest of the business. This particular form of management style is often useful in complex, major decision-making processes.

Bureaucratic

Bureaucratic management is found primarily in public sector bodies and many large corporate businesses, particularly those that are regulated. There is a need in these organizations for accountability and transparency to gain public confidence, the support of stakeholders and shareholders and the confidence of industry regulators. In such organizations the risks of contravening the law, regulations, policies and procedures are relatively high and could lead to critical or disastrous consequences, in particular for large private-sector enterprises or health and social care bodies. To protect the public or other stakeholders, it is necessary for such organizations to have in place efficient and effective recording processes and procedures to minimize mistakes, ensure adherence to any governing laws or regulations and achieve quality outputs. Such systems may mitigate any wrongdoing and have the foregoing benefits, although they are not foolproof. Other advantages include more reliable decision-making and safeguarding from abuse by employees or managers. Disadvantages of bureaucratic systems include slow decision-making and delivery, and they tend to be resource intensive and, therefore, costly.

Consultative

Although this type of management style implies worker involvement in decision-making, in effect it is dictatorial and similar to the autocratic style. The communication is usually from senior management to lower levels within the management chain for the purpose of seeking views and feedback on proposals. However, frequently the decisions have more or less been made, so the purpose of consulting is primarily to obtain the commitment of employees and maintain staff morale. The prime advantage of this style is that it can engender loyalty, although you should not underestimate the ability of employees to view the consultation as a pointless exercise. The disadvantages of this style are similar to those of the autocratic management style.

Persuasive

The persuasive management style is another that has similarities with the autocratic style, but with more emphasis on employee engagement. The persuasive manager maintains full control of the decision-making process but will spend a considerable amount of time trying to convince work groups of the benefits of the decisions and allaying any concerns they may have. The style excludes staff from the decision-making process. It enables decisions to be made quickly and provides employees with a full understanding of the background to the decision and how it is likely to affect their day-to-day jobs. On the negative side, use of the style is not guaranteed to gain employee support for the decisions. More importantly, such an approach fails to capitalize on the valuable views of those delivering the work on the front line. The adoption of this style could lead to lack of initiative and a fall in productivity due to resentment from people with no power over the decisions that are affecting them. This management style may be appropriate in difficult and challenging situations or when it is necessary to drive forward change to which the workforce is resistant.

Laissez-faire

A laissez-faire manager leaves staff to get on with their work with little interference. This sort of people manager tends to act as a mentor and stimulator. They rarely get involved in the detail and delivery of work objectives, preferring to work at a distance, engaging with people as necessary to offer them encouragement. These managers are known to be complete delegators of work on the basis of their view that employees are more motivated and committed if they feel they have full control and responsibility. This people management style is only really effective in teams that are made up of strong and competent members who need little guidance and minimal developmental support. They will feel trusted and empowered by the laissez-faire manager. It is most suitable for use in creative and entrepreneurial companies or teams made up of highly qualified professionals. There are clear risks to this type of management style, which lacks focus and direction and avoids involvement in day-to-day work.

Management by walking around (MBWA)

People managers who manage through walking around among team members and others within the organization are usually good listeners and use the information they gather from conversations to minimize challenges and avoid possible crises. They recognize that formal communication processes do not necessarily capture workers' concerns and suggestions or maintain morale. The MBWA manager can act upon the information obtained or use it to inform decision-making higher up the management chain. These managers act as coaches and counsellors. They are not necessarily involved in controlling and delivering the work objectives, and leave decision-making to the workers. There are risks around the loss of authority for those who adopt this type of management style, although it can lead to quick response times.

Paternalistic

Paternalistic people managers are generally regarded as managers who care about the people for whom they are responsible in a way that aims to achieve a balance between management decision-making and the well-being of employees. They are the sort of managers who take account of the impact of business decisions on the staff. Even though they may take decisions without involving others in the same way as an autocratic manager, their internal decision-making process analyses and takes account of the implications of those decisions on the workforce and strives to ensure their welfare is safeguarded. This management style of caring for others helps motivate workers, increases their loyalty and minimizes staff turnover. The downside is that it can create high dependency on the manager and if he or she makes an error or makes the wrong decision, staff may feel let down. There is also potential for dissent in the work group.

Summary of management styles

A management style incorporates your people management skills and provides a framework for decision-making, taking action and controlling work groups. We each have a natural management style that reflects who we are and our personal characteristics and behaviours. This may or may not be suitable for many of the situations you are faced with as a people manager. Your management style can be developed and adapted by improving your understanding of yourself and how you respond to certain individuals and people. Below is a table summarizing the features of the management styles we have discussed today together with their advantages and disadvantages.

Management style	Features	Advantages	Disadvantages
Autocratic	Unilateral decision-making Clear instructions	Rapid decisions Perception of strong and competent management	Employees feel disempowered and not trusted Fosters dependency and resentment Creates divisions between managers and workers
Democratic	Involvement of workers in decision-making	Staff ownership of decisions Improved job satisfaction and work quality Team-building Cooperation and good two-way communication between management and staff Creates culture for ideas to come forward	Lengthy decision-making process Decisions may not be in the business's interests Workers may not have the necessary skills and experience to make sound business decisions

Bureaucratic	Established rules and procedures to follow	Inspires confidence of stakeholders Reliable decision-making Mitigates business risks	Slow decision-making Demotivating for staff Costly
Consultative	Top down communication and decision-making Consultation with employees	Maintains morale of staff Could gain the commitment of workers	Staff feel disempowered
Persuasive	Unilateral decision-making Time spent allaying work group's concerns	Quick decision-making Staff provided with full information on the implications of decisions	Staff feel excluded from decision-making Fall in productivity Lack of initiative among the workers
Laissez-faire	Staff left to make decisions Complete delegation of work Manager at a distance, uninterested and hands-off	Competent and skilled staff could feel empowered and trusted	Lack of focus and direction Resentful staff
MBWA (management by walking around)	Good listening Visible and accessible manager Manager acts as coach and counsellor	Useful informal information is gathered Quick responses to issues Helps ward off any crises or prepare for any forthcoming challenges	Loss of authority and respect Reliance on team to deliver with limited direction and control
Paternalistic	Communication is downwards Decisions are autocratic Account is taken of the personal and social needs of the group	Staff involved in decisions, which could result in high morale Staff turnover low Employee loyalty	High dependency on manager Slows decision-making process If manager makes wrong decision, staff can become disenchanted and dissatisfied

Summary

An organization's success or failure can be influenced significantly by the people manager's style of managing. Your choice of management style, therefore, is likely to impact greatly on the performance of your staff.

The type of management style you choose to employ will usually reflect your personal characteristics.

As we have illustrated, each management style has its own pros and cons. A good people manager will be aware of his or her propensity to adopt one particular style and the benefits and disadvantages of using this in certain situations. Effective people managers will adapt their management approaches both to the individuals and the situations they face. It has been shown that there are significant benefits to be gained from adopting a people management style that involves listening, talking, supporting and working with your team on work objectives.

Fact-check (answers at the back)

1. In times of crisis, which management style should be used?
   a) Bureaucratic ❑
   b) Persuasive ❑
   c) MBWA ❑
   d) Autocratic ❑

2. A disadvantage of the democratic style is:
   a) Can lead to conflict ❑
   b) Resistance to decisions ❑
   c) Could result in poor decisions ❑
   d) Staff resentment ❑

3. The bureaucratic style is appropriate for:
   a) Creative organizations ❑
   b) Times of crisis ❑
   c) Regulated businesses ❑
   d) Team building ❑

4. Quick decisions require:
   a) A laissez-faire style ❑
   b) Autocratic management ❑
   c) MBWA ❑
   d) Staff involvement ❑

5. Which management style leads to sound decision-making?
   a) Paternalistic ❑
   b) MBWA ❑
   c) Bureaucratic ❑
   d) Consultative ❑

6. A consultative manager:
   a) Involves staff in decisions ❑
   b) Decides unilaterally ❑
   c) Lets staff decide ❑
   d) Takes the majority view ❑

7. The advantage of MBWA is:
   a) Quick decisions ❑
   b) Prepared for threats ❑
   c) Involves staff ❑
   d) Clear direction ❑

8. A disadvantage of paternalistic management is:
   a) Over-reliance on the manager ❑
   b) Employee uninterest ❑
   c) Creates conflict ❑
   d) Loss of commitment ❑

9. Which management style involves unilateral decision-making?
   a) Laissez-faire ❑
   b) Persuasive ❑
   c) Democratic ❑
   d) Bureaucratic ❑

10. Which management style is suitable for creative workers?
    a) Autocratic ❑
    b) Paternalistic ❑
    c) Laissez-faire ❑
    d) MBWA ❑

SUNDAY MONDAY TUESDAY WEDNESDAY THURSDAY FRIDAY SATURDAY

THURSDAY

Tools for people management

Over the past four days we have covered what is meant by people management, the role of people managers, motivational theories and the features of various people management styles together with their advantages and disadvantages. It is now time to focus on tools to support you in your task of managing people.

There are numerous tools available which primarily relate to people management, performance management, quality management, strategy development, project management, process and organizational change, and environmental management. Some of these are linked to accreditation processes, to which we will refer briefly.

Today we are going to discuss the basic aspects of the main tools that a people manager can access under the management components listed above. Some of these are inter-related, such as people and performance management.

You will gain a knowledge of:

The main tools that are available to support you in becoming an effective people manager

How these tools will improve the overall performance of your team, and your credibility and reputation within the business

Management tools and techniques

People managers develop primarily through learning on the job. However, there are numerous tools and techniques available to help them deal with particular issues or develop certain areas within the work group. These can be useful for developing people, managing change, developing strategies and plans, managing projects, delivering quality-assured goods and services, and ensuring good environmental management.

People development tools

A people manager can access a number of psychometric tests to inform him or her on how a staff member should be motivated and managed, and the role he or she should play in the work group in order to benefit the team and the business as a whole. These tests are also useful for assessing development areas and deciding how these should be tackled. We will be discussing the training and development of people on Saturday, but today we are going to explore how the knowledge of psychometric testing can help in this respect.

There are two types of psychometric tests: those which assess an individual's numerical, verbal or reasoning ability, frequently referred to as aptitude tests; and those which focus on personality to uncover a person's preferred style of behaviour or motivation. You may wish to use psychometric tests in relation to recruitment for vacancies in the team, to inform coaching sessions, for team building or for career development purposes. There are many testing tools available so the people manager needs to be clear about what is needed from the test in order to select the most relevant type.

Numerical, verbal and reasoning tests are helpful in assessing the particular aptitudes, abilities and intelligence of candidates for employment or promotion. There are a wide range of tests available which, in effect, are structured, systematic ways of assessing a person's numerical, logical and verbal reasoning. They are usually used as part of the overall assessment process for recruitment or promotion. These tests are administered under examination conditions and can involve solving problems, undertaking tasks or answering multiple-choice questions. The most common form of tests are:

Test	Method and ability assessed
Numerical reasoning	A number of arithmetical problems and mathematical questions, possibly presented in charts and graphs that need interpretation. These are used to assess people's ability to handle and interpret numbers.
Logical reasoning	These tests expect the candidate to identify rules and patterns from information provided in diagram sequences containing various shapes in order to find the next one in the sequence. The ability to think logically and analytically is tested.
Non-verbal reasoning	Diagrams and pictures are used to assess the candidate's capability of analysing and solving problems through this means.
Verbal reasoning	This type of test consists of a number of relatively short paragraphs of written text, from which the candidate is expected to assess the accuracy of a number of statements based on the information. It is used to assess abilities in understanding, analysing and interpreting complex written information.
Verbal logic	Verbal logic tests involve solving a number of puzzles of different types. They test ability to think logically, analytically and numerically, and extract meaning from complex information.

Personality tests are very useful for people managers to understand their own behaviours, motivations and empathy, as well as those within the work group. Understanding your personality and that of others is fundamental to motivating teams in order to capitalize on their strengths and needs. People are all different and information from personality tests helps build appreciation of individuals' values and special strengths and qualities, along with understanding of their behaviour traits.

A number of personality tests are based on the theories of the psychologist Carl Jung, who developed concepts of psychological types. He identified two types of attitudes in humans i.e. introverted and extroverted. The latter tends to be objective and outwards focused, while the former is subjective and inwardly motivated. It is acknowledged that both characteristics are present in everyone to varying degrees and that many people have a healthy balance of the two aspects.

Jung developed a framework of four functional types which he related to extroversion and introversion. These were thinking and feeling, which enable the taking of decisions and forming of judgements rationally because they reason, decide and make judgements; and sensation and intuition, which are irrational acts based on the gathering of information and perceptions. On this basis, Jung developed eight personality types, from which the popular Myers Briggs personality test, known as MBTI (Myers Briggs Type Indicator), was developed. This test is widely used for understanding and interpreting personality and preferred ways of behaving in the workplace. It is useful for:

- understanding and developing yourself and others
- understanding what motivates others
- understanding others' strengths and weaknesses
- building effective teams
- allocating tasks and responsibilities
- agreeing roles within a work group
- identifying your own and others' development needs.

More recently, a psychologist named Eysenck developed a test that measures personality on the two scales of:

- introversion–extraversion
- stability–instability (unemotional–emotional).

His tests provide a valuable additional perspective to the work of previous psychologists by assessing through detailed questioning whether individuals' temperaments are stable or not and whether they fall within the introversion or extroversion category. His theory produces four main types of personality.

Stable extrovert (unemotional extrovert)	Stable introvert (unemotional introvert)
Sociable, outgoing, talkative, responsive, easy-going, lively, carefree leadership	Calm, even-tempered, reliable, controlled, peaceful, thoughtful, careful, passive
Unstable introvert (emotional introvert)	Unstable extrovert (emotional extrovert)
Moody, anxious, rigid, sober, pessimistic, reserved, unsociable, quiet	Touchy, aggressive, excitable, changeable, impulsive, optimistic, active

People can display a mixture of these characteristics. As a people manager it is helpful to use this model to understand your own and others' personality types.

The US company Inscape developed a system known as the DISC model, which is frequently used for organizational development purposes. It is based on the assumption that the foundation of personal and professional success lies in knowing yourself, understanding others and realizing the impact of your action and behaviours on others. The method assesses Dominance, Influence, Steadiness and Compliance (DISC). Dominance and compliance relate to things, and influence and steadiness to people. The model provides a personality description based on determination of a person's dominant preferred style and supporting styles.

A well-used team building assessment tool is Belbin's team roles based on the research undertaken by Dr Meredith Belbin. This has shown that teams balanced with people of different but complementary competencies perform more effectively than less well-balanced teams. This model is used by many of the UK's top companies and a significant number internationally. A set of nine team roles have been identified, including a specialist role. The particular strengths, styles and functions associated with the roles are specified as:

Role name	Strengths and styles	Functions and tasks
Coordinator	Confident, mature with ability to motivate everyone to achieve shared goals	Clarifies group objectives, sets agendas, establishes priorities, identifies problems, sums up and is decisive, does not dominate discussions
Shaper	Energetic, assertive, competitive, motivated, achievement driven	Shapes the team's efforts, looks for patterns in discussions and identifies practical considerations. Gets results. Can steam-roller the team
Planter	Creative, unorthodox, innovative, inventive, imaginative, problem-solving	Source of original ideas, puts forward radical, original ideas, suggestions and proposals
Monitor-evaluator	Analytical, prudent, serious, critical thinker	Provides a measured and dispassionate analysis through objectivity. Stops the team being committed to a misguided task
Implementer	Reliable, loyal, structured, systematic, practical, dependable, efficient	Turns decisions and strategies into defined and measurable tasks, sorting out objectives and pursuing them logically.

Resource investigator	Good communicator, networker, outgoing, affable. Quick, negotiator, seeks and finds options	Brings in ideas, information and developments from outside the team. Salesperson, diplomat, liaison officer and explorer
Team worker	Supportive, sociable, flexible, adaptable, perceptive, listener, calming influence, mediator	Operates against division and disruption in the team, cements members together in times of stress and pressure
Completer-finisher	Accurate, attention to detail, high standards, quality-orientated, delivers to schedule and specification	Maintains a sense of urgency with relentless follow-through
Specialist	Technical expert, highly focused capability and knowledge driven by professional standards and dedication to subject area	Contributes detailed technical and specialist advice

The roles of coordinator, shaper, planter and resource investigator are noted as requiring extrovert tendencies. In small teams people frequently assume more than one role. The method is useful in helping teams improve their behaviours and performance when issues such as conflict, failure to meet targets or continual mistakes arise. In such circumstances it would be necessary to assess whether the team has the right skills in terms of coordinators, resource investigators and evaluators. The interaction between different personalities within a team leads to conflict on occasions so applying the Belbin model can assist each team member to understand and value their differences.

Another well-used personality test is the 'Big Five' factors. This trait theory has been fully researched by a number of psychologists. It measures traits by scoring them on the following scales:

● Extroversion versus Introversion
● Confidence versus Sensitive

- Detail-conscious versus Unstructured
- Tough-minded versus Agreeable
- Conforming versus Creative.

The higher the score, the more likely the candidate will be to exhibit the behaviour and the less able to show behaviours at the lower end of the scale. The factors need to be combined to indicate how people operate and their underlying preferences. The five factor model is best used to assess non-managerial staff. It is quick to use and provides accurate results. It is effective at enabling an understanding of someone's key drivers. There are a number of other personality tests that are closely linked to the Big Five factors. These include Belbin's team roles and others known as 16PF, Occupational Personality Questionnaire (OPQ), Fundamental Interpersonal Relations Orientation–Behaviour (Firo–B), the Birkman method and the Lumina Spark system.

People managers should have a basic understanding of a number of personality tests and assessment tools such as these so that they can consider their use in particular situations. Tests are useful for building self-awareness, personal development, motivation, training, selection and recruitment, and people management. They help the people manager understand team members and manage communications, relationships and behaviours more effectively. They are a valuable aid to motivation and management.

Strategic development tools

Every business needs to scan the external environment and look ahead for planning purposes in order to remain competitive and survive. The two most widely used tools for deciding the strategic directions of a business are known as PEST and SWOT analyses.

PEST is an acronym for Political, Economic, Social and Technological factors. Generally, it is used in a marketing context. It encourages more lateral thinking. PEST provides a framework for looking at situations, reviewing and updating strategies or plans, establishing direction, considering a marketing proposition or assessing whether a new product or service is likely to be viable. The model is sometimes expanded to include legal and environmental factors (PESTLE). In use, appropriate questions or prompts are developed for the market issue under consideration. These are aligned to the four PEST quadrants. The issue needs to be clearly defined so that those contributing to the exercise understand fully the purpose and implications of the PEST model. In carrying out the PEST analysis, you can score the issues listed in each section. This is particularly useful if you are comparing more than one option for market entry purposes or business development opportunities. An example of the model to be followed is given here.

Subject (e.g. market, business proposition etc.)	
Political	**Economic**
Current legislative framework	Current domestic economic situation
Planned legislation	Economic forecasts
Government and regional policies	International economic outlook
International situation	Taxation issues
Trading conditions	Seasonal and climate impacts
Grants available	Market cycles
Pressure or campaigning groups	Specific sector outlook
Environmental issues	Interest and other bank charges
	Exchange rates
	International trade implications
Social	**Technological**
Demographics	Technology developments
Social trends	Research and its funding
Consumer attitudes, opinions and	Dependent technologies
buying habits	Technology solutions
Brand image	Production capacity
Product trends	Information and communications
Media coverage	technology
Selling channels	Consumer use of technology
Diversity	Innovation
PR and advertising	Licensing and patents
Ethical issues	Intellectual property
	Global technological issues

Note: the issues listed are given solely as a guide.

SWOT is an acronym for analysing the Strengths, Weaknesses, Opportunities and Threats for assessment of a business or proposition. It follows on from a PEST analysis, which provides you with market assessments from the standpoint of a particular proposition or business. SWOT assesses the strength of a business or proposition in the context of its competitors. The analysis is carried out under the headings of strengths, weaknesses, opportunities and threats, and the factors that appear in each of these quadrants are similar to those given above for the PEST assessment.

Finally, it is worth touching upon the concept of the Balanced Score Card, which has been defined as 'a strategic planning and management system used to align business activities to the vision statement of an organization'. Alternatively, it can be viewed as an attempt to embed an organization's vision and mission statements into practical implementation across the whole business. The Balanced Score Card is aimed at improving efficiency and joining up the interdependent, internal operations in relation to finance, internal processes, learning and development, and customers or clients. Prior to developing the score card you need to be aware of the business's vision, mission and strategic plan, and know its financial situation, its structure and operating procedures, employees' skill levels, customer satisfaction levels and other areas that may be identified for improvement. The following is an example of the areas that could possibly be improved under these headings.

Department	Areas
Finance	Return on investment Cash flow Return on capital employed Profit levels and other financial results
Internal business processes	Number of activities for each function Duplicate activities across functions Allocation of processes to the right department Blockages and delays in processes Computerization of processes

Learning and development	Appropriateness of employee skills levels
	Employee turnover
	Sickness absences
	Job satisfaction
	Training and development
Customers/clients	Delivery performance
	Quality performance
	Customer satisfaction
	Complaints/returns
	Percentage of market
	Retention rates

Measurements need to be set for each of these factors which are SMART (see the Monday chapter) and clearly aligned with the organization's strategic plan. The process can lead to more effective and relevant information systems, efficient processes, highly motivated and skilled employees, improved financial management and greater customer satisfaction.

Decision-making tools

All people managers have to solve problems and make decisions. These are closely linked tasks and there are systems available to improve the quality of your decision-making. The strategic development tools above can help in decision-making, but brainstorming is also another way of solving problems and making decisions. It is effective at unleashing creativity and identifying options. Workshops can also be useful for taking major decisions that require the commitment and support of all staff. A simple, straightforward method is to write down the pros and cons of particular options. This involves assessing the advantages and disadvantages, the points in favour and those against.

The steps to be followed for solving problems and taking decisions are:

● define and clarify the issue
● collect all the facts and build up an understanding of the reasons for the problem
● consider all possible options and solutions
● analyse the advantages and disadvantages of each option

- select the best option and make the decision
- explain your decision to those affected and ensure effective implementation.

This method, which can be scored, is best applied to routine decisions that are unlikely to have a major impact on the business. For example, buying a relatively inexpensive new piece of equipment or travelling to a meeting. A scored example is:

Should I travel to a meeting or handle the matter by video-conferencing?			
Pros (for – advantages)	Score	Cons (against – disadvantages)	Score
Face-to-face contact	3	Cost and time involved	5
Opportunity to build relationships	3	Difficult issues may be raised	3
Could visit other suppliers in the area	3	Not available to manage staff	4
Ability to assess operations on site	2		
Total: 4 pros	**11**	**Total: 3 cons**	**12**

When decisions involve a number of options and choices, the brainstorming method can be the most effective option. This is also suitable for use in a workshop setting. The method identifies and helps solve problems by developing decision-making options. It is suitable for use when there are more than a couple of options available and the decision is likely to have a relatively high impact on the business, for example selection of a new site for location of the business or deciding on new markets.

The process is:

- identify options and on a sheet for each, write the option concerned together with a pros and cons column
- write down as many impacts and implications as possible in each of the columns
- weight these on scores of 1 to 3, or 1 to 5, with 1 being the lowest
- compare the total scores and choose the most attractive option.

Some people are natural decision-makers, others may be better at analysing problems. Regardless of whether you are good at decision-making or problem analysis, these tools should help you and your team improve your decision-making capability and the quality of those decisions.

Quality management tools

All people managers need to be concerned about the quality of their staff, the work they undertake and the team's outputs. Quality management involves planning, control, assurance and improvement of a product or service. Processes are crucial to ensuring total quality management, which is defined as 'a set of coordinated activities to direct and control an organization in order to continually improve the effectiveness and efficiency of its performance'. A wide range of Total Quality Management tools are available to identify, measure, prioritize and improve processes. The best-known is probably the ISO 9000 standards; others include Kaizen, Six Sigma, EFQM and many more. It is likely that these will be organization-wide so as a people manager you will need to have a basic understanding of the concepts and the implications for you and your team.

   Quality management is based primarily on the following eight principles, which form the basis of the ISO (International Organization for Standardization) 9000 quality management system.

- An understanding of the needs of current and future customers, and meeting or exceeding their expectations. The focus should be on both external and internal customers.
- Strong leadership which is directional and motivational, and creates and maintains an internal culture of quality improvement.
- Involvement of people at all levels of the organization to capitalize on their abilities for the benefit of the organization.
- Process approach bringing together activities and related resources.
- All inter-related process are identified, understood and managed as a system in order to achieve quality objectives to contribute to the organization's efficiency and effectiveness.
- Continual improvement of overall performance.
- Decisions are based on facts from analysis of data and other information.
- Mutually beneficial supplier relationships in order to add value.

ISO 9000 quality management standards are aimed at delivering performance improvement through certifying an organization's processes and systems. One of the criticisms of it is that it is not concerned with the quality of the product or service.

Kaizen originated in Japan, where total quality management was pioneered. The word means continuous improvement. It is a way of thinking, working and behaving in accordance with the values and culture of an organization with the aims of being:

- profitable, stable, sustainable and innovative
- focused on eliminating waste and increasing productivity
- proactive in identifying potential problems in systems, processes and activities, and rectifying them before they arise
- creative in establishing a harmonious and dynamic organization in which everyone participates and is valued for their contribution.

It involves every aspect of the business all the time as well as full participation and empowerment of everyone. It uses a range of analytical tools and techniques to review systems and improve processes. There are close connections between the Kaizen philosophy and those of motivational theorists such as Maslow, Herzberg and McGregor, covered on Tuesday.

Six Sigma is suitable primarily for large manufacturing enterprises, but more recently has been applied to the service industry. It aims to improve the quality of process outputs by identifying and eradicating the causes of any defects or errors. It relies on statistical information and experts. The process involves a defined order of steps to be taken and has quantified financial targets aimed at cost reductions and/or increased profits. Recently the system has been developed in the light of lean manufacturing ideas to create the methodology known as Lean Six Sigma which aims for business and operational excellence by combining a focus on process flow and waste issues with the original Six Sigma focus on variation and design.

There is some debate about the effectiveness of Six Sigma in securing tangible business growth. Some regard it as no more than a basic quality improvement system that does not give rise to new products or technological innovation and which stifles creativity and innovation. Another criticism is its attention to reducing variation rather than robustness of systems to eliminate any need to reduce variation.

The **EFQM** (European Foundation for Quality Management) Excellence Model is a management framework which takes a holistic view of an organization. It is suitable for use in organizations of all sizes and from all sectors. It is widely used in both public and private sector organizations. The model is a self-assessment tool which uses nine criteria for identification and analysis of a body's strengths and weaker areas in order to develop an improvement plan aimed at sustainable growth and enhanced performance. The nine criteria are:

Enablers
{
1 Leadership
2 Strategy
3 People
4 Partnerships and resources
5 Process, products and service

Results
{
6 Key results
7 People results
8 Society results
9 Customer results

The first five criteria are regarded as 'enablers' because they cover what is done and how, while the remaining four are classified as 'results' because they are focused on what an organization achieves or delivers.

The model is based on the following eight Fundamental Concepts of Excellence.

1 Achieving balanced results

Excellent organizations meet their mission and progress towards their vision through planning and achieving a balanced set of results that meet both the short- and long-term needs of their stakeholders and, where relevant, exceed them.

2 Adding value for customers

Excellent organizations know that customers are their primary reason for being and strive to innovate and create value for them by understanding and anticipating their needs and expectations.

3 Leading with vision, inspiration and integrity

Excellent organizations have leaders who shape the future and make it happen, acting as role models for its values and ethics.

4 Managing by processes

Excellent organizations are managed through structured and strategically aligned processes using fact-based decision-making to create balanced and sustained results.

5 Succeeding through people

Excellent organizations value their people and create a culture of empowerment for the balanced achievement of organizational and personal goals.

6 Nurturing creativity and innovation
Excellent organizations generate increased value and levels of performance through continual and systematic innovation by harnessing the creativity of their stakeholders.

7 Building partnerships
Excellent organizations seek, develop and maintain trusting relationships with various partners to ensure mutual success. These partnerships may be formed with customers, society, key suppliers, educational bodies or non-governmental organizations (NGOs).

8 Taking responsibility for a sustainable future
Excellent organizations embed within their culture an ethical mindset, clear values and the highest standards of organizational behaviour, all of which enable them to strive for economic, social and ecological sustainability.

Although there is evidence of the success of organizations that have implemented the EFQM model in respect of both performance and outputs, it has been criticized for not supporting the remedying of problems. There is also a view that the model is best suited to transactional environments.

Project management tools

Project management tools can be useful for the people manager in a number of situations. They are primarily used for planning and managing change, but can be applied to a number of tasks, projects of all sizes and in a number of functional areas, including people management. A similar process is followed for all projects.

- Agree the specification (terms of reference) for the project.
- Plan implementation in terms of timescale, financial and staff resources, and milestones.
- Communicate to those involved and all those with an interest.
- Agree and allocate project actions.
- Manage the project through communicating, encouraging and enabling team members.
- Monitor implementation, review progress, adjust plans as necessary and communicate.

- Complete, review and report on performance.
- Follow up to ensure effective implementation through training, support and reporting of benefits.

The specification, or terms of reference, should provide a clear and accurate description of the project aims and generally cover its background, objectives, scope, constraints, assumptions, reporting and management arrangements, dependencies, estimates and timescales. The various stages of the project should be carefully planned, involving the team wherever possible. There are a number of tools available for detailed project planning which are relatively easy to understand. An example is a Gantt chart, which presents a separate timeline for each component part of the project, detailing the activity and costs. Another example is a Critical Path Analysis flow diagram, a linear flow diagram of the timeline that shows the anticipated timing of the use of resources and when activities will be carried out. The latter illustrates what needs to be done and when.

Most projects involving expenditure will require a spreadsheet such as MS Excel for planning, monitoring and reporting expenditure. Project timescales and costs should be realistic and not overambitious, and some risk assessment should be undertaken, including planning for contingencies. As regards the project team, this should be made up of committed individuals with the relevant skills and experience. Communication within the team and to relevant interests is vital in order to keep everyone informed and to secure their support, agreement and cooperation. The project activities delegated to the relevant team member need to be clear and accord with the SMART concept (see the Monday chapter).

Managing the project and motivating the team requires the people management approach we are covering this week, in particular what we learnt about managerial roles on Monday, and motivation and management styles on Tuesday and Wednesday. Once the project is completed, a review and report is necessary, together with follow-up, which may involve training and change management.

Project management is a specialized area of management, in a similar way to quality management, so it is not necessary for you, as a people manager, to have in-depth knowledge of the various techniques unless you are leading or are closely involved in a major project. Apart from Gantt charts and Critical Path Analysis, there are numerous software packages for project management purposes. In day-to-day work as a people manager, you will usually only need to apply the principles of project management.

Environmental management tools

Environmental management is likely to be an organization-wide function. As a people manager you would not normally be involved in detailed implementation unless you work in the functional area. However, all managers need to have an understanding of the environmental management tools and techniques used in their organization as they will be expected to ensure that their teams comply with the necessary requirements. With the increasing emphasis on the environmental impact of businesses of all types, organizations are now becoming aware of their responsibilities in relation to environmental sustainability. The best-known environmental management models and processes are EMS (Environmental Management Systems), ISO 14001 and EMAS (the Eco-management and Audit Scheme).

EMS is a comprehensive, systematic, planned and documented way of managing an organization's environmental policy and improving its environmental performance. It covers the organizational structure together with planning and resource allocation for developing and implementing environmental programmes to minimize the impact of an organization's whole range of activities on the environment. EMS is concerned with evaluations of practices, processes and procedures with a focus on continual improvement. The model follows a Plan-Do-Check-Act (PDCA) cycle.

ISO (International Organization for Standardization) 14001 is an environmental management standard which sets out the specific standards to be met in order for an organization to be certified. It has been adopted globally. EMS may incorporate ISO 14001, the aim of which is to improve environmental performance and legal compliance across a range of relevant aspects in order to save costs through waste minimization and efficient use of energy and water, ensure compliance with environmental regulation and manage risks effectively.

The Eco-Management and Audit Scheme (EMAS) is a European Union voluntary certification scheme which incorporates ISO 14001 but is more comprehensive and robust. It demands strict adherence to the measurement and evaluation of environmental performance targets against set targets in relation to six environmental indicators. These indicators cover efficiency in the use of energy, materials, waste and emissions as well as protection of biodiversity. The system has been shown to lead to significant business cost savings.

Summary

Today we have covered briefly the various tools that are available to you as a people manager to support you in managing the performance of your staff, developing or contributing to strategy formulation, project managing tasks and understanding quality and environmental management systems. These tools can be useful in enabling you to become more effective in your role as a people manager.

People management is a highly variable role. It is impossible to be prescriptive about how to carry out the task because of its many variables. Knowledge of people management, strategy development, project management, and environmental and quality management tools and techniques should contribute to your efficiency and effectiveness in your multifarious people management tasks.

SUNDAY
MONDAY
TUESDAY
WEDNESDAY
THURSDAY
FRIDAY
SATURDAY

Fact-check (answers at the back)

1. People's aptitudes can be tested through:
   a) SWOT ❏
   b) EMAS ❏
   c) Verbal reasoning ❏
   d) MBTI ❏

2. Team-working roles are established through:
   a) ISO 14001 ❏
   b) Belbin ❏
   c) Brain-storming ❏
   d) Logical reasoning ❏

3. Psychometric tests are used for:
   a) Decision-making ❏
   b) Recruitment ❏
   c) Planning ❏
   d) Market assessment ❏

4. Which of the following is one of Belbin's team role names?
   a) Coordinator ❏
   b) Leader ❏
   c) Strategist ❏
   d) Manager ❏

5. Firo–B is a type of:
   a) Strategic tool ❏
   b) Environmental system ❏
   c) Personality test ❏
   d) Decision-making tool ❏

6. PEST means... Complete the words.
   a) P...... ❏
   b) E...... ❏
   c) S...... ❏
   d) T...... ❏

7. SWOT is used for:
   a) Market assessment ❏
   b) Decision-making ❏
   c) Strategic planning ❏
   d) Quality management ❏

8. The Balanced Score Card is used for:
   a) Project management ❏
   b) Environmental management ❏
   c) Decision-making ❏
   d) Strategic planning ❏

9. EFQM is a:
   a) Environmental system ❏
   b) Quality management system ❏
   c) Project management system ❏
   d) Decision-making system ❏

10. A Gantt chart is a tool for:
   a) Personality assessment ❏
   b) Team-building ❏
   c) Project management ❏
   d) Strategic planning ❏

FRIDAY

How people managers manage performance

We should now have a sound understanding of people management, what people managers do, how to motivate staff, people managers' various management styles, and the tools and techniques that are available to people managers to help them do their jobs. Today it is time to look at how people managers can performance manage their teams effectively in the wider organizational context.

We are going to discuss the meaning of performance management and how this is done in practice. A sample work plan aimed at improvement is provided as an illustration of how you can compile a plan for your team in order to monitor and review performance against targets and objectives on a regular basis.

We cover the performance management process and the performance management tools that are available at organizational, team and individual levels. Finally, we conclude by summarizing the benefits of effective performance management.

By the end of today you should have developed:

an understanding of performance management

an understanding of how to implement it in practice

Performance management

Performance management is a process at the heart of people management. It is about ensuring that the goals of the organization, division, team or unit and individuals are realized in the most effective and efficient manner. In effect, it takes place at all of these levels. Effective performance management is dependent on having the right systems and people in place. It needs to be integrated into day-to-day management tasks. Generally, all businesses of a reasonable size have a strategic plan underpinned with annual business plans, which are reviewed throughout the year. On Thursday we covered performance management tools that relate to the implementation of these plans and are suitable for use at organizational, divisional and team level, such as EFQM, Six Sigma and the Balanced Score Card.

Performance management should take a long-term view of the development of teams and individuals in line with business requirements. It needs a structure which provides a framework to enable people to understand what is required of them. The corporate strategic goals are a starting point from which departmental and team performance and development goals can be developed into a work plan suitable for regular review. In order to manage performance successfully at a team and individual level, the people manager needs to have a clear work plan covering the financial year which is linked to the overall organizational plan. It is important to have input into the plan from staff responsible for delivering the work objectives.

Performance management at all levels follows a cycle which involves planning, taking action, reviewing and revising. Each team or unit should have a delivery plan which relates to higher-level business plans and strategies. Team members should have had an opportunity to contribute to the plan and the individuals concerned should have an annual performance plan which sets out their expected contribution to the delivery of the plan. The individual performance plan is a tool for managing both someone's behaviour and outputs. It is aimed at developing people and improving their performance by aligning personal goals with those of the wider organization. A people manager can use performance management for maximizing the performance of the team or individual or to deal with poor performance. Although the principles are the same, the former is often a more collaborative, informal process, while the latter involves confronting performance issues and recording formally the steps in the process because it can lead to disciplinary proceedings or termination of employment.

In performance managing staff, a people manager should ensure that individuals understand clearly what is expected of them in terms of output, contributions, behaviours and development. You should also ensure that people have the necessary knowledge, skills and abilities to deliver; if these are deficient in any way, provide support to address any knowledge or skills gaps or any behavioural issues. Sensitive feedback is an important part of this, which should be a two-way conversation so there is understanding and clarification of perspectives and perceptions. It provides an opportunity for staff to communicate their needs and wishes regarding how they are managed. People managers need to be aware of the impact of their own behaviour on others and be concerned to demonstrate positive behaviours.

Performance management is, therefore, a two-way process for developing successful relationships between the people manager and the individual as well as the team. It is a continuous process which covers all aspects relevant to running a successful business and forms part of day-to-day management. Successful people management is dependent on effective performance management, which brings together people with systems and processes in an environment shaped by leadership and culture.

The right organizational culture is critical to improving performance management. It is difficult to describe a culture. It is best explained as the sum total of the beliefs, values and behaviours of individuals within a given group. An organizational culture is the means by which norms of acceptable behaviour are established, although it is not

Example of a team performance plan

Organizational aim: To increase the levels of manufacture and sales of high-value cheeses by 20%							
Divisional aim: To market a range of high-value cheeses and increase sales by 20%							
Team aim: To market the cheeses and increase the number of customers leading to 20% increase in sales Staff resources: 1 marketing manager (MM), 1 assistant marketing manager (AMM) and 2 marketing assistants (MA) Financial resource: £1 million							
Objective	Tasks	Staff resource	Financial resource	Milestone	Target	Outcomes
To develop a marketing campaign	Undertake market research Market segmentation Prepare marketing plan	MM 0.2 AMM 0.3 MA 0.5	£50,000	05 April 12 April 25 April	30 April	Agreed marketing plan for implementation
To attend trade and consumer shows in order to increase customer base by 20%	Identify appropriate show Make booking Organize stands and staffing arrangements Attend shows Follow up actions	MM 0.4 AMM 0.2 MA 0.5	£250,000	14 April 30 April 6 weeks before show On show days Within 5 days	4 shows annually	£1.5m of new orders 20 new customers

To organize advertising campaign in order to generate new leads	Commission agency	MM 0.2	£500,000	30 April	Peak viewing figures	Two campaigns generating 50 new leads
	Agree advertisement copy etc	AMM 0.3		31 May	1,000 social media mentions	
	Approve campaign	MA 0.5		30 June		
	Monitor implementation			Ongoing		
To organize PR to create greater brand awareness	Draft and issue press releases	MM 0.2 AMM 0.2 MA 0.5	£200,000	Minimum of 1 a week	15 annually	Increase in media coverage
	Updating of website			Daily	Up-to-date website	Increase in website hits
	Twitter comments and monitoring			Daily	Daily comment	Increase in Twitter comments
	Facebook updates and monitoring			Daily	Daily update	Increase in number of Facebook hits

Note: on average an employee works for about 44 weeks a year (220 days). One day of a five-day working week is 0.2 days, half a day is 0.1.

unusual in larger organizations to have a number of sub-cultures. In some organizations a culture of performance improvement may exist where the ethos of continual improvement is embedded among all staff who are keen to provide the best possible products/services to its customers and clients. In others, a performance management culture is found where the emphasis is on management through the development of systems and processes to measure and report on performance with the aim of improvement.

Managing performance requires the striking of a balance between nurturing and developing people and ensuring that the team's goals and objectives are achieved, and that a valuable contribution is made to the overall performance of the business. A people manager has to achieve this balance according to the particular situation they face and doing so is challenging. For example, a people manager may be under pressure to deliver work objectives for which he or she is accountable, but this is affected by a key member of staff underperforming due to personal circumstances outside the control of the people manager. The people manager will need to assess many such challenging situations and adopt the most appropriate managerial response as there is an inextricable link between good people management and good performance.

The performance management process

The role of the people manager in relationship to performance management is to show leadership and be an exemplar in terms of his or her performance and behaviour. Through his or her own performance the people manager should achieve the following.

● **Set out a clear vision for the team's performance in line with the wider organizational goals and culture.**
Individuals need to know how their work fits in with the rest of the business and how their contribution can make a difference to the business's success or failure.

- **Communicate to the team and individuals what is expected of them in terms of quality of work, quantity of work, timescales, milestones and behaviours.**
Poor or ineffective communication is frequently the reason why people fail to perform to the expected standards. People need to know, without doubt, what expectations there are of them and these expectations need to be reasonable in terms of the ability and capacity of the individual. It is always worthwhile seeking the agreement of staff to what is required of them.
- **Motivate staff and continually monitor performance.**
The importance of motivation of staff was covered on Tuesday and the role of the people manager in monitoring and controlling performance was discussed on Monday. It needs to be emphasized that people managers should support and help staff in meeting the standards and expectations the organization has of them. Seeking agreement to performance expectations provides an opportunity to explore with a staff member what help or support is needed. It is important to ask in order to test out perceptions and avoid presumptions. People need to know for certain what is to be done, why and how.
- **Engage staff in planning; seek and act upon their views on performance improvements.**
The people manager should work in harmony with team members. He or she should not normally act in isolation from the team, particularly in respect of work planning and performance improvement. Individual team members can make a valuable contribution to preparation of a challenging but achievable plan and are well-placed to suggest ways in which performance can be improved at individual and team levels.
- **Provide regular praise and feedback on areas for improvement.**
People need to know how they are performing. They value positive feedback and expressions of appreciation. Equally, they would prefer to have immediate feedback on areas for improvement, rather than be informed at a later date or not be told at all. Negative feedback should be delivered in a supportive and non-judgemental way, focused on an area referred to as less strong rather than as a weakness.

- **Support the performance and development of staff.**
  The majority of people will need support at some time. This may relate to help in completing a task because the timescale is too tight, clarification of a problem, the need for advice in dealing with a difficult customer, time off to deal with an unexpected domestic problem, and numerous other issues that crop up from time to time that may impact on a person's performance. It is part of the role of a people manager to support his or her staff in dealing with any difficulties that arise. We will touch upon people development in more detail on Saturday, but this is a good point to flag up that many people are keen to learn and develop. Some will become disenchanted with their jobs if they are not challenged, stretched and given development opportunities. The people manager needs to know his or her staff sufficiently well to understand their motivations and identify those that need continual development and those that need developmental support to carry out their jobs to a satisfactory standard.
- **Facilitate learning and development.**
  Following on from the above, businesses that have people learning and development embedded in their cultures are often the most successful. A people manager should identify staff who would benefit from learning and development initiatives and facilitate this through providing the time and/ or financial resources to allow it to take place for the good of the individual and the benefit of the business.
- **Be a model of exemplary behaviour in terms of good performance management.**
  If you are respected as a people manager by demonstrating your commitment to excellent performance, showing empathy with team members and displaying ethical behaviours in accordance with the norms of the organization, people will want to emulate your commitment and behaviours. This will have a beneficial effect on the work and reputation of the business. Conversely, if you say the right words but do not act them out, people will soon note your lack of authenticity and will be less inclined to perform to the best of their ability.

Performance management tools

Performance appraisal

Performance appraisal, sometimes known as a performance review or performance evaluation, is an important component of performance management. Performance management is a strategic, holistic process which brings together all the activities that contribute to the successful management of people and teams in order to achieve high levels of performance. Performance appraisal is one of a number of performance management tools. It is focused on the individual and adopts a relatively short-term approach. The process provides an opportunity for the people manager to talk to individual team members about their performance, development needs and the extent of managerial support needed. It is about reviewing past performance, identifying areas which have been done well and those where improvement is needed. The appraisal process also considers and agrees an individual's development needs.

Performance appraisal is another tool for people managers to use to successfully manage their teams, with a focus on improvement, development and behavioural management. An individual performance plan should, therefore, cover the many aspects of successful people management such as goal achievements and behaviours, as well as learning and development.

The people manager carries out the appraisal process, which should be concerned with an individual's overall job performance, in particular the quality of their work and their outputs in line with pre-agreed criteria and targets. The exercise is usually carried out annually, but it is advisable to undertake mid-year reviews. Its main purpose is performance improvement, but it can serve the purposes of identification of talent, disciplinary action, termination of employment and application of pay and reward systems, and provides the opportunity for one-to-one communication.

Generally, performance appraisal follows six steps.

1 Measurement of performance against previously agreed targets and objectives, which should correlate with the team's work plan – an example of which has been given earlier in this chapter.
2 Evaluation of behaviours and attitudes against the organization's espoused values.
3 Positive feedback in terms of what has been done well and where measurable targets and objectives have been met or exceeded.
4 Constructive criticism on areas where there is a need for improvement, offering support and advice as to how this could be achieved.
5 Listening to the appraisee's perspective, support requirements and needs together with their career aspirations.
6 Agreement on and recording of future targets and objectives, and what needs to be done to improve performance.

Many organizations have developed forms for taking staff through the appraisal system, covering achievement of objectives/targets, levels of competence for the role, training and development requirements and agreed actions.

There are a number of benefits to be gained from conducting a performance appraisal. These include a focus on improving performance, the gaining of useful two-way information, promotion of trust, collaboration on goal-setting and determining training requirements. On the other hand, performance appraisals are viewed by some as unnecessary if businesses already have a total quality management system in place. They are sometimes viewed as negative experiences and can lead to inflated ratings, as well as legal action if not carried out properly.

In carrying out a performance appraisal, the people manager needs to be honest, clear and specific, to give praise as well as criticism and to be sensitive to how his or her messages are likely to be received by those being appraised.

360-degree feedback

Another form of staff performance appraisal is 360-degree feedback, which collects views and feedback on an individual's performance from a range of people with whom the individual interacts on a day-to-day basis. It is claimed that this method provides a more rounded, accurate and less prejudiced view of the individual's performance. Normally, the views of between eight and ten people are sought through the use of questionnaires. These include customers as well as internal staff. The questionnaires include a series of statements which are rated on a scale, usually one to five. The feedback should be anonymized and conducted by someone skilled in the process.

Learning and development

Businesses that are concerned to develop their people and establish learning cultures are those which are more likely to be successful. It is beneficial for every team member to have a personal development plan (PDP) which sets out a list of time-bound actions to develop their knowledge and skills in the job as well as developing their competencies for career progression or specialism. Although the focus of PDPs is on the individual, the aim should be closely related to developing organizational capability.

Objectives, performance standards and measurement

The individual team member's objectives or targets should relate to a work plan similar to the one illustrated at the beginning of this chapter. They can be either results-orientated, relate to personal development objectives or both. Objectives and targets should be clearly defined and measurable, and agreed with the person concerned.

The benefits of good performance management

There are many benefits to be accrued from effective performance management at organizational, divisional and team levels. A transparent, challenging but achievable set of performance measures communicated effectively to a valued and involved workforce results in sound management control that is likely to lead to increased outputs/sales, improved delivery times, cost reductions, projects delivered on time and to budget, and the meeting of top-level strategic goals.

Summary

Performance management is a key part of the people manager's job. It involves having the right people and processes in place as both are fundamental to achieving an organization's objectives. It should take place at all levels of the business, from director of board level down to individuals. The existence of effective processes enables the people manager to set out and monitor work processes against targets and goals, and behaviour and development expectations of team members in line with the business's wider strategic objectives.

Performance management is useful for identifying areas of poor performance and those areas where the development of staff is needed.

We have touched upon the importance of culture and leadership in order to improve or manage performance, pointing out that some organizations have embedded cultures of continual performance improvement, while in others there is a reliance on systems and processes.

The benefits of good performance management were highlighted.

SUNDAY
MONDAY
TUESDAY
WEDNESDAY
THURSDAY
FRIDAY
SATURDAY

Fact-check (answers at the back)

1. Performance management takes place at:
   a) Organizational level ❏
   b) Team level ❏
   c) Individual level ❏
   d) All levels ❏

2. A team plan is used for:
   a) Setting strategic goals ❏
   b) Personal development ❏
   c) Performance management ❏
   d) Monitoring profit levels ❏

3. An organizational culture relates to:
   a) The industry sector ❏
   b) Management style ❏
   c) Country links ❏
   d) Values, beliefs and behaviours of an organization ❏

4. The performance management process involves:
   a) Leadership ❏
   b) Sales ❏
   c) Project management ❏
   d) Environmental management ❏

5. A performance management tool is:
   a) A workshop ❏
   b) 360-degree feedback ❏
   c) Critical Path Analysis ❏
   d) EFQM ❏

6. Performance appraisals relate to:
   a) Management ❏
   b) The performance plan ❏
   c) The team ❏
   d) Individuals ❏

7. The benefits of performance appraisal are:
   a) Increase in sales ❏
   b) Quality management ❏
   c) Work control ❏
   d) Determination of development requirements ❏

8. 360-degree appraisals seek the views of:
   a) Subordinates ❏
   b) Management ❏
   c) Peers ❏
   d) A range of contacts ❏

9. A personal development plan:
   a) Lists job tasks ❏
   b) Includes strategic aims ❏
   c) Focuses on learning and development ❏
   d) Identifies required behaviours ❏

10. Benefits of good performance include:
    a) Cost reductions ❏
    b) New market entry ❏
    c) Setting of strategic goals ❏
    d) Increase in staff turnover ❏

SUNDAY

MONDAY

TUESDAY

WEDNESDAY

THURSDAY

FRIDAY

SATURDAY

SATURDAY

How people managers develop their teams

On our final day, we are going to cover ways in which people managers can develop their teams. Team development is a fundamental part of the people manager's role, but often the most neglected due to pressure to meet work targets or personal ambitions.

However, there are obvious advantages to the people manager if he or she focuses on bringing together a cohesive, motivated and committed team. Such teams generally produce good quality work first time around, work tirelessly to achieve targets, come up with ideas and embrace change. They are also likely to have a low staff turnover and low sickness absenteeism.

We are going to explore the usefulness of a well-known group development model and the various ways in which team members can be developed. By the end of today you will have an appreciation of:

The importance of training and development

A well-known group development model

The various ways of training and developing staff

Building successful teams

Building a successful team is another major challenge faced by people managers. Work teams bring together groups of people with different personal characteristics, backgrounds and life experiences. Furthermore, the individuals are likely to have differing abilities and capacities for the tasks they are expected carry out. A people manager may either inherit a team that has been in existence for some time, be expected to bring together a new team, introduce new team members or drive forward change within the team. In each of these cases, team members need to learn to work together to function at maximum performance levels. It is the people manager's role to facilitate and encourage the efficient and effective functioning of the team.

The group development model

Almost half a century ago, Bruce Tuckman put forward a model of group development that comprises the stages of forming, storming, norming and performing. It is useful for the people manager to know about this model to develop an appreciation of group dynamics and their role in ensuring that the team works to maximum effect. It can also be helpful for the people manager to share their knowledge of the model with the team so that they can also understand the dynamics of the process.

The first stage of team development involves the initial forming of the team and can take place when a new team is set up or someone new joins an already established team. In this situation, people generally display their best behaviour because they are keen to be accepted and fit into the group. Every effort is made to avoid any conflict or disagreement by not dealing with any issues that may need to be addressed and ignoring any feelings that may arise. During this phase people tend to be more concerned about routine processes and procedures than outputs, while spending time gathering views and impressions of the other members of the team.

In the forming period, the people manager needs to support the team or new team member(s) in learning about the challenges and opportunities they face. Agreement also needs to be reached on team and/or individual goals and objectives prior to working on the tasks. Often there is a need for the people manager to adopt a directive management style during this phase, which gives him or her an opportunity to assess how the team members work individually and together and their responses in particular situations, such as those that are stressful.

The forming stage is followed by the storming stage where people open up and the contentious issues and disagreements avoided during the first stage are brought out into the open. It is a stage during which there is competition between different ideas and views that need to be reconciled. Some team members will find this phase particularly hard and try to evade addressing any disagreements by focusing on detailed, inconsequential tasks. This is a particularly difficult stage for the people manager because it is one of confronting issues, which inevitably gives rise to conflict. It is also the phase when team members make up their minds about the sort of management style that will be acceptable to them. The people manager will need to exercise tolerance and patience during this period, which is important if the team is to develop into an effective unit. He or she will probably need to continue with a directive management style, but be more available to team members to ensure sound decisions are made and professional behavioural standards upheld. It will also be important to be non-judgemental during this time and encourage individuals to accept their differences.

The norming stage is when the team's plans and goals have been agreed and accepted, and individuals settle down to take responsibility and carry out their particular tasks in pursuit of successful achievement of the team's goals. This is an easier stage for the people manager to handle and will require a more permissive management style.

The final stage is that of performing, which occurs when the team operates smoothly and functions efficiently and effectively. During this stage team members are highly motivated, skilled and knowledgeable, and are able to resolve any differences that may arise. The people manager's style in this phase should primarily be permissive. The Tuckman model is discussed further in the Sunday and Thursday sections of Week 3.

Developing team members

One of the main functions of a people manager is the training and development of staff to grow a high-performing team that is making a valuable contribution to the achievement of organizational goals and targets. In developing staff, people managers need to take account of individual learning styles and decide on the most appropriate means of development for the individual and the team. It is important, therefore, to have an appreciation of learning styles and the main means of developing teams. These aspects are discussed below.

Learning styles

People have different ways of learning and these rarely vary throughout their working lives, so it is important for people managers to understand the various learning styles of the staff for whom they are responsible. People handle information in different ways. For example, some like information provided in a formal, structured way, some prefer to have a degree of independence in collecting and analysing information, while others enjoy processing complex information and developing theories. Some people, particularly extroverts, need a high level of involvement and participation in gathering and learning new information and theories. The majority of people have a dominant learning style or technique, but generally they have a mix of styles that they adapt for different circumstances.

Knowledge of your own learning style and those of the people you manage will help in the design of the most appropriate learning methods for individuals. The most commonly mentioned styles are the following.

- Visual learners learn through seeing and watching others, and respond best to pictures, diagrams, videos etc.
- Auditory learners learn through lectures, presentations and discussions with others. They prefer to talk things through and listen to others' views.

- Linguistic or verbal learners gain knowledge primarily through reading and writing or through listening to information.
- Physical or kinaesthetic people learn best through a hands-on approach and active exploration.
- Logical people learn through analysis, reasoning and logic.
- Social or interpersonal learners learn most effectively in groups or through interactions with other people.
- Solitary or intrapersonal learners work things through on their own through self-study.

The people manager has a number of methods available to him or her for training and developing staff to achieve a high-performing team. The main methods include on-the-job training, coaching, mentoring and formal training and education.

On-the-job training

On-the-job training, which involves staff being trained while remaining in the workplace, is considered to be one of the most effective means of training. It takes place in the normal working environment and can involve an experienced member of staff or the people manager working alongside a new staff member to pass on their knowledge and skills. The people manager has a valuable role in providing this training by selecting the most appropriate form of on-the-job training for the individual, or possibly delivering the training himself or herself. He or she should check that the staff member has received sufficient training to carry out the required tasks.

The most popular methods of on-the-job training include:

- demonstration or the use of instructions
- following manuals or operating procedures
- coaching, which is referred to in more detail below
- hands-on practice under supervision.

The advantages of on-the-job training are its cost-effectiveness and the fact that an employee is also productive while undergoing the training. Disadvantages are the possibility of disruption to work flow and the effectiveness of the training being dependent to a degree on the quality of the trainer.

Coaching

In recent years there has been a significant interest and growth in coaching as a means of developing staff and teams. Coaching is about helping to identify people's skills and capabilities and enabling them to use these to the best of their ability. Coaching in the workplace involves the individual being supported in learning to achieve a result or goal, or for personal or professional development purposes. Coaching may be done with individuals or with groups, either in person, over the phone or through online contact. Generally, it takes place for a limited amount of time.

Many organizations now expect people managers to coach their teams to achieve higher performance levels, personal growth and career development. As a people manager there is, therefore, merit in you developing the basic skills of coaching to improve your management and leadership abilities, and to be more effective in facilitating team meetings.

There are a number of models and styles of coaching; the most common involves asking questions and challenging the coachee to find the answers himself or herself. Coaches may also use inquiry, reflection and discussion to help those being coached to identify personal or business goals and develop action plans to achieve them. These goals may be many and varied, such as handling interpersonal relationships, improving behaviours, dealing with conflict or developing competence in particular areas.

Mentoring

Although there are close similarities between coaching and mentoring, and a coach can act as a mentor, there are differences between the two concepts. Mentoring involves a developmental relationship between an experienced individual and someone less experienced who would gain from the interactions between them. It uses the same models as coaching and demands the same skills, such as listening, questioning, clarifying and reframing. Mentoring is generally a longer-term relationship than coaching. It provides a learning opportunity for both parties.

As a people manager you are expected to act as a mentor to your staff. This is one of a number of ways in which you can help their development and improve their and the team's performance. Mentoring is an effective way of achieving higher productivity and growth. Generally, people value the opportunity to learn from others who are more experienced than them and those that actively seek mentoring are more likely to be successful. A mentor shares his or her own experiences with the mentee so that he or she can benefit from this in pursuit of his or her personal development. The aim is to share experience, encourage and ask pertinent questions in order to get mentees to learn for themselves. Showing interest in the person as well as the particular issue should form a part of the mentoring process. It is about listening and helping them rationalize their plans and can involve delivering unpopular messages that the mentee may not want to hear. Mentors transfer their knowledge and experience to others and do this willingly.

Apart from your role as a mentor to your staff, there would be value in selecting a mentor for yourself in order to have external, objective support in becoming a successful people manager.

Training and educational courses

There are usually costs associated with training and educational courses; the costs of the course itself and the costs to the business of not having a productive member for staff available for the course time. As a people manager you need to be certain that the training or educational course is in the organization's interest and that the contents of the proposed course cannot be delivered in a different and more cost-effective way. You also need to be certain that you have the budget to cover the costs and that other necessary team training will not suffer as a result. It might be worthwhile sending one team member on a course with the aim of them passing on their learning to others in the team.

There are several other ways in which a people manager can develop staff. These include secondment to another team or department, work shadowing, project work and job rotation. As a people manager, it is a prime task of yours to focus on the training and development of staff in order that the team can produce the best work possible in terms of quality and output. Identifying the need for training and development can be achieved through day-to-day observation or the performance management tools that were discussed on Friday. Once the need has been identified it is important to consider the most appropriate means of delivery of the training or development. This should be in accordance with the nature of the training or development required, the learning styles of the individual concerned and the team's overall budgetary and time constraints.

Summary

Finally, we have discussed the importance of people managers developing their teams and the various ways in which this can be done. The need to recognize and take account of differing skills levels and learning styles was stressed.

The well-known Tuckman group development model was explained, in particular the various stages of forming, storming and norming.

It was pointed out that the people manager should have knowledge of various learning styles so that he or she can assess the best way to develop individuals according to their preferred learning method.

A number of training and development methods were outlined, such as on-the-job training, coaching, mentoring, and training and educational courses.

SUNDAY
MONDAY
TUESDAY
WEDNESDAY
THURSDAY
FRIDAY
SATURDAY

Fact-check (answers at the back)

1. Which stage is not included in Tuckman's model?
   a) Norming ❏
   b) Performing ❏
   c) Reforming ❏
   d) Storming ❏

2. Conflict and disagreement emerges in which stage?
   a) Performing ❏
   b) Reforming ❏
   c) Norming ❏
   d) Storming ❏

3. A directive management style is suitable for which stage?
   a) Performing ❏
   b) Norming ❏
   c) Storming ❏
   d) Forming ❏

4. Which management style is appropriate for the performing stage?
   a) Permissive ❏
   b) Autocratic ❏
   c) Bureaucratic ❏
   d) Directive ❏

5. Which is not a recognized learning style?
   a) Visual ❏
   b) Coaching ❏
   c) Physical ❏
   d) Solitary ❏

6. On-the-job training does not involve:
   a) Mentoring ❏
   b) Coaching ❏
   c) Educational courses ❏
   d) Guidance ❏

7. Logical people learn through:
   a) Interactions ❏
   b) Seeing ❏
   c) Discussions ❏
   d) Reasoning ❏

8. Social people learn best:
   a) Through analysis ❏
   b) Lectures ❏
   c) In groups ❏
   d) Practical exploration ❏

9. On-the-job training involves:
   a) Lectures ❏
   b) Self-study ❏
   c) Mentoring ❏
   d) Group discussions ❏

10. Mentoring differs from coaching by:
    a) Being longer term ❏
    b) Questioning ❏
    c) Reflecting ❏
    d) Challenging ❏

SATURDAY

FRIDAY THURSDAY WEDNESDAY TUESDAY MONDAY SUNDAY

WEEK 3
Managing Teams
In A Week

Introduction

'There is no "i" in team but there is in win.'

Michael Jordan

The recent 2012 London Olympics displayed many excellent winning teams showing brilliance in how they worked together. We saw great team coordination, team spirit, focus on collective goals and a unity in how they worked to achieve their goals. Some of the teams had outstanding individuals in their teams who were also great team players. When watching such teams perform, we are awestruck by the beauty and efficiency of these Olympian teams' performances. After reading Week 3, you will be able to create and lead a team full of such Olympian types with an Olympic team spirit!

Very few people can succeed in their careers without having to manage, supervise and lead other people. Exceptions might include specialists in their fields who are able to grow in their chosen careers without needing to manage anyone. But virtually everyone is part of a team, and at some point in their working lives they must take a leadership role – if only to chair a team meeting or a project in their boss' absence.

Leading a group of people in a team involves many variables, including each team member's personality, expectations, experience and ambitions. Putting a group of people together can produce all kinds of outcomes – sometimes negative (such as conflicts, arguments, poor performance etc) and sometimes positive (great synergy, alignment, great results etc). The role of a team leader or manager is to minimize any potential negative outcomes while maximizing the positive potential of the team.

Week 3 will walk you through the entire process of successfully leading and managing a team, showing you the key dos and don'ts and spelling out where you need to put special attention and focus. These seven chapters will cover:

How to get started with a team, exploring what a great team looks like and how it performs, and how to create a new team from scratch with individuals who bring their own habits, skills and expectations

The stages of development of a team and how a new manager can gain the respect and understanding of a team

The importance of aligning a team and setting common goals and expectations with clear agreement on a mission, vision and values.

How to create a team culture and processes of excellent communication, with clearly understood expectations, well-run team meetings and discussions, and the minimizing of any conflict and gossip

How to work with remote or virtual team members where face-to-face meetings are difficult to arrange

How to identify and work with problematic and non-performing members of your team and how to balance fairness and discipline

How to ensure that each team member's job role is clear and that the work is efficiently delegated and shared among the team members

How to grow your team through excellent training and development, including coaching, mentoring and on-the-job training

Turning a good team into a team with a culture of excellence

How to create a self-functioning team which can operate in your absence and in which you have groomed a successor to take over from you if needed.

SUNDAY

Getting started with your team

The first step in learning to successfully lead and manage a team is to understand the secrets of being a team leader, whether of an existing team or a team you are creating from scratch. Often you will face a combination of the two, taking over an existing team while also being expected to change its members.

To create a great team, one must first be able to visualize what a high-performing team is like, what goals and objectives such a team aims to achieve, how it works towards achieving these goals and what makes it appear successful.

A second key aspect of creating a new team or joining a team as its leader is understanding that a team grows and develops over time and that its issues, challenges and performance will be strongly influenced by the stage that it has reached in its development.

This chapter will show you how to:

- Understand what teams are and why we need them
- Think through what team excellence looks and feels like
- Create a new team from scratch, exploring the key dos and don'ts
- Apply Tuckman's 'stages of a team' model
- Take over an existing team, gaining its respect and understanding

What are teams and why do we need them?

'Talent wins games, but teamwork and intelligence wins championships.'

Michael Jordan

'Overcoming barriers to performance is how groups become teams.'

Katzenbach and Smith

A team can be defined as a group of individuals who are brought together and organized to work together to achieve common collective aims, purposes, objectives or goals. One could argue that if the team has no common objectives or goals, it is simply a group of individuals who just happen to be sharing the same office or job titles.

What makes a team great?

Take a moment to think of a great team, perhaps one you watched during the Olympic Games or a team you have worked in.

What makes your chosen team appear to be a great one?

- Is it because of what they have achieved? Do they achieve far more than other similar teams? Do they always achieve perfect results?
- What skills and knowledge do the team's members possess which might make them stand out?
- Is it because of who is in the team? Does it comprise some high-performing individuals?
- Is it because of how they work together? Do they appear to be aligned? Do they appear to work very positively together?
- Is it because of how they are led and managed? Has the team's leader been in the same role for a long time?
- Is it a team that you wish to be part of? Do you think that you would excel in such a team?

How do you like being managed?

In addition to exploring what makes a team appear like a great and successful one, it is helpful to think about your experiences of being in a team and how those teams were led and managed. Think back and reflect on the bosses you have had in the recent past and then answer the following two questions:

1 In what ways were you and your colleagues managed which inspired and motivated you to want to be in the team, to work harder and generally to feel valued?
2 In what ways were you and your colleagues managed that you did not like and which did not motivate you or inspire you to want to work hard and be in the team?

Answers typically include the following kinds of responses:

Q1: Positive ways of being managed	Q2: Negative ways of being managed
Recognized members of the team for their good performance	Showed too much favouritism to certain members of the team
Openly communicated and talked with all of us	Team meetings were too long and boring

(Continued)

Listened well to our ideas and concerns and gave credit where due	Took credit for all of our effort and work
Recognized the individuality of each of us in the team	Always seemed to delegate all of his/her work to us without ever really explaining what we had to do

Keep a list of your answers to serve as a reminder ensuring that you only repeat the positive habits of your current and past bosses and not their negative ways of managing their teams.

The aim of Week 3 is to ensure that your staff will view you very positively as their boss and, if asked to answer the same two questions, would give a list of positives far longer than any list of negatives!

Understanding the stages of a team

We all change and evolve over time and it is to be hoped as we grow through childhood into adulthood that we will grow not only in age but also positively in terms of our personality, experience and skills.

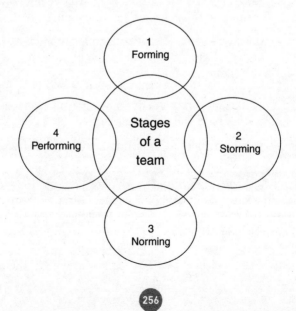

Given that a team is made up of individuals, it should not surprise you to learn that teams also go through different stages of development, from being created through to becoming a mature and, hopefully, high-performing team.

One model of such team development is key to your understanding of teams. It is called the Tuckman model and it is made up of four stages describing a team's development:

Stage 1: Forming

Sometimes called the infant or child stage of a team's development, Stage 1 occurs when a team is newly created or 'born'. During this stage the new team's members are learning their way together and it is sometimes called a period of testing and dependence where the necessary processes, norms and common understandings are not yet in place.

A leader of a forming team may typically observe and experience the following happening among the team members:

● not knowing who to ask for help or what to do
● cautiousness as people test what is acceptable and needed
● beginning to develop trust in each other
● complaints that things are not what they are used to
● anxiety
● getting to know the common goals and expectations.

Have you experienced working and/or leading a team that is moving through the forming stage? What do you recall about this period?

Stage 2: Storming

Some refer to this stage as the rebellious teenage years of a team's growth and development. This is the most difficult stage for a team and the most challenging for the team's leader. Sadly, many teams get stuck at or revert to this stage. The stage is often identifiable through conflicts and arguments as team members try to assert what they think should be done or said. One could view it as the time when the members think they know what needs to be done and each grows in confidence as their egos clash.

Team members of a storming team may typically:

● express of all kinds of differences
● question the way the team is being led and managed
● attempt to assert their individuality and independence
● exhibit a team performance that declines and slows down
● experience conflict, arguments and fallings out
● form rival groups and engage in office politics
● wish to leave the group, or even resign.

When were you last in a team or leading a team that was passing through such a difficult and turbulent phase of development? How did you respond and cope?

Stage 3: Norming

This is sometimes called the early adulthood stage of the team's development and is typically evidenced by the team becoming more cohesive after having worked through some of the storming-period challenges. There is an emerging understanding and acceptance of the team's goals and working styles, and each person's role and personality.

The following might be visible within such a team:

● consensus-building and decision-making
● confiding and sharing with each other

- pulling together to achieve the team's goals
- a performance that begins to be good and consistent
- the boundaries of the team having been established.

Has a team that you have been part of ever reached such a stage of maturity and performance? Did you see any evidence of the earlier stages still evident in the team?

Stage 4: Performing

This is the optimal stage and could be called a mature adult stage of development. Not all teams will reach this level, and those that do often relapse into the other stages over time.

A high-performing team is identified by:

- the unique identity it has established
- interdependence between team members
- how well everything seems to flow
- people seeking new challenges as they sense that everything is straightforward and becoming easy to do
- the team being given more to do, so workloads increase
- a lot of work being accomplished and goals achieved
- members caring about and supporting each other.

Have you ever led or worked in a team that has reached this optimal stage of its development? What do you recall about this time?

It is possible to take an online assessment to work out which stage your team has reached; results usually show a team being at all four stages, although one particular stage is normally dominant.

Based on the description of the four stages of development, at what stage (or stages) is your existing team?

New and existing teams

Are you taking over an existing team or are you being asked to create a completely new team?

- If you have been asked to create a completely new team, your team will be in the 'forming' stage and you might not face the complexity of being simultaneously at different stages.
- If you have been asked to take over an existing team, especially if the team has previously been underperforming, it is likely that the team will be mainly in the 'storming' stage.

In the latter case, what do you think will happen to such a team when you join it as its boss? Typically the team will partially go into a 'forming' stage as you bring new and unknown expectations, working style and goals to the team.

When taking over an existing group of people you need to explore at what stages they are working. Combined with this, as you and any other new team members join the team, there will be a partial return to the 'forming' stage as the whole group is working together for the first time. As a result, such a team is never static and you will be kept very busy as the manager.

A successful leader of any team must continually ensure that the entire team quickly and effectively moves from the 'forming' stage into the 'norming' and 'performing' stages, without getting stuck in the 'storming' stage. Much of Week 3's advice is focused on ensuring that your team does not become stuck at the 'storming' stage.

Creating a brand new team

1 Hire the ideal talent

You can create the ideal new and optimal working culture (habits, norms etc) through hiring the ideal kinds of individuals.

Do not rush this important process and plan well what kind of team you wish to create. What mix of personalities and skills does your new team need in order to ensure that it succeeds?

2 **Allow time for your team to understand your expectations**
Give the new team members time to get to know your own expectations regarding goals, aims and objectives. Give them more time if they are joining your team from other organizations rather than moving internally within your company. (Monday's chapter explains how to set goals and objectives for your team.)

3 **Be careful with experienced new team members**
Many of your new team will have left established teams to join yours. Such individuals may quickly start to act as if they know what to do (a kind of 'been there, done that' mentality) and as a result your team could very quickly enter the 'storming' phase. Be ready for this and be firm when you observe unacceptable behaviour.

Taking over an existing team in your organization

1 **Be clear about what is unacceptable**
You will be taking over a team with many good and bad habits and working styles which will have been created by the team under their previous manager(s). Your task is to observe quickly and listen well to understand what is happening, and then to map out which habits you wish to either:
  – strengthen and support, e.g. good team spirit and communication
  – lessen and reduce, e.g. writing long email reports
  – stop altogether, e.g. wasting time in meetings
  – have the team start doing, e.g. follow a new reporting style.

2 **Be ready for resistance**
The existing team may not readily accept you as their new boss, making comments such as: 'But this is not the way we used to do things ... we used to operate very well.' Remember that people find any kind of change or disruption hard to accept so a new boss can create anxiety and concern

and they will fight to hold on to the past (i.e. ways in which they were previously managed). Be patient, explain clearly your rationale for any changes but be firm when necessary.

3 **Be ready to communicate clearly**
The team will be used to working in a certain way and now they have a new boss. As a result you will need to be especially mindful of the need to communicate clearly about what you are observing and expecting of the team. (Such communication challenges are covered in Tuesday's chapter.)

Taking over a team in a new organization

When you move to a new company as a team manager, all of the above advice applies, and there are a few additional points to remember as well.

1 **Adapt to the new culture and working norms**
You will need to align your own working and leadership styles with the norms and expectations of your new organization and of your own new boss. Do not go charging into your role using your previous style. You may need to alter, tone down or emphasize certain aspects of your management style. Observe what is different in your new company compared with your previous experiences.

2 **Work to gain your team's respect and acceptance**
You must remember that you are the new person in the team and you may face resistance to being accepted. Be ready to be patient, listen exceptionally well and ask as many questions as possible to ensure that you are understood and also that you truly understand the norms and expectations of your new organization and its culture.

Summary

You now understand what a team is and what makes a team great.

We have explored how you like to be managed and led, which can help guide you in how you choose to manage others, e.g. not copying a past boss's bad habits!

You can now use the Tuckman model, which helps you to understand which of the four stages of development your team has reached – forming, storming, norming or performing.

You now understand the key challenges of starting to manage a completely new team and taking over an established team.

We have also discussed the challenges of taking over a team in a new organization that you might have joined.

Now that you understand how to start managing a team, you are ready to learn how to become a successful manager and in the Monday chapter we will explore how you can ensure that your team is aligned with a clear mission, vision, value and goals.

SUNDAY

MONDAY

TUESDAY

WEDNESDAY

THURSDAY

FRIDAY

SATURDAY

Fact-check (answers at the back)

1. Which of the following is *not a* stage of the Tuckman model?
a) Norming ❏
b) Feeling ❏
c) Storming ❏
d) Forming ❏

2. Which of the following is *not* a characteristic of a group that is a team?
a) A team has common goals ❏
b) A team is aligned ❏
c) A team works together ❏
d) A team does not communicate together ❏

3. How would you best describe a team at the forming stage of development?
a) It has been established a long time ❏
b) It has very few members ❏
c) It is a newly created team ❏
d) It is a virtual team ❏

4. What is a key difference between teams at the storming and at the norming stages?
a) A storming team is not performing well but a norming team is ❏
b) A norming team is more recently formed than a storming team ❏
c) A storming team is more productive than a norming team ❏
d) Both are very similar ❏

5. What are the challenges of starting to lead a team in a company that you have just joined?
a) You have less time to perform your work well ❏
b) You don't know the company's and the team's culture and norms ❏
c) You have no specific challenges ❏
d) Members of your team do not know each other ❏

6. Which stage of a team's growth and development should you be aiming for?
a) Storming ❏
b) Performing ❏
c) Forming ❏
d) Norming ❏

7. Which of the following is *not* a characteristic of a performing team?
a) Everything seems to flow well ❏
b) A unique identity has been established ❏
c) Arguments between members ❏
d) Interdependence has been created ❏

8. Which of the following is very unusual in a team in the storming phase?
a) People trying to assert their individuality and independence ❏
b) Performance of the team declining and slowing down ❏
c) Conflicts, arguments and falling out ❏
d) The team is in alignment and agrees on most things ❏

9. Which of the following would you expect of a newly created team in the forming stage?
a) Complaints that things are not what they are used to ❏
b) Anxiety ❏
c) Getting to know the common goals and expectations ❏
d) All of the above ❏

10. When taking over a new team, why is it important to listen and ask questions?
a) Because you need to truly understand what is happening and what members of the team are thinking and doing ❏
b) Because people only like a boss who listens and does not tell them what to do ❏
c) Because you have no time to do anything else ❏
d) Because you do not know what else you could do ❏

MONDAY

Alignment and goal-setting for your team

The Sunday chapter introduced you to the various stages that your team may have reached. It is now time to explore how you will align your team around a particular direction, purpose and goals. It is no good creating a team and then leaving it to do its own thing without a clear idea of where it is heading or what its goals are.

This chapter will explain how to:

- Create mission and vision statements that show the purpose and direction of the team
- Set clear and achievable goals, both for the team as a whole and for individual team members
- Understand why and how your goals or objectives should be **SMART**, **CLEAR** and **PURE**
- Use the goal-setting process to give a new team some quick wins that will help the team-bonding process
- Create a team charter to outline your team's purpose and clarify how the team will work together
- Emphasize the importance of alignment within a team to ensure that individuals' goals and aims are in line with yours and those of the organization
- Ensure that your team's understandings and expectations are in alignment with yours.

Setting a direction for your team

'The trouble with not having a goal is that you can spend your life running up and down the field and never score.'

Bill Copeland

'If everyone is moving forward together, then success takes care of itself.'

Henry Ford

Imagine being asked to lead a team of people in a company that you have just joined. Now imagine if nobody in the company had answers if you asked the following questions.

- What are the goals for my team this year?
- How will we know if my team has done a good job this month?
- What are the aims and the objectives of my team?
- What is the mission and vision of my team and of the company?
- What values are expected or need to be exhibited by my team?
- What kind of culture does my team have?

Often, managers are not clear about their team's direction, just doing the work and tasks that seem urgent and important and responding to other colleagues' and stakeholders' requests and needs. Do you know what I mean? Being very busy, but not really being productive or having a clear direction to your work?

A successful team manager must set the direction of the team, specifically by:

- creating the mission and vision of the team
- developing a set of team values
- developing an optimal team culture
- setting the goals and objectives that the team needs to achieve
- formulating a team charter.

Creating a mission and vision for your team

What is a team's mission? This is a statement of purpose about why the team exists. Here are some examples of possible team mission statements.

- We are a team of SAP implementation experts working to roll out SAP in a timely and cost-effective manner in the company (a SAP implementation team in a company's IT department)
- We exist to ensure that the company's internal audit processes and controls are optimized and robust (an internal audit team)
- We are a top-performing marketing department able to successfully help roll out and support all of our company's existing and new product lines (a multinational's marketing function).

What is a team's vision? It is often seen as a description of what the team wishes to become in the future. Here are some examples of team vision statements.

- To become the leading accounting and finance support team in the entire company (a finance and accounting team)
- To be the highest-performing sales team in the industry (a regional or product sales team)
- To be the team that everyone turns to for advice and help on taxation (a taxation team in a company's finance function).

Often the mission and vision are merged into one statement or paragraph.

Do you have such statements for your team? Why not work with your new team to develop mission and vision statements.

Team mission and vision statements should be aligned with the organization's own purpose and direction to avoid your team pulling in the wrong direction.

Developing a set of team values

A team's values show what the team stands for and believes in. They are the attitudes, beliefs and behaviours that matter to the individuals in the team. We all have values but the question is: are we conscious of what our values are and are they optimized to help the team to succeed?

Studies show that organizations and teams that have thoughtful, positive and aligned sets of values are able to operate and perform more successfully. Not surprisingly, a team that is poorly managed or led often develops negative or unproductive values which can impact badly upon the team's performance. Examples of such values might include:

● that it is OK to be late
● that there is no need to take responsibility
● not listening to others

- keeping others under pressure
- not sharing information unless asked.

What are your own values? And what values do you wish your team to have and to live and work by? Does your organization or your boss have a list of core values that they expect you and your team to live by?

Here are some typical examples of values that various organizations and teams aspire to work and live by:

- honesty and integrity
- open communication
- taking full responsibility
- thinking out of the box and being creative
- being persistent and never giving up
- always helping and giving time to others
- working with passion and enthusiasm
- always being willing to listen and be open-minded
- being technically up-to-date and knowledgeable.

Do aim to develop a list of values for your team, and be ready to work with team members in turning the values into habits which form part of how you work together each day.

Developing an optimal team culture

Culture and values are interconnected; the culture could best be defined as the collective behaviour and patterns of the individuals in the team. It is normally made up of their values as well as their habits, behaviours, beliefs, working norms, expectations and communication styles. Put simply, it is how the team chooses to act, think and operate.

I strongly advise you to ensure that the culture you create, support and grow within the team that you lead is consciously developed and is optimized to ensure your team's success.

Setting team goals and objectives

Having set the direction for your team, it is now key to set the team's goals and objectives. Goals and objectives are much the same things, and often goals are expressed as Key Performance Indicators (KPIs).

271

Sometimes the goals for your team are set by your boss or others in your organization. In this case, you would normally still have the responsibility of breaking down the team-wide goals to create individual goals for each member of your team. Have you done this before, and how easy was this for you?

When setting goals for individuals in a team it is important to demonstrate that you did so thoughtfully and objectively. I like to use the following framework, which comprises 14 requirements of optimal goals: **SMART, CLEAR** and **PURE**. This model is attributed to the British leadership coach John Whitmore.

Do use this framework as a checklist when you next need to create or to review the goals of your team:

Optimal goals are **SMART**:

Which means the goals are:	How do you ensure this?
Specific	Goals should be clearly stated and relate to specific aspects of the team's work
Measurable	Goals should be as objective and quantifiable as possible
Attainable	Bear in mind the saying: 'If a goal is unattainable there is no hope, and if it is not challenging it is not motivating.'
Realistic	Goals should be relevant and realistically related to the team's work
Timely	Goals should be achievable in the time frame set for achieving them

Optimal goals are **PURE**:

Which means the goals are:	How do you ensure this?
Positive	Goals should be expressed, as far as possible, as positive rather than negative achievements
Understood	Goals should be understandable by your team, otherwise they will never be able to accept them
Relevant	Goals should be relevant to what your team are employed to do
Ethical	Goals should not force your team to question their integrity, e.g. having to consider cheating to achieve the goal

Optimal goals are **CLEAR**:

Which means the goals are:	How do you ensure this?
Challenging	Goals should be challenging to motivate your team
Legal	Goals must be legally acceptable, just as they should be ethical
Environmentally friendly	Goals should not involving wasting resources or adversely affecting the environment
Agreed	Goals should be agreed and accepted by those asked to achieve them
Recorded	Goals should be written down and shared, with people signing off on them as needed

Do not let the goal-setting model complicate your thinking. Remember the popular acronym K.I.S.S. ('Keep it simple, Stupid!'). If in doubt, keep the goal simple – it is better to achieve something rather than nothing at all.

Goal-setting with a new team

When setting goals with a new team for the first time, you need to be especially careful and mindful of the fact that you may not yet have built up high levels of mutual trust, understanding and rapport. Bear in mind the following.

1 **Have some quick-win goals**
Try to set some collective team goals which can be achieved relatively easily and quickly. These wins will enable your team to celebrate some success together quickly and show team members that under your leadership the team is on the right track. This should help you bond with the team and gain their respect and confidence.
2 **Spend extra time explaining your proposed goals**
Be ready to spend extra time explaining the logic and rationale for the goals or objectives that you are setting or accepting (from your boss or others in your organization). Remember that some people will not openly say that they do not agree with or buy into your goals.

Formulating a team charter

A team charter summarizes the scope of the team's work, what the team needs to achieve and how it will do so, including establishing the boundaries of the team's work.

There are no fixed rules for a team charter's content, but I would suggest as a starting point a structure such as the following.

Ideal headings within your team charter	Details
What is our team purpose?	This is your team's mission and vision
What are our desired end results and goals?	These are your team's goals and objectives
How will the team work together?	List how the team members will interact, work and communicate together
Who are our key stakeholders?	Listing out all the key stakeholders and how the team needs to work with each of them

Do consider spending a few hours with your new team creating your first team charter.

Aligning your team

Visualize a rowing team – it might be one of the teams in the annual Oxford and Cambridge University Boat Race. Perhaps there are eight or even 12 rowers, with a cox steering the boat. How can the team ensure that it wins the race?

Scenario 1 – By each person rowing at his own pace and as fast as he can, ignoring the others in the boat, including the cox?

Scenario 2 – By each person rowing at the same rate and in perfect formation, with the oars entering and leaving the water at the same time, and being guided by the instructions of the cox about when to speed up or slow down?

I do hope that you chose the second scenario as the correct answer!

A team's alignment can be defined as having a group of individuals who all understand and agree to:

- the team's direction and purpose, e.g. mission statement, vision statement, values and/or strategic direction, team charter (already covered in this chapter)
- the team's goals and objectives for the current and/or next financial year or period – I hope after reading this chapter you have a clear idea of how and why goal-setting is so important
- individual job responsibilities, duties and goals (see the Tuesday chapter)

- the team's working style and norms, e.g. communication styles, meeting protocols etc (other chapters will explore these in more detail).

Why is team alignment so important?

A team that is not aligned could also be called a dysfunctional team. Such teams exhibit a range of unproductive working styles and behaviours, including:

- wasting time and other resources – the team may be working unproductively, e.g. work may being replicated or may be taking too long to complete
- arguments and misunderstandings – different members of the team may have widely divergent beliefs and expectations
- sabotage and deception – team members might play games, e.g. withholding information from one another.

If you take over an existing team and you spot any of the above behaviours and outcomes, you will need to analyse why the team is not aligned and then decide how to rectify the causes of any misalignment.

A final question on this alignment topic is related to you as the team's leader: are you really and genuinely aligned with your boss and your organization?

- Do you agree with and buy into your boss's and organization's directions, values, culture, goals etc?
- Are you willing and able to change your own beliefs, values, goals etc so that they are in alignment with what your boss and your organization ask and expect of you?
- Are you then able to create and develop the optimal direction and goals for yourself and for your team, which are in alignment with your boss's and your organization's needs and expectations?

You might welcome the help of an executive coach or mentor, or relevant training courses, to help you to understand how to align your own thinking and beliefs so that your team can literally follow your lead, rather than being expected to 'do as I say and not as I do (or believe)'.

- You cannot expect people to always complete their work on time if you leave tasks unfinished.
- You cannot ask your team to always arrive early for client presentations if you are often late.

If you wish to change your team's behaviours, culture etc, try to follow the words of Mahatma Gandhi:

'Be the change that you want to see in the world.'

SUNDAY

MONDAY

TUESDAY

WEDNESDAY

THURSDAY

FRIDAY

SATURDAY

Summary

As the working world becomes ever more complex, with a 24/7 culture of Blackberries and emails, a team could easily find itself overwhelmed, overworked and not knowing what to do next. As their manager it is your role to give your team clarity of purpose and direction, and to keep them all aligned with clear goals and expectations of the values and culture that they must aspire to work by.

You are now in a good position to create a direction and purpose for your team in the form of mission and vision statements; develop the required values and culture within your team; and decide if you wish to work with your team to create a team charter.

You can appreciate the importance of being aligned as a team and all rowing your 'boat' as one team.

You understand the importance of you, as the team's leader, 'walking the talk' and doing what you expect of others in your team.

The next stage is to assign responsibilities and delegate work within your team and to ensure that the work is optimally allocated so that the team is as productive as possible. This is the subject of Tuesday's chapter.

SUNDAY

MONDAY

TUESDAY

WEDNESDAY

THURSDAY

FRIDAY

SATURDAY

Fact-check (answers at the back)

1. What is a mission statement?
   a) A statement of past performance ❏
   b) A statement of purpose ❏
   c) A statement of working hours ❏
   d) All of above ❏

2. What is a vision statement?
   a) A statement of what you wish to become in the future ❏
   b) A statement of the future planned budget forecast ❏
   c) A statement summarizing feedback from the team members ❏
   d) None of the above ❏

3. Why is alignment important?
   a) It makes a team more productive ❏
   b) It reduces duplication and wasted effort ❏
   c) It avoids arguments ❏
   d) All of above ❏

4. A team charter might include:
   a) Goals ❏
   b) Purpose ❏
   c) Working norms ❏
   d) All of the above ❏

5. What is the culture of a team?
   a) An organigram ❏
   b) Behaviours and habits ❏
   c) Salary and remuneration scale ❏
   d) Working hours and overtime rules ❏

6. Which of the following are possible values of a team?
   a) Honesty ❏
   b) Good listening ❏
   c) Persistence ❏
   d) All of the above ❏

7. Which of the following is *not* a SMART goal requirement?
   a) Creative ❏
   b) Timely ❏
   c) Measurable ❏
   d) Realistic ❏

8. Which of the following is *not* a CLEAR goal requirement?
   a) Agreed ❏
   b) Recorded ❏
   c) Detailed ❏
   d) Legal ❏

9. Which of the following is a PURE goal requirement?
   a) Short ❏
   b) Written in English ❏
   c) Complex ❏
   d) Relevant ❏

10. What does K.I.S.S. mean? ❏
    a) Be loving and kind ❏
    b) Keep it simple, Stupid ❏
    c) Know Information Simply Stated ❏
    d) None of the above

TUESDAY

Delegating and managing the work within your team

The Sunday and Monday chapters have discussed how to take over a new team, the different stages of team development and how to set your team's direction and goals. This has created a framework that allows you to get the team as a whole into an optimal shape or alignment. We will now explore how to ensure that each individual member of your team is able to perform his or her role optimally.

This chapter will show you how to:

- Place the right people in roles that suit their interests, personality, skills and experience
- Use a model to understand the typical kinds of work-role preferences that different people might have
- Delegate and allocate work to your team to ensure that the work is completed and that the work is shared fairly
- Ensure that individuals' goals and key performance indicators are in alignment with the team's and organization's goals
- Engage with, empower and motivate your team so that they will succeed in ways above and beyond what is expected of them.

Managing the individuals in your team

> *'An empowered organization is one in which individuals have the knowledge, skill, desire, and opportunity to personally succeed in a way that leads to collective organizational success.'*
>
> Stephen Covey

A participant in a management training course that I was leading recently said that he would rather be in charge of 100 machines than be in charge of just one person. That may sound extreme but many managers, even those with many years of experience in leading others, can feel overwhelmed by the prospect of having to manage and deal with the individuals in their team.

A key role of anyone leading a team is to ensure that each member of the team:

- is placed in the optimal job role
- understands what to do
- knows why it needs doing
- understands how to do it
- is able to do it
- actually wants to do it.

I have developed the following six-step framework to help you ensure that each person in a team is given every possible chance of being a successful performer and contributor who will hopefully stay with the team.

The six-step team talent management framework

In many ways being a great manager is learning to ask the right questions, rather than knowing the answers. The 'six steps' are in the form of six questions which you are strongly encouraged to ask yourself whenever you face challenges in managing members of your team.

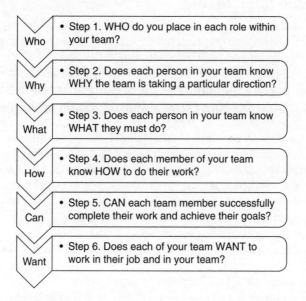

Who	• Step 1. WHO do you place in each role within your team?
Why	• Step 2. Does each person in your team know WHY the team is taking a particular direction?
What	• Step 3. Does each person in your team know WHAT they must do?
How	• Step 4. Does each member of your team know HOW to do their work?
Can	• Step 5. CAN each team member successfully complete their work and achieve their goals?
Want	• Step 6. Does each of your team WANT to work in their job and in your team?

The remainder of this chapter will walk you through this important model.

Step 1. WHO do you place in each role within your team?

Before determining what work, task and goals each team member needs to complete, you must first ensure that you have the ideal people in each job role.

I once hired an accountant to work in my team and for a couple of years she did a great job. She was a highly qualified accountant with a stellar track record. Then one day she made a serious mistake in a spreadsheet that she had created. When she came to apologize we began talking about how tedious and sometimes boring being an accountant can be. She then revealed that she did not enjoy her job any more and that was probably why she was making mistakes. She spoke of preferring job roles that would be more people-focused and customer-facing. Luckily I was able to offer her a customer service role which she enjoyed and performed well. She is not unique; so many people work in jobs that they either do not enjoy and/or are not very good at. Can you imagine how unproductive your team would be if it were filled with such people?

As a manager you must ensure that each role is filled by the ideal individual – someone who is able, motivated and willing to perform well in that role. You must decide the criteria team members must meet in order to perform well in your team as well as in specific roles.

- What are the required hard skills, such as work experience, technical and academic experience and skills? How suitable is the person?
- What kind of soft skills or attitudes, behaviour and personality are needed? How suitable is the person?
- Do you need to analyse further the required tasks and responsibilities of the role? Do you have job descriptions that are sufficiently detailed?
- Do you wish to adjust the job role to fit a potentially strong member of your team?

When hiring people or considering changes to an existing member's role, you should draw up a list of key job requirements. You can then carry out a gap analysis to understand where the individual may fall short and where they are strong. Examples might include:

- lacking certain technical experience or certification
- not having enough product or industry exposure
- not possessing the ideal soft skills, e.g. not sufficiently persistent or details-oriented.

Then ask yourself:

1 Do their strengths and potential outweigh their weaknesses?
2 Can I help to develop their areas of weakness while strengthening their strengths?

Suitability is a key success or failure factor

I have come to realize that a major weakness of most under-performing teams is having people in roles for which they are not suited. The reason is that each of us has a natural preference for the kind of work we enjoy doing, e.g. some like to plan, others like to move around, while others prefer to delegate work.

To be a successful manager, you need to ensure that each person is ideally suited to the work you wish them to do. How can you do this? You need to understand the individual's work preferences, and this can achieved through observation, interview or using an assessment tool. There are many assessment tools, including the Belbin Team Roles Inventory, Harrison Assessment, Gallup's Strengths Finder and SHL's OPQ; we shall look at the Belbin model.

Exploring preferences using the Belbin model

This model, created by the psychologist Meredith Belbin, is used to discover what kind of work tasks we like to do. It demonstrates that we all prefer one or more of the following nine kinds of roles.

Role title	Role description
Shaper	Prefers roles in which they can seek improvements and challenge others to improve
Implementer	Prefers work in which ideas and plans have to be put into action

(Continued)

Completer finisher	Prefers work which involves finishing things, often thoroughly and in a timely way
Coordinator	Prefers to act as someone coordinating others' actions and often likes to take charge of meetings
Team worker	Prefers roles that work closely with others and would not like a solitary role
Resource investigator	Prefers work that involves research and gathering information
Planter	Prefers work that involves having to develop new approaches and ideas
Monitor evaluator	Prefers work involving analysis and analysing information and options
Specialist	Prefers work that enables them to be an expert in a certain area or field

Based on the nine Belbin roles, what are your preferred work role preferences? What are those of your team members?

As you use such a model, you will make all sorts of discoveries. A typical example might be discovering that the person in your team who never completes their work on time might have the 'Completer finisher' role very low in their preferences profile. When faced with such an example of what I call a misfit, you can:

● encourage the person to develop and change
● change the role for the person
● change the person, i.e. replace him or her.

You can find a free version of the Belbin model on the internet. Do explore using such an assessment to understand your team members and yourself better.

Step 2. Does each person in your team know WHY the team is taking a particular direction?

Monday's chapter showed you how to ensure that your team has a clear direction through having a stated mission, vision, team charter, and team goals and objectives. But do your team members understand how each of their roles and work can contribute towards helping the team to achieve these things?

Your team may claim to know and agree but there is no harm in checking. In your next team meeting, ask your team questions such as:

● How would you describe our team's objectives, purpose and goals? Are they clear enough?
● Can you recite our team mission and vision statements? Do you like them? How can we word them differently?
● How does your role contribute to the team's and to the organization's success?

Step 3. Does each person in your team know WHAT they must do?

Individual and shared goals

Monday's chapter showed you how to create goals for your team. You might also create Key Performance Indicators (KPIs) for each team member – these are goals written in the form of measures against which performance can be measured.

As a manager you need to decide:

● which of the team goals are shared by the entire team
● which team goals can be broken down into individual goals
● how to ensure that individual goals are aligned with the overall team goals that your boss or organization may have given you.

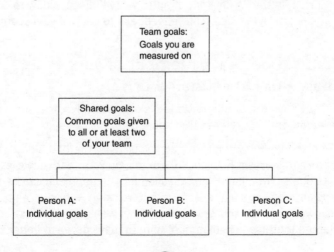

The kinds of goals that you set will vary by the function, industry and organization that your team is part of.

- How difficult should the goals be to achieve? Much is written about having challenging goals and it is your task to decide how easy or demanding the goals should be. My advice would be to make them difficult but also achievable – so-called stretch goals
- How will you motivate your team to achieve their goals? This would be through a combination of monetary and non-monetary incentives, which we explore later in this chapter.

Job description, responsibilities and duties

The goals given to an individual should correlate with their job description. Does each of your team have a clear job description which enables them to understand what is expected of them in terms of performance?

A great job description should include at least two things.

1 A detailed description of the responsibilities and tasks
2 A description of the needed competencies, i.e. knowledge, skills, behaviours and attitudes.

Be ready to update and adjust the job descriptions of your team members when you are reviewing their performance and setting their goals and objectives for the following budget year or period. In the Wednesday chapter we will discuss how to evaluate performance and give feedback to each of your team.

Step 4. Does each member of your team know HOW to do their work?

Do they have the right knowledge, skills, attitudes, training and development? There are three aspects to this question.

1 You should know what strengths your team members possess and aim to make full use of them to help your team achieve its goals. This strengths-based leadership approach can be a positive and motivating approach to working with your team.
2 Do your team members have areas of weakness and/or areas that need development to help them perform better

in their roles? You will need to share, diplomatically, your opinions with your team members and help them to plan how they will bridge the gaps.

3 Your team has four options with respect to how they use any of their competencies (their hard and soft skills, knowledge and behaviours etc). These are shown below.

You can be successful as a manager by learning how to evaluate and then communicate to each of your team what they need to do to perform to their maximum potential:

- continue and do more of, e.g. to continue being persistent and detail-oriented
- continue but do less of, e.g. to continue replying to all emails in a timely fashion but to write shorter emails
- stop doing, e.g. to stop interrupting colleagues during their presentations
- start doing, e.g. to start learning about project management and how to lead projects.

Step 5. CAN each team member successfully complete their work and achieve their goals?

Your team might be qualified and very eager to complete their work and to achieve their goals. However:

- do they have the necessary tools, resources, systems, processes and people network?

- even if they have everything they need, are they empowered and allowed to do all that they must to achieve their goals?

I recently coached an individual who complained about not being able to do his job well. He said that, although he had been working in his company for over three months, he had not yet been given a computer or his own work station.

If your team members had no computer or work station, could they succeed in their roles? Does your team have everything it needs to succeed? What might you be overlooking? Such issues will be specific to your team, but here are some examples:

- Do team members understand how to operate your company's enterprise resource planning and other software systems?
- Do team members have a copy of any employee handbook?
- Do team members know who to contact to seek help and assistance within your team or in other departments?

Step 6. Does each of your team WANT to work in their job and in your team?

Are your team members sufficiently engaged and motivated to stay in their roles and to perform well? This is a very important question.

Do you understand what motivates your team (and you)? Much has been studied and written with regard to motivation. The two best-known theories of motivation are:

- Maslow's hierarchy of needs – this states that once the basic human needs (such as food and shelter) are satisfied, a person then seeks things like meaning and to be valued.
- Herzberg's two-factor model – this explains that some things offered to employees, so-called Hygiene Factors such as a person's salary and working conditions, are not positively motivating and are necessary simply to prevent dissatisfaction. According to Herzberg, the things that truly motivate individuals, Motivators, are such things as being valued and being given responsibility.

AT BLOGGS AND SON, THEY GET APPLES AND A PAT ON THE BACK

I think that there is truth in both of these well-known models, but what motivates one person may not motivate another. Everyone is unique, and it is your key task as their manager to explore, learn and act upon what will (or might) motivate each of your team members. What are you offering your team to motivate them to perform well? Here is a list of the kinds of things that might motivate a typical employee. It is not an exhaustive list, but it serves to show you that virtually anything can serve to motivate or demotivate someone in your team:

- monetary rewards
- base salary
- bonuses
- other benefits – statutory and optional
- working hours and overtime
- holidays
- equipment – PC, car, phone
- office space
- office facilities – kitchen, smoking room
- social events and outings
- delegation
- mentorship
- induction programme
- connecting with leaders
- travel
- expenses' reimbursement policy
- overseas postings
- early responsibility
- annual remuneration review
- quality of food in the canteen
- management and supervisory opportunities
- job description and KPIs
- culture
- environment
- responsibility

- challenge
- communication
- growth of business and opportunities
- learning, development and training
- freedom and openness to ideas
- feedback and listening culture
- performance reviews
- promotions
- career path
- equitable workplace
- fair recognition and reward of performance
- diversity and lack of discrimination
- termination process and outplacement

Seven basic needs

When I coach individuals and teams, I am often astonished to discover what is causing individuals to be demotivated (sometimes called disengaged). I have come to believe that all human beings have seven basic needs which have to be met to truly fulfil and motivate them.

Basic needs	Description
To have certainty	People like to know what is happening and what they have to do. We dislike change and the unexpected.
To have variety	People rarely like to do the same monotonous work each day and will become bored.
To be valued	People like to be acknowledged and thanked for their work and contribution.
To connect with others	People rarely like to work completely alone without being able to communicate with others.
To be able to contribute	People want to feel that their efforts and work are worthwhile and for a greater good.
To be able to grow	People like to grow in their careers and roles and to learn more.
To leave a legacy	People like to do things that will make a difference and leave a lasting impression.

I think that you can quickly become a successful manager if you bear in mind these seven needs and try to ensure that what you offer and promise your team members fulfils these.

Do note, though, that not every person will exhibit all seven needs at any one time.

If you are not sure what might motivate your team to perform well, a good starting point is to think about what motivates you. I would also encourage you to ask your team what they seek in life and why they work in your organization and within your team. The answers might surprise you!

Over time, as you become a more experienced manager, you will get a better sense for what can successfully motivate people in your team.

9. Which of the following describes the need to connect with others?
a) People rarely like to work completely alone without being able to communicate with others ❑
b) People want to feel that their efforts and work are worthwhile and for a greater good ❑
c) People like to grow in their careers and roles and to learn more ❑
d) People like to do things that will make a difference ❑

10. Which of the following describes the need to have variety?
a) People like to know what is happening and what they have to do. We dislike change and the unexpected ❑
b) People rarely like to do the same monotonous work each day and will become bored ❑
c) People like to be acknowledged and thanked for their work and contribution ❑
d) People rarely like to work completely alone without being able to communicate with others ❑

WEDNESDAY

Optimal communication within your team

Your job as a manager is to lead a team with passion and belief, and to inspire them to great performances. Systems and procedures alone are not enough to achieve this and what you need to develop and nurture will be all forms of excellent communication both with and within your team.

All successful managers understand that, no matter the size of their team or business, only through constant and varied types of communication with their staff can they maintain the performance and reputation of their business.

This chapter will show you how to:

- Understand the different styles of communication that each of us can use in different situations
- Realize the importance of listening skills to help ensure that people feel that they are being heard
- Ensure that you choose the ideal form of communication for your purpose
- Ensure that meetings are necessary and well-run, with structured agendas and good chairing
- Deal with the challenges of managing virtual and remote teams where communication may be constrained
- Successfully manage a multicultural team and ensure that you have an optimal working culture.

You are a full-time communicator

'The single biggest problem in communication is the illusion that it has taken place.'
George Bernard Shaw

'To effectively communicate, we must realize that we are all different in the way we perceive the world and use this understanding as a guide to our communication with others.'
Anthony Robbins

How often in the day are you communicating with other people? Think about how you spend your working day and of all the different kinds of information, data, decisions and news you need to share with others in some form of communication:

- good news or bad news
- expected or unexpected
- straightforward or complicated
- for certain people only or for many
- to be told to others
- to be learnt from others
- to be shared
- to be discussed
- conclusions to be reached
- information to be combined
- gaps to be filled
- decisions to be made
- appreciation and thanks.

Some might say that when you are silently doing some work (e.g. testing some equipment or reading a manual), you are not communicating. But you are communicating something to those who observe you through your silent non-verbal communication.

I have come to the conclusion that everything you do as a manager is a form of communication. I am not suggesting that you are always wanting or needing to communicate but rather that other people will constantly receive all kinds of verbal and non-verbal messages from you. For example, the time you leave your office to go home is a form of communication – it shows others your work ethic and potentially suggests to others your expectations of how long people should stay in the office each day.

Communication styles

'She never listens to me and always shouts at me so loudly ... he always wants the last word ... she never clearly explained it to me ... my boss is so annoying and argumentative ... she always skim-reads everything I give her ... never likes to speak to me in person and always sends me requests by email ... she is so quiet and never speaks up even when you know she has something to say ... I do not understand what he wants us to do ... he jumps to conclusions and stops listening...'

Do such opinions and thoughts sound familiar?

A successful manager needs to create a working environment for his or her team where each team member clearly communicates any needed or necessary information, ideas and decisions to those individuals who need to know, and to have this information shared in such a way that it is received and understood by the other parties.

We are all unique and have developed our own communication styles and preferences, some of which may be positive and productive, while others might impact negatively upon the team. Some of us are extroverts, others very quiet; some like to write, others enjoy speaking in public; some are very loud and can seem aggressive, others speak too much.

What is your style like? Ask your team what they think of your style – what is good and what is not so good? What could be changed and improved?

The importance of listening skills

> *'I listen very well. I never interrupt. I never deflect the course of the conversation with a comment of my own. People, if you pay attention, change the direction of one another's conversations constantly. It's like having a passenger in your car who suddenly grabs the steering wheel and turns you down a side street.'*
>
> Garth Stein

The next time you are having a conversation with a group or an individual, observe how each of you communicates.

- Who is truly listening?
- How often are people interrupting each other?
- Is more than one person speaking at the same time?
- Is the flow of the discussion often being changed?
- Are people concentrating and paying attention?
- Is there a pause between people speaking?

I suspect you would not be impressed with what you observe, and I have come to realize that the biggest hurdle to good team performance is the failure to listen well to what others are trying to communicate.

Do people not listen to you? How do you feel about this? If we do not hear what the other person is trying to communicate, we face:

● demotivating and disengaging the other person
● wasting time and resources, because we may repeat things or miss opportunities or dangers
● failing to grow through learning from other people's ideas and points of view.

The complexity and information overload that we face in our 24/7 interconnected world, so full of noise and information, does not make listening easy but it does actually make it more essential that we listen well.

How can you be a team boss who listens effectively?

Pause and reflect before you speak and always remember a very useful abbreviation: W.A.I.T. This is to remind you of a very important question: *'Why am I talking?'*. It might encourage you to listen and observe more and speak less. After all, you have two ears and two eyes but only one mouth!

After someone has spoken to you, acknowledge that you have heard them before rushing to respond. Likewise, when responding to a written idea, comment or opinion, always try to show you have read and absorbed what has been shared with you before giving your own ideas etc.

Remember to be empathic and develop the mentality of wishing first to understand and then to be understood by others. I believe as a team head that it is sometimes better to really understand what your team is thinking and saying than to obsess over making sure they hear what you want them to hear.

Encourage your team to share their thoughts, opinions and ideas with you.

Discuss with the team your expectations of how the team should communicate between themselves and with other stakeholders. Also, ask them about their expectations.

Forms of communication

When you have some information to share with all of your team or with just one member, how do you decide the form of communication? Do you choose to:

- write a short or long email? Who do you copy the email to?
- write a memo or report?
- pick up the phone?
- arrange a video conference or Skype call?
- send a fax?
- speak face to face?
- call a formal or informal team meeting?
- send an SMS?
- post something on the company's social media pages?
- ask someone else to pass on your message?
- keep quiet and use non-verbal body language to pass on a message?
- do nothing, assuming the other person already knows?

Do you have preferred ways of communicating? Do you prefer emails, phone calls or meetings? Many things will influence your choice from the options: common sense, your working environment, working culture norms, the location of the other person, how urgent the matter is, the time of day, the type of job, the expectations of your boss or company etc.

Here is some advice to help you in your choice of communication.

- Keep it clear and concise.
- Indicate the urgency and importance of what you are communicating.
- Be ready to follow up (e.g. call after sending an urgent email).
- Be explicit about whether you are communicating in expectation of a reply, other action or simply to share some information.

I realize that some people prefer to write things down and others prefer to speak. No matter what your normal style is, be prepared to alter your style to ensure the greatest effectiveness, e.g. if you typically avoid calling people on the phone and only email, be ready to make a phone call when an email may not be appropriate (e.g. not urgent or personal enough).

Allow how you communicate to win over your staff and to motivate them to listen and to follow your lead. Be genuine and authentic. Show that you are thoughtful, that you care and that you are human.

Managing emails

How many emails have you received in your inbox so far today? So far this week? We all receive and send many emails and you might wish to set some guidelines with your team to ensure that they only send out emails that are appropriate and useful in helping you all to achieve your goals.

You might set team rules about:

- who you should typically 'cc' when writing emails
- which emails to reply to
- how long or short your emails should be.

Meetings

Meetings are a key aspect of leading a team. You may not enjoy spending hours in meetings but, like it or not, in many organizations they have become a key part of ensuring that teams can be successful. As a manager it is your role to ensure that any meetings you arrange with your team (and others) are appropriate and necessary as well as being well-organized and well-run.

The five secrets of successfully chairing and leading team meetings

> *'If you don't know where you are going, you will probably end up somewhere else.'*
>
> Lawrence Peter

1 Determine the desired outcomes and translate them into an agenda

Why do you need to hold a meeting? What are the desired outcomes you have in mind? It is important that you are clear about this before planning a meeting, and definitely before you share details of the meeting with your team.

- Do you need to share information about some plans? Is the desired outcome that all of the attendees should be given some specific plan of action, some specific knowledge etc?
- Do you need to have a debate or discussion and then to make a decision? Is the desired outcome that all the attendees are party to a decision?
- Do you need a meeting for team-building purposes, e.g. to bring the team together to share some common challenges and issues? Is the desired outcome a more aligned team?

The ideal agenda is a document that sets out the expectations of the meeting. It should include:

- issues and topics for discussion, each as a separate agenda item
- the names of who will present each issue or topic
- proposed timings, i.e. the time to be spent on each agenda item.

2 Decide who should attend and how they should prepare

On my training programmes, participants often complain about having to attend too many meetings where they feel their attendance is of no value and that they are wasting their time having to sit through hours of discussions. Have you ever had this feeling? If you or any of your team were not in a meeting, what more productive tasks could they be doing (this is the so-called 'opportunity cost' of attending the meeting)?

You might wish to have an entire group or team attend a meeting for reasons of team cohesion, common understanding, team unity etc. But if this is not the case, be selective about who should attend and for how long – people can be asked to attend only for specific agenda items to avoid taking up so much of their time.

You must also be careful not to burden your team with too much pre-meeting preparation – only ask of them what is really needed and important to ensure that the meeting can achieve its aims. Do you share in advance a detailed proposal which is to be voted on in the meeting without much time spent on discussion? Or do you share a short summary beforehand and use the meeting to present and discuss the proposal?

309

3 Plan the form and style of meeting professionally

Consider the nature of the meeting.

- Is it a regular meeting (e.g. monthly sales review meeting) or a special one-off meeting?
- Is it a formal meeting with an agenda and in which minutes will be taken, or is it an informal meeting?

Should the meeting be face to face or by video-conferencing or telephone? Or using software to allow information to be shared on each participants' computer screen. Should it be a meeting at which everyone stands rather than being seated? Is a meeting the best communication tool to achieve your desired outcomes? Sometimes an email or memo might suffice and would be less time-consuming and costly than a meeting, particularly if attendees must travel to the meeting location.

4 Chair the meeting like a great leader

> *'Effective chairing will ensure that a meeting achieves its aims and objectives. Chairs should facilitate, encourage, focus and clarify.'*
>
> University of Winchester (UK) website

If the meeting is one that you have organized, you will probably wish to lead and chair the meeting and your leadership skills will be put to the test.

Based on my experience, here are some tips on how to
ensure that meetings you chair are successful.

- Understand the issues and information being discussed;
  you must at least read the preparation materials and
  come prepared.
- Allow everyone to express their opinions, do not talk too
  much yourself and do not allow anyone to ridicule or
  belittle another person's ideas and contribution.
- Keep the discussions on topic and on time and do not
  allow people to talk for the sake of it.
- Show respect for values, think of all attendees and do not
  criticize or try to push your own opinions too much – if you
  wish to impose your opinion, do not ask for others' opinions!
- If you wish to seek a decision from the group, through a
  vote or majority consensus, be sure you enable everyone
  to share their views.
- Try to keep the entire meeting positive and civil and as
  short as possible, and listen well to all that is shared as
  well as that which is not shared.

5 Have clear and actionable minutes
Minutes are a written record of the meeting and they
should record the decisions made at the meeting, including
details of who will action and follow up the decisions and
actions agreed upon, and within what time frame. As with
goal-setting, the actions required after a meeting must be
clearly recorded and shared with all attendees to ensure no
misunderstandings.

How to work with remotely located team members

Do you have team members who are located away from your
office – perhaps in another town or even overseas? This is now
common in our increasingly globalized world. You may also have
a virtual team under your leadership, with members scattered
around the world and only coming together for specific reasons
(see the project teams section later in this chapter).

If you have a remotely located team member or members, you will need to work out how to maintain communication, sharing and general interaction. This can be a real challenge if the person cannot easily attend team meetings or just walk into your office or grab you for coffee to discuss something informally.

In such cases you may need to make an extra effort to connect with the team member, e.g. arranging weekly video-conference catch-ups.

Managing a multicultural team

Another challenge arises when you have team members who come from different cultures. The different cultures might be ethnic, religious, geographic or the working culture of an employee's former company.

As a team leader your role is to:

- ensure that anyone joining you from a different culture is able to fit in and settle into your team without negatively disrupting your working culture and norms
- identify and appreciate the cultural differences within your team and work with your multicultural mix
- educate the rest of your team about accepting diversity, helping them to understand that just because someone thinks or acts differently, that does not make them wrong or a poor performer.

The following are examples of cultural differences that you might experience with staff from different parts of the world.

Some people:	Whereas others:
Do not question authority (e.g. their bosses)	Would actively question and challenge
Work best through informal structures	Need formal rules and processes
Are individualistic and want their own success	Like being in groups and having group success
Are interested in people and connections	Focus on systems, procedures, products etc
Are materialistic and focused on remuneration	Care about quality of life and well-being

| Are happy to work long hours without breaks | Need a formal lunchtime and go home on time |
| Keep quiet and do not rush to give opinions | Never seem to keep quiet and always share |

If you would like to delve deeper into this subject, look at the work on workplace culture by Hofstede and Trompenaars.

Leading temporary, short-term or project teams

Sometimes teams are created that will have only a short lifespan, perhaps working on a short project that will last only a few weeks or months. Leading such teams presents the following challenges.

- The team members may never have worked together before.
- They may have never worked with you before.
- There may be little time to become familiar with one another.
- High performance may be expected immediately.
- There may be no budget and no time for team bonding or team building.
- The work might be stressful as there may never be enough time and manpower to do everything that needs doing.

The key to success in such a situation is for a manager to show in an open and honest way that he or she understands the team's challenges and issues, and that together the team will seek ways of ensuring that they achieve their goals without getting burnt-out.

I have recently been working with a project team that faced all of the above issues. With coaching, the team's manager worked very hard to ensure that the team could be aligned with common expectations and she made sure that they regularly socialized together. Each week she would also have a short team meeting where she would explore how the team members were feeling, connecting and communicating together. Topics such as stress, overwork and pressure were discussed and the team members learnt to try to help each other. The team was very successful in completing its project and the team's manager was highly rated by her staff and company.

Summary

This chapter has shown you all of the communication issues that a successful manager must master to ensure that they can create and maintain a high-performing team.

You now understand that communication is a full-time role; today, a manager who remained holed up in their office without speaking with their staff would be very lucky to keep their job!

You appreciate each person's communication style and realize that listening is the main communication style for any high-performing team leader.

You can choose the ideal form of communication for use in different situations.

You are able to organize and chair all kinds of team meetings, including those involving remotely located staff.

You understand the challenges of working with short-term or project teams where you lack time to create an ideal team working environment.

SUNDAY

MONDAY

TUESDAY

WEDNESDAY

THURSDAY

FRIDAY

SATURDAY

Fact-check (answers at the back)

1. What does W.A.I.T. stand for?
   a) Why am I thinking? ❏
   b) Why am I talking? ❏
   c) Wait, act, indicate and talk ❏
   d) None of the above ❏

2. An ideal team meeting agenda should include:
   a) Issues and topics for discussion ❏
   b) Names of who will present each topic ❏
   c) Proposed time to be spent on each topic ❏
   d) All of the above ❏

3. Which of the following might influence your choice of the form of communication?
   a) The expectations of your boss or company ❏
   b) The location of the other person ❏
   c) How urgent the matter is ❏
   d) All of the above ❏

4. A workplace culture is:
   a) The habits of the group ❏
   b) The thinking and norms of the group ❏
   c) The behaviours and styles of the group ❏
   d) All of the above ❏

5. Ideal communication should be viewed as:
   a) A minor part of your role ❏
   b) A full-time task ❏
   c) Left to your team ❏
   d) None of the above ❏

6. Which of the following is *not* the trait of a good listener?
   a) An empathic person ❏
   b) Seeks to understand rather than be understood ❏
   c) Tries to speak first in meetings ❏
   d) Acknowledges what others say ❏

7. In a meeting, what should you do when someone else is speaking?
   a) Interrupt them ❏
   b) Not listen ❏
   c) Think of what you want to say ❏
   d) Listen to them and then acknowledge what they have shared ❏

8. How should you manage your emails?
   a) Decide who you should typically copy emails to ❏
   b) Decide which emails to reply to ❏
   c) Decide how long or short your emails should be ❏
   d) All of the above ❏

9. Which of the following is a problem of working with remotely located team members?
   a) They may be from another culture ❏
   b) You cannot easily meet them face to face ❏
   c) You cannot easily see what they are doing ❏
   d) All of the above ❏

10. Which of the following is *not* one of the secrets of holding successful meetings?

a) Invite as many people as possible to attend ❏

b) Determine the required outcomes ❏

c) Set a clear agenda with topics for discussion ❏

d) Chair the meeting well ❏

THURSDAY

Managing poor performers in your team

Managing staff who are not working and performing to the optimum can be your most difficult task and is the topic I am most asked about in my coaching and training work, regardless of whereabouts in the world my clients are located.

This chapter will show you the typical performance issues that you might face and how to think through your response to different situations. Each challenge will be unique and you will need to find a suitable response for the precise circumstances of each case.

This chapter will show you how to:

- Explore what performance problems can look like and learn how to understand the possible causes of poor or underperformance
- Explore the team performance issues associated with older as well as younger staff
- Recognize the problems that toxic people can create within a team
- Understand that performance issues can be caused by the entire team rather than by an individual's problems
- Understand each person's different decision-making styles and how these can impact upon a team's performance
- Ensure that 'groupthink' is not occurring
- Give and receive feedback to help to improve your team's performance.

What does poor or underperformance look like?

Members of your team can fail to meet targets and goals that you have set for them. They can also have a negative effect on others in the team which might affect the performance of other team members or their willingness to stay in your team.

How can you spot team members with potential performance issues *before* the problems manifest themselves in goals not being achieved? This would give you a chance to rectify things before it is too late. Here are some key questions to help you spot who may have performance issues.

- Who complains and gossips?
- Who seems to create conflict and is argumentative?
- Who is acting selfishly and not sharing?
- Who answers back, and does not seem to respect or listen to you?
- Who in your team do other team members not like to work or communicate with?
- Who seems to be lazy and often absent or having long coffee breaks?
- Who never seems to start or finish their work on time?
- Who often asks for help and says they do not understand what you have already told them?

Possible causes of poor or underperformance

It is important as a manager to seek out the root causes of why someone is not working and performing to the optimum in your team. Sometimes what you see is only a symptom of some underlying issue. For example, Person A acts lazily and spends his time gossiping and complaining rather than focusing on his work. The possible causes might be a combination of:

- not having clear objectives or goals
- not having the tools to complete his work
- not being incentivized or motivated
- not having the skills or knowledge to know what to do
- being bored by their work
- being afraid of making a mistake.

It is not enough to simply stop the person complaining and gossiping. It is your task to find out what is happening and to try to help solve the underlying issues. Sometimes a few performance issues are linked and you need to tackle a few things to arrive at the root cause. The diagram below shows how one problem (Issue 4) has underlying causes, the key one being that the person is not interested in their work (Issue 1).

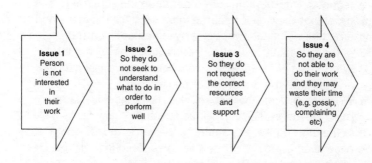

Often, such flows become downward spirals. In the scenario above, the person is likely to lose interest even more if they are not in a position to do their work well.

A very useful framework for seeking the reasons for performance issues (and one which complements the six-step model in Tuesday's chapter), is the widely used Gilbert's Six Boxes, where any reason for an individual's poor performance would fall into one or more of the following six 'buckets':

Necessary feedback and expectations	Needed resources available	Appropriate incentives
Required knowledge and skills	Optimal ability to do work	Attitude and motivations

The top three boxes relate more to what you and the organization needs to provide and do, while the bottom three relate more to the individual.

Based on these six boxes, explore the reasons for any performance issues in your team by asking yourself these six sets of questions.

1 Do I need to give the individual or individuals feedback to help them improve their performance? How strong or firm do I need to be? Have I neglected to do so? How can I alter my communication and leadership style to help?
2 Is the individual lacking anything in terms of resources (support, information from other sources, equipment and time) that they need to perform better? Are the goals and direction not ideal or not clearly stated and communicated?
3 Is the individual correctly incentivized to perform better? What kinds of incentives or motivators are missing or not aligned with the required performance?
4 What knowledge, experience or skills is the individual lacking or misusing that is affecting their performance? How can I solve this?
5 Is the individual really suited to the work and tasks that they have been given? Are they able to succeed in their role if given help or have they reached a ceiling?
6 In what ways is the individual not motivated to perform well? What factors are holding them back and demotivating them?

Is it a team-wide performance problem?

If one of your team has an issue, be careful about jumping to conclusions and assuming that it is just that individual's problem. It could be that this individual is reacting to problems within the whole team, e.g. others not sharing information with him or her.

Is the team stuck in the 'storming' phase (remember Tuckman's model from the Sunday chapter) so the team's performance has declined? The graph below is a reminder of the development stages of a team and how teams can fall back into the storming phase.

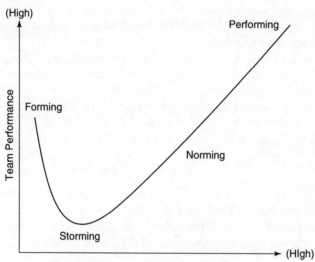

Beware of individuals blaming others

Some individuals may try to blame others in the team or to blame you for their poor performance, even when it appears clear to you that it is the individual who is at fault. You need to know your team well and be able to observe what is really happening, which is something that becomes easier with time and experience. If you initially blame the wrong party or reason for a performance problem, be ready to apologize and be open with those involved. We all value honesty and humility in those we work with. People can be very forgiving even if falsely accused of something.

If ever in doubt, pause and take a calm step back. Look for the bigger picture, what is sometimes referred to as a 'balcony' or 'helicopter' view, of what is happening.

Giving feedback to your team

When coaching individuals I often hear comments such as: 'But no one ever told me that I was not performing well ... I did not realize that my boss was not happy with my performance until the day he fired me.'

It is not enough simply to give your team goals and objectives; it is essential that you provide excellent feedback which forms part of your evaluation of their performance. Too often, managers only give feedback at the time of the company's annual performance appraisal review. At other times there is typically no structured sharing and communication.

Here are some key dos and don'ts about how you should give feedback.

- You should remember to give feedback as often as possible about all the good work that your team members are doing and not give feedback only when there is a problem.
- Feedback should be timely and should be given immediately after the performance issue has occurred.
- Feedback should be as clear and specific as possible, and you should give your own opinion rather than quoting what others might think.
- Try to describe what you observe about the person's performance, not simply making accusations or judgements.
- Always try to give positive feedback first before moving on to any potentially critical or negative areas of discussion.
- Allow the person to listen and to respond.

'I praise loudly. I blame softly.'

Catherine the Great

Teach your team to receive feedback and overcome blind spots

It is not enough to give feedback; your team members need to be encouraged to hear and to listen well, so learn to share with them. Tell them that they do not need to immediately respond and try to justify everything that is being discussed about their performance.

Sometimes team members may have difficulty hearing and agreeing with your feedback because they do not believe or accept that they might have a particular weakness. This could be called the individual's blindspot and you need to encourage them to be open-minded and understand that we all have weaknesses and issues that we may not be aware of but which others are.

Types of performance issues

Here are some of the common people issues that you are likely to face when you start managing a team.

Older, long-serving staff

Often there is no problem in working with older and long-serving people, and their knowledge, experience and wisdom can really help you and the rest of the team. However, sometimes older staff may not be willing to listen and work with you, particularly if you are introducing new ideas and changes. Such people can be negative and cynical, and will often speak slightingly about what you are trying to do and will appear to undermine you.

How can you work with and manage such people?

- Were they so used to a previous management style that now they are not willing to adjust to your leadership? Perhaps initially you can give them some leeway and time, but you need to set clear expectations and be ready to be firm.
- They may feel that they know how to do your job better than you do. This is never easy to deal with but you must not let them undermine you.

- They may feel threatened by the changes you appear to represent and they may fear for their jobs. Try to win them over and reassure them.
- Do they resent you being appointed as their manager because one of them was passed over for the role? By slowly trying to gain their respect you can hope to win them over.
- Are they unable to understand or do what you are asking of them? Perhaps extra sharing, communication or training is required.
- You may need to be firm and ask them to stop being negative or speaking unpleasantly about you. A point may be reached where you will need to give warning letters and threaten to dismiss someone. You will need to make sure that you have kept your boss informed along the way and also sought advice about employment law from your human resources team.

Generation Y staff

You may need to hire staff aged in their twenties, part of the so-called Generation Y. This age group brings with them expectations that can create problems; these include wanting responsibility immediately, not wanting to work long hours, wanting to be promoted quickly and not connecting well with older staff in the team.

How can you ensure such young people succeed in your team?

- Teach and show them what is expected of them in their work and be open with them about the realities of how much responsibility you can give them and of the probable timings of future promotion.
- Spend time understanding their motivations and expectations.
- Guide and mentor them, encouraging them to accept what needs to be done in their jobs and careers.
- Be ready to be firm if they are not adjusting to what is expected of them.
- Be aware that younger people may not be as loyal as older staff so they might resign if they feel you are pushing them too much or if the work (in their opinion) is boring or not challenging enough. In Friday's chapter we cover the topic of staff retention.

Bad examples

You are likely to have at least one team member who may be setting a bad and unacceptable example to the rest of the team, and you will need to intervene in some way. What could someone do that is unacceptable? Here are some examples I have come across:

- often being late for work
- spending too long away from their desk
- being slow and lazy
- being selfish and not sharing
- preventing other people from doing their work
- not listening to what you are communicating
- not doing as they are asked
- being dishonest and lying
- speaking unpleasantly about other people
- criticizing you and/or the organization
- openly talking about leaving
- not being willing to learn new things.

Dealing with unacceptable behaviour

Here is a three-step approach to follow.

1 **Find out why**
   Explore the underlying reasons for the individual's behaviour; typically this is linked to the individual's motivations, attitudes, behaviours and values. Gather feedback from other people (while also responding to people's complaints about the individual's actions).

2 **Agree a plan**
   Have a meeting with the individual. Ideally this should be a face-to-face confidential meeting – although your boss or human resources manager may need to be present – in which you explain your concerns in detail.
   - Listen to the responses and opinions of the individual.
   - Be ready to explain again why there is a problem, if necessary talking about the organization's values and culture.

327

- Try to agree a written action plan of required changes and a time frame for improved performance.
- Warn the person of the consequences of not changing their behaviour.
- Agree when you will meet again, if this is appropriate.

3 Follow up and monitor the individual

Follow up and monitor the individual's performance. Give the individual feedback, letting them know what changes you are observing. If the changes are not positive, you will need to consider disciplinary action, including giving warning letters as well as considering dismissal, in line with your company's rules and your country's employment laws and regulations.

Dealing with a high performer with negative issues

Sometimes negative behaviour is exhibited by someone who is achieving their goals and objectives and who may be viewed as a high-performing member of the team. This can create a dilemma for you as you will probably not wish to lose such a person. From my experience, I would strongly encourage you to:

- talk with the individual openly, sharing your concerns about their attitude and behaviour. Do not keep quiet for fear of losing them.
- consider disciplinary action and even dismissal if the individual will not acknowledge their need to improve and will not change how they are acting. You cannot keep such a 'toxic' person in a team without negatively affecting the entire team.
- explain to the team what led to a person's dismissal – this will counter any inaccurate gossip or rumours.

Letting such a person go will demonstrate to the rest of the team that you are serious about creating and maintaining an ideal working environment and culture based on certain values. Such firm action is all part of creating a culture of excellence – this is explored in more detail in the Saturday chapter.

Poor decision-makers

Humans are creatures of habit and we can become lazy about thinking through everything that we do in our work. How does your team deal with and think through problems and solutions in its daily work?

- Do some members always seem to jump to one conclusion or idea and refuse to listen to other ideas?
- Do others float various solutions and never seem to agree which is the ideal way forward?

- Do team members seem to follow the same style in every interaction you have with them?
- What are your own decision-making habits?

According to Ken Brousseau's famous decision-making model, optimal decision-making in any given situation revolves around two questions.

1 How much information should ideally be analysed in making a decision?
2 How many ideas and solutions need to be optimally considered before a final decision can be made?

Your challenge is ensure that you teach your team to think well and to make correct decisions. Make sure that they avoid making the following common mistakes:

- using too little information or ignoring information
- being overwhelmed by too much information
- jumping at the first solution or idea that is suggested and not looking any further
- implementing someone else's suggestion without thinking it through sufficiently.

You must also be ready to review their work and provide feedback and advice when they may be going astray in their decision-making.

- Sometimes you can leave your team to make mistakes, allowing them to learn from such mistakes.
- At other times, the potential mistake might be too costly and you must guide them to another solution, explaining to them your rationale and logic.

Avoiding the problem of 'groupthink'

Sometimes a group jumps to collective decisions and conclusions which may prove to be wrong and lead to performance problems. 'Groupthink' occurs when a team discusses an issue and agrees on a way forward while ignoring lone voices that may have other suggestions to make.

This is a common problem within teams where there is a culture of not speaking up and of not questioning what others are saying. In certain cultures, if a team leader makes a suggestion, it is highly likely that the group will support it and will ignore other ideas. This can be very dangerous. As well as leading to potentially wrong decisions being made, it can also be very demotivating to those in your team, particularly those who are creative and innovative, who may feel they are not being listened to.

Are you the cause of the problem?

In what ways might you be directly contributing to the poor performance of your team members?

- Are you delaying any decisions or communication, e.g. a difficult conversation with a poor performer?
- Are you ignoring what is in front of you, e.g. are you reluctant to admit that someone in your team is at fault or not being a good team player?
- Are you biased in some way, e.g. always favouring certain members of your team and being blind to their weaknesses?
- Are there any trust issues involved? Are people in your team reluctant to share with you their ideas and concerns? Do they not trust that you will use what they share in a fair and objective way (i.e. do they fear you will use it against them)?

One solution is to build up as much trust and rapport with your team as possible. As you grow your management career, do 'walk the talk', ensuring that what you think, what you say and what you do are all in visible alignment.

Remember that as the head of the team, you are ultimately responsible for the entire team's performance. You cannot ever say that it was not your fault if your team performs badly!

Summary

This chapter has been a guide to the thinking and solutions that can help you to understand and solve poor performance problems that might arise in your team.

You are now able to understand the kinds of possible performance problems that you may face.

You can use the Six Boxes questions to discover the possible reasons for team members' problems.

You know that there are some common patterns of poor performance, particularly when you have some older, more experienced staff or younger Generation Y staff in your team.

You know that sometimes problems that may appear to come from one or two individuals might actually be a team-wide issue.

You understand the ideal decision-making process and why poor decision-making might lead to poor performance.

SUNDAY

MONDAY

TUESDAY

WEDNESDAY

THURSDAY

FRIDAY

SATURDAY

Fact-check (answers at the back)

1. Which of the following is *not* one of the Six Boxes model?
   a) Needed resources available ❑
   b) Amount of holidays given ❑
   c) Optimal ability to do work ❑
   d) Attitude and motivations ❑

2. Which of the following could be viewed as unacceptable behaviour?
   a) Often being late for work ❑
   b) Spending too long away from desk ❑
   c) Being slow and lazy ❑
   d) All of the above ❑

3. How should you respond to anyone exhibiting unacceptable behaviour?
   a) Find out why ❑
   b) Agree a plan with the individual ❑
   c) Follow up and mentor the individual ❑
   d) All of the above ❑

4. A team-wide performance problem suggests the team is in which stage of the Tuckman model?
   a) Norming ❑
   b) Performing ❑
   c) Forming ❑
   d) Storming ❑

5. Why might older staff cause performance issues?
   a) Fear of change ❑
   b) Thinking they know more than you ❑
   c) Jealousy over your appointment as manager ❑
   d) All of the above ❑

6. Good feedback should be:
   a) Clear and timely ❑
   b) Only in writing ❑
   c) Given only over phone ❑
   d) Given only at end of year ❑

7. What is 'groupthink'?
   a) People have different ideas ❑
   b) People agree to one idea too easily and quickly ❑
   c) People never agree ❑
   d) It is what your boss thinks ❑

8. Why should we not jump to conclusions when investigating a performance issue?
   a) The causes may not be what you initially think or see ❑
   b) There may be more than one reason ❑
   c) It might be a team-wide issue or an individual's issue ❑
   d) All of above ❑

9. Which of the following is a common mistake when making decisions?
   a) Using too little information ❑
   b) Ignoring information ❑
   c) Jumping at the first solution or idea that is suggested ❑
   d) All of the above ❑

10. Which of the following is the ideal way to receive feedback?
    a) Listening well ❑
    b) Not rushing to speak ❑
    c) Not feeling compelled to justify what you are being told ❑
    d) All of the above ❑

SUNDAY

MONDAY

TUESDAY

WEDNESDAY

THURSDAY

FRIDAY

SATURDAY

FRIDAY

Managing high performers in your team

Having created and built up a team, you need to ensure that you encourage and manage those in your team who are performing well and maximize the chances of them performing even better in the future. You will also need to ensure that you retain and keep these high performers.

This chapter will help you to:

- Understand who in your team is performing well and who has the potential to perform even better in the future
- Differentiate between those in your team who are performing well and those who are not, objectively measuring your team members' performance
- Rank your team members by their performance and by their potential
- Deal with high-performing staff who may not be exhibiting the values, behaviour and attitudes that you expect of them
- Be an excellent situational leader, adapting your management style as needed, and balancing how directive and how supportive you need to be
- Understand the importance of retaining key staff and having a talent retention strategy
- Create a strategy based around the six secrets of retaining high-performing staff.

Who is performing well in your team?

> *'Teamwork is so important that it is virtually impossible for you to reach the heights of your capabilities or make the money that you want without becoming very good at it.'*
>
> Brian Tracy

How many of your team are performing well? Who is outstanding? Which of your team has the potential to perform even better in the future?

Each organization has its own model for monitoring and evaluating its employees' performance. Do you know and understand your own organization's model? Typically there would be a combination of:

- setting performance goals, and also goals based on certain soft skills and values
- creating a timetable for discussing and evaluating the achievement of the goals
- having a series of discussions between each employee and his or her line manager to evaluate the actual performance of the employee, with most organizations grading their staff based on:
  - achievement of their work goals
  - how well the individual reflects certain values or core competencies.

Differentiating among your team

Many managers have difficulty in being honest and open with all members of their team about each team member's performance and potential. Why is this so? It is because some managers find it hard to tell some of their team that they are not performing well, fearing that it would upset them and demotivate them. As a result, a manager might give similar performance rankings or gradings to their team members. However, by not being honest and differentiating between different levels of performance, you may demotivate your better performers because they feel that you are not valuing their hard work and good performance.

Some organizations insist upon what is called 'forced ranking', which was first popularized by General Electric. With forced ranking, a manager must give a range of performance gradings to their team members based on certain percentages. A typical example might be as follows.

Typical grades	Typical grading definitions	Example percentage of staff to be given each grade
A	Excellent	10%
B	Good	35%
C	Average	35%
D	Below average	10%
E	Not performing	10%

In this example, you would only be able to give one in ten of your team an 'excellent' grading.

You must learn to be very objective in grading your team members and in giving them feedback on their performance. Keep notes about how you arrive at each of your team member's gradings and be ready to justify your decisions to others. It is important that you are seen by your team to be fair, understanding and objective.

Performance versus potential

Some of your team might have performed well in the year to date, but how do you know if they will continue working well and whether they could take on more work and responsibilities in the future? In other words, do they have a high potential to grow in your team in your organization?

How would you define potential with your team members?

- To keep performing well in their current role with their existing goals?
- To be able to grow and take on more responsibilities, and possibly be promoted into a more senior role?
- To be able to consistently live by and demonstrate your team's values and core competencies?
- The degree to which they want to take on more responsibility?

It can be easy to communicate what you think of their potential to a team member with high potential – they would be only too happy to be told that you think they have great potential to grow and succeed in your team and in your organization. Your difficulty comes in telling someone with limited potential what you think of them. As with poor performers, the best practice is that you must be honest, but diplomatic!

I would encourage you to use a table such as the one shown below to rank your team members in terms of *both* their performance and their potential.

		Low	Medium	High
Potential (in future)	High	Low performers with high potential		High performers with high potential
	Medium			
	Low	Low performers with low potential		High performers with low potential
		Low	Medium	High
		Performance (to date)		

How would you lead your team members depending on their performance and potential rankings? As you gain more experience of managing teams, you will develop your own style of working with each team member, but here are some ideas to get you started:

High performers with high potential
These are the stars of your team and you should make sure that you retain and support them. Retaining such

high performers is a key role of any successful manager. It is also important that you do not let their success go to their heads and they must be encouraged to be good team players, helping the entire team to succeed. These issues are discussed in more detail later in this chapter.

High performers with low potential
They may have peaked and reached their maximum potential in their current role. Are they comfortable being thought of as having low potential with limited promotion possibilities? You could try to retain them in their current role in which they are performing well.

Low performers with high potential
Why are they currently underperforming? Would they be able to perform better in a different role or even in a different team? The key is to try to create a role for them in which they can flourish and perform well.

Low performers with low potential
Are you able to develop and grow such team members? If they have been performing poorly and also have poor potential to perform well in the future, then it is possible that you will need to let these staff go to make room for better performing people.

Individuals with average or medium levels of performance and/or potential

Only you can decide how you work with and manage such individuals, who are often referred to as the 'backbone' of a team. It would be unusual to have a team without such members and your task is to work to improve both their current performance and also their future potential.

But be careful not to push all of your staff to improve; some people are genuinely happy to remain 'average' performers and do not have the desire and ambition to be pushed to perform better or to improve their perceived potential.

Performing well, but...

Have you ever known someone who performs well (in terms of achieving their goals) but they may not be someone you wish to work with? For instance, they might be sexist, lazy, arrogant, deceptive, not communicate well, not listen, be selfish etc.

You will at some point have team members who are achieving their goals and are deemed to be high performers, but they may have some attitude and behaviour problems and are not exhibiting the expected values of your team. This will be a challenging situation for you. On the matrix below, people like this would sit towards the bottom right; as a manager, you need to try to move them to the top right corner (shown by the arrow).

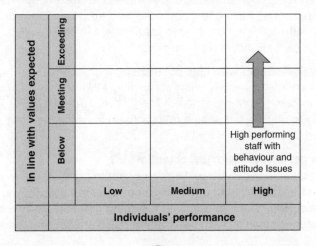

How can you do this?

- Have you spoken with the individual in question to discuss your concerns? You need to do so, and during such a conversation try to discover whether the individual agrees with your opinion. Ask them why they are acting this way.
- Are they demotivating others in your team and organization? You may hear complaints from others.
- How willing and able are you to try to change their unacceptable behaviour(s)? You must decide how firm you will need to be and choose how you will manage them – see the section below on being a situational leader.
- 'To keep or not to keep them?' Are you afraid of losing them from your team if you push them too hard to change? You will need to understand how difficult it would be to replace such an individual with an equally strong performer.

A high performer whose performance declines

You may have to deal with a high performer whose performance is starting to decline. If you view the decline as a temporary blip, you might not enter into much discussion with the individual. However, if it is not a temporary decline, you need to investigate the cause(s). There might be a number of factors involved, such as:

- boredom with their work
- loss of interest in their work
- not getting on with you as their manager.

To help get such a good performer back on track, you will need to be a good situational leader.

Situational leadership

Would you manage a high performer in the same way that you manage a poorly performing member of your team? Do you ever consciously alter your management style depending on the situation and the person you are talking about?

343

Being able to alter your management style to the circumstances is a key skill of a top performing team leader. Ken Blanchard's Situational Leadership model, shown below, is a good demonstration of why this is so important.

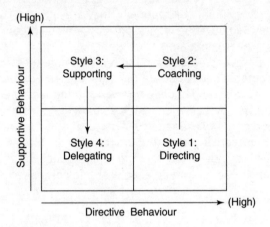

With any member of your team, you can choose to be a combination of:

- **directive** – telling and showing a person in your team what they have to do and then closely supervising their performance
- **supportive** – actively providing guidance, feedback and support to a person when they are working under you and encouraging them.

The Situational Leadership model shows four possible management styles that you could adopt in any given situation. Each is explained below, with an indication of when each style might be appropriate.

Style 1: Directing
This is sometimes called a 'I will decide what you do' style and is a style of offering a little support while being very directive. You would come across as being very decisive and clear.

You would normally use such a management style with new staff or with staff who have some serious performance issues. In both cases you need to explain clearly what needs to be done or achieved. It is a useful style when you have no time to allow the individual to learn for themselves what they need to do or to change. Be careful not to overuse this style, though, as it can be viewed as being too strong and could be seen as micro-managing.

Style 2: Coaching

This is sometimes called a 'Let's talk and I will decide' style. It is a style of being very engaged or involved with an individual in your team, and being both very decisive and very supportive.

This style is typically used when you need to be very actively involved in helping someone to achieve their goals and to improve their performance. An underperforming but established member of your team might need to be managed in this very hands-on way. If you manage someone in this way for too long, however, they might feel micro-managed and unable to make their own decisions.

Style 3: Supporting

This can be called a 'Let's talk and we both decide' style. It is still quite a hands-on style, where you feel you do not have to be directive but still need to provide a lot of feedback, discussion and support.

Typically this style is used with staff who are experienced but still need active support and help. They do not need or expect you to direct them but still need your active support and involvement.

Style 4: Delegating
This can be called a 'Why don't you decide?' style. It is a style of offering very little directive and supportive support. It does not mean that you are not managing someone, but it does mean that you are not having to provide a hands-on and involved style and as a result you are giving an individual a lot of space in which to work and perform.

This is the ideal style that can be adopted with high-performing staff who know what they have to do and require less of your time compared to new staff or underperforming staff.

The three arrows in the diagram show the ideal flow in how you would change your style of managing an individual over time – from when they join your team (Style 1) to when they become a consistently high performer (Style 4).

I encourage you to start being very conscious of how you manage and communicate with each of your team. Decide if your style is optimal in each case, remembering to adjust your style as needed.

Retaining top performers

Having identified your top performers as well as those who have high potential, you must decide how you ensure that you retain such individuals and keep them in your team.

A good manager needs a talent retention strategy for those team members they wish to retain. The strategy can be quite simple and could start with answers to two questions:

1 Why do your staff choose to stay and work in your team?
2 What do they seek in their job, career and workplace?

These two questions link to discussions elsewhere in Week 3 about employee motivation, and I would encourage you to ask your staff for their opinions in the form of an employee satisfaction survey. Ideally this should be anonymous so that your team are more comfortable with sharing and being honest. Such surveys can be very helpful in revealing what your team members really feel and think about:

- their work
- being in your team
- being managed by you.

Do not be offended if they surprise you by being critical and a little negative – it is better to know the truth than to be left in the dark thinking everything is fine. Facts are friendly, and once you know the truth you can act upon it.

Six secrets of retaining key staff

Here are six key areas that you could focus on as part of your talent retention strategy.

1 Be a leader that team members trust and want to work with
Communicate well with your team and, most importantly, listen to them. Ensure that you meet their expectations and when you cannot meet them, have an honest and open discussion about why not. I would add that you must 'walk the talk' and make sure that you do what you promise.

Also, do develop your leadership styles to inspire and motivate your team – the Saturday chapter explores this in more detail.

2 Reward team members fairly

Make sure that your team's remuneration model (including bonus and commission structures, salary review processes etc) is fair, open and transparent, while also ensuring that you pay your staff at competitive market levels. Humans like to compare things with others, so it is imperative that you show no favouritism or lack of objectivity in how each person in your team is evaluated, judged and rewarded.

3 Support team members' career and life plans

Understand what your team members' ambitions and career goals are and try to work with them in achieving their dreams. Part of this involves having a good succession planning model so that high performers can be groomed for more significant roles and can be promoted. Another aspect involves you having honest and open dialogue about what job opportunities may exist in your team or in the wider organization, and supporting your team members in moving to new roles. This may mean you have to let them join another team in your organization to give them the needed career growth.

4 Give team members work that they enjoy

Make sure that you try to match the work roles given to each of your team members with what they would like and enjoy doing. It is also advisable not to let your staff overwork and become burnt-out; they may enjoy what they do, but you must support them in having a good work–life balance.

5 Recognize team members' good work and efforts

How often do you say: 'Thank you', 'Well done', 'Good work' or 'Great performance'? When did you last publicly acknowledge the good work of members of your team? Remember that humans yearn for and need to be recognized. If in doubt, do not keep silent.

6 Create and maintain a positive environment

Try to ensure that within your team there is a healthy and open culture with no tension, anxiety, undue stress, negative gossip and rumours. You need your staff to be happy to come to work.

In my experience, following these six secrets will keep members of your team motivated and wanting to continue working with you.

Summary

This chapter has shown you how to successfully work with and retain your high-performing and high-potential staff.

You are now able to define who in your team is high-performing, understanding the importance of differentiating between those in your team who are performing well and those who are not.

You can analyse your team members by both their performance and by their potential.

You understand how to think through why your high-performing staff may have some behaviour or attitude issues and are not living up to the values expected of them.

You can vary your leadership style depending on the situation and on which of your team members you are communicating with and trying to manage.

You understand how to successfully retain your high-performing talent to ensure that you do not lose them to the competition.

SUNDAY

MONDAY

TUESDAY

WEDNESDAY

THURSDAY

FRIDAY

SATURDAY

Fact-check (answers at the back)

1. Which of the following is *not* one of the six retention secrets?
   a) Being a good leader ❏
   b) Firing staff who do not listen well ❏
   c) Rewarding staff well ❏
   d) Helping your staff to plan their careers ❏

2. Situational leadership involves:
   a) Varying the style of management ❏
   b) Being directive at times ❏
   c) Being supportive at times ❏
   d) All of the above ❏

3. In the situational leadership model, coaching is being:
   a) High in directive and low in supportive styles ❏
   b) High in both directive and supportive styles ❏
   c) Low in both directive and supportive styles ❏
   d) None of the above ❏

4. Why is a talent retention strategy important?
   a) Losing staff is costly and disruptive ❏
   b) Good talent is hard to replace ❏
   c) It's not easy to keep your staff ❏
   d) All of the above ❏

5. Why is it important to say 'Thank you' and 'Well done' to your staff?
   a) It makes them feel valued ❏
   b) It makes them feel that they have been recognized ❏
   c) Both of the above. ❏
   d) None of the above ❏

6. Which is it better to have in your team?
   a) A high performer who is not in alignment with your company values ❏
   b) A high performer who is in alignment with your company values ❏
   c) A low performer with low potential ❏
   d) A potentially high performer who is not in alignment with your values ❏

7. Why is it key to give your staff work that they enjoy?
   a) They will be more successful ❏
   b) They will burn out ❏
   c) They will have no work–life balance ❏
   d) None of the above ❏

8. Being a leader that others trust can help you to:
   a) Retain your staff ❏
   b) Motivate your staff ❏
   c) Lead to better performance by your team ❏
   d) All of the above ❏

9. Which is the ideal style of managing a team member who is experienced and high-performing?
   a) Delegating style ❏
   b) Coaching style ❏
   c) Directive style ❏
   d) Supportive style ❏

10. The 'I will decide what you
    do' style in the situational
    leadership model is the

a) Delegating style ❑
b) Coaching style ❑
c) Supportive style ❑
d) Directive style ❑

SATURDAY

Creating and maintaining a culture of excellence

It is not difficult to learn how to manage a team so that it performs to an acceptable level. But to lead a team to a level of performance that makes other people say: 'Wow, what a brilliant and amazing team!' is a little harder.

This chapter will help you to understand what you can do to raise your team members to a level of excellent performance combined with excellent potential. In terms of your role as manager, this chapter will help to elevate you from being a good team manager to one who is truly outstanding and admired.

This chapter will show you:

- What a culture of excellence is and why it worth aspiring to create such a culture in your team
- The seven key understandings that are the foundation for creating a culture of excellence within your team

What is a culture of excellence?

'When a team outgrows individual performance and learns team confidence, excellence becomes a reality.'

Joe Paterno

Any team, consciously or unconsciously, agrees a set of understandings around which all of its thinking and activities are organized. This is your team's culture.

What are your team's understandings? Are they optimal? Ideally, such understandings should be centred on achieving and maintaining excellence in all aspects of the team's work and workings.

I think the most helpful definition of excellence is optimizing the 'what we do' with the 'how we do it', i.e. choosing to do the optimal tasks and actions while also ensuring that such work is completed optimally.

The diagram below shows this pictorially. Which box would you define as excellence?

What tasks and actions Does your team undertake?		How does your team perform its tasks and actions?	
Right ones		Doing the right things badly	Doing the right things well
Wrong ones		Doing the wrong things badly	Doing the wrong things well
		Not well / Badly	Well

Hopefully, you chose the top right-hand box! This is the correct answer: where your team are doing the right things well.

Note that understandings are linked to your team's written and unwritten goals, objectives, rules, norms, stated values and the content of your team charter (covered in the Sunday chapter).

Components of a culture of excellence

Seven key understandings seem to be essential to high-performing teams around the world. I would encourage you to explore how you could apply each of these to your own team, refining them as needed over time to suit the make-up of your team and the challenges your team is facing.

As the manager of the team, it is your role to take the lead in creating and sharing the required understandings, and to work with your team to refine them as necessary.

1 Outstanding leadership is key to the team's success

No manager can expect to go into work each day and to act in exactly the same way each time. Your staff must know and accept this – one day you will be firm and strong, another quite relaxed. In addition to becoming a great situational leader, there are many other key leadership styles that you may wish to adopt as needed. Here are three styles that you might choose to learn more about and to use at appropriate moments with your team:

- **Servant leadership:** This style puts the manager in a supporting role, providing support for the needs of the team, without taking an active leadership role.
- **Transformational leadership:** This is an inspirational style, focusing upon helping a team to achieve a vision which is created and formulated by the team's boss.
- **Adaptive leadership:** This style involves encouraging and inspiring a team to recognize, adapt and learn new things to help deal with new challenges facing the team.

You must learn to decide when you should join your team 'on the shopfloor' to help them with their daily operational challenges and when you should step back to take a 'balcony view', seeing the whole picture and thinking strategically about the challenges facing your team.

2 The team always lives up to the highest of values

It is your role as the team's leader to ensure that all of the team aspire to live and work by the highest of values. I cannot tell you what values you should choose, but there are four values that many of today's successful leaders strive to follow with their teams.

- Working with total honesty and integrity
- Working as a single team where individual performance is supported but not at the expense of the overall team
- Only allowing acceptable behaviour and attitudes, with nothing offensive or abusive being tolerated
- Challenging each other to excel and to achieve the most that each person is capable of.

This links to the earlier discussions about culture, and you must allow yourself to lead in creating the optimal environment with the highest of values being maintained.

3 The team maintains a strong culture of learning and development

A successful manager knows that each member of the team is on a personal career path and should wish to help each member to maximize and grow their careers. In addition to gaining experience in their work, a team member needs to grow and develop in many ways. They require your help through:

- assessing what skills and competencies they need to develop
- providing the time and funds for the training they need
- providing them with mentoring and coaching.

Your role as a successful manager will be one of continually helping and encouraging each member of your team never to stop learning, growing and developing.

4 The team changes direction as often as needed

As a manager you must truly accept the need for constant change and help your team to also understand and accept this. Change is inevitable, but failure and poor performance within teams can arise from fighting this need to change and to adapt. Change is not hard if you can create a mindset within your team of acceptance and understanding. Be ready to spend as much time as necessary on communicating with

your team about any need to change or adapt that you plan
to introduce.

Help your team to understand that they may need to
change either *what* they are doing as a team or *how* they
are doing things as a team in response to any number of
events and actions.

5 No single team member is greater than the whole team
I love the following quote from the American baseball player
Babe Ruth, which captures the essence of this understanding:

> **'The way a team plays as a whole determines
> its success. You may have the greatest bunch
> of individual stars in the world, but if they don't
> play together, the club won't be worth a dime.'**

A great manager must ensure that the team's drive for
excellence is never derailed by an individual in the team – it
is better to lose someone from your team if that can serve to
maintain the team's overall success.

You will recall the discussion in Friday's chapter about
high performers with attitude problems. An excellent

manager will not tolerate such staff for long; either the high performer's attitude must quickly improve or they should be asked to leave the team (and organization).

6 The team maintains an optimal work–life balance

A manager must create and maintain a healthy working environment. It is no good if a team achieves its goals through the team members working 18 hours a day and then being off work with stress and heart disorders!

You must also remember to look after your own work–life balance and health. Great managers often work very long hours but take the time to have holidays and to recharge.

7 The team members wish to leave a legacy

What legacy do you and your team members wish to leave behind? Working in a team is not just about earning a salary. We work for about half of the time that we are awake. How can you help make your work together as a team more meaningful and fulfilling? Do discuss such questions with your team.

Encourage your team to help those in the community, bringing your combined skills and experience to benefit those in need. Encourage yourselves to work together in your spare time to do voluntary work of some kind and to have a CSR (corporate social responsibility) impact on your organization and community.

What kind of team do you wish to leave in place? One day you will move on to a new role and/or to a new organization. Will your team members be proud to have worked in your team? What will they recall about the experience in years to come? As you work in your role, try to ensure that you lay the foundation for your team having great memories of being managed and led by you!

What will you do now?

What additional understandings have you thought of implementing? I would encourage you to create an Action Plan for becoming a more successful manager, creating a document such as the following, adding more rows as needed:

What activities and actions must I focus upon? (Include insights, discoveries, knowledge, theories etc)	Why is a change in this activity or action important for me, my role and/or my team?	How will I practise and ensure this action or activity is improved or implemented? (Include a time frame)

Do seek the support and mentoring advice of your own boss as you strive to become an outstanding leader of your team. Good luck!

Summary

This chapter has shown what you must focus on in order to create a truly sustainable and excellent team.

You must now develop your own style of managing others.

Here are three pieces of advice to help you progress in your management career:

Never stop knowing and changing yourself. Be self-aware and observe how you manage others, seeking feedback and being ready to adjust your style as needed.

Always listen to your team. Being a team's manager does not mean that you have all the answers – be ready to humble yourself and to listen to and to learn from your team. They may have more to teach you than you might imagine.

Develop managers within your team. Inspire those in your team to aspire to become great managers themselves in the future. Share what you have learnt from reading this book.

SUNDAY

MONDAY

TUESDAY

WEDNESDAY

THURSDAY

FRIDAY

SATURDAY

Fact-check (answers at the back)

1. What best describes excellent performance?
   a) Doing the wrong things well ❑
   b) Doing the right things well ❑
   c) Doing the wrong things badly ❑
   d) Doing the right things badly ❑

2. What is servant leadership?
   a) Supporting and letting your team lead ❑
   b) Helping your team to achieve a vision ❑
   c) Helping your team to adapt to changes ❑
   d) None of the above ❑

3. What is adaptive leadership?
   a) Supporting and letting your team lead ❑
   b) Helping your team to achieve a vision ❑
   c) Helping your team to adapt to changes ❑
   d) None of the above ❑

4. What is transformational leadership?
   a) Supporting and letting your team lead ❑
   b) Helping your team to achieve a vision ❑
   c) Helping your team to adapt to changes ❑
   d) None of the above ❑

5. Why is a culture of learning important?
   a) Most people want to grow and develop ❑
   b) People will feel valued if their boss supports their learning ❑
   c) It will help your staff to perform better ❑
   d) All of the above ❑

6. What was my final advice to you?
   a) Remain self-aware ❑
   b) Listen to your staff ❑
   c) Help your staff to grow and become managers one day ❑
   d) All of the above ❑

7. What should your Action Plan focus on?
   a) Testing what you remember after reading this book ❑
   b) Planning what you wish to focus on developing ❑
   c) Giving feedback to your staff ❑
   d) None of the above ❑

8. Leaving a legacy might involve which of the following?
   a) Meeting your budgetary target ❑
   b) Hiring new staff ❑
   c) Having your team do voluntary work ❑
   d) None of the above ❑

9. No one being bigger than the team means what?
   a) A team must be large and structured ❑
   b) You must hire new staff ❑
   c) Mindset and soft skills are important ❑
   d) One person cannot be allowed to derail a team's performance ❑

10. What can you learn by really listening to your team?
    a) Humility ❑
    b) New ideas ❑
    c) The team's thoughts ❑
    d) All of above ❑

WEEK 4

Successful Appraisals
In A Week

Introduction

Appraisals are often seen as an isolated and time-consuming round of paperwork which everyone has to engage in and few see any point to. The aim of Week 4 is to help people to see how they can play a useful part in the development of the organization as a whole, and to make them a worthwhile and useful part of the staff development process. The aim of this final week is to summarize the main themes that make a difference to the practice of appraisals.

It has become accepted practice in organizations to have a yearly round of appraisals. When we join a new place of work, we may be lucky enough to be trained in its appraisal system, which usually means being shown how to fill in the forms, or we may just learn how it's done by seeing how our line manager appraises us.

The consequence of this is that, for many of us, appraisals are just another set of paperwork to be completed, another time-consuming task to be fitted into our busy schedule. It's not a task we can rush through, either, as it requires us,

367

as managers, to spend time with each person on our staff, working through the form and agreeing it with them.

Yet, if we were to truly recognize the potential and intended value of appraisals, they would be regarded completely differently.

The original intention of an appraisal system is to encourage and develop the staff of the organization, so that they all perform to their highest potential. Properly implemented and used, appraisals will help you, if you are a manager, to ensure that your staff are as effective as possible in their work, and thereby to make your area of work a powerful contributing factor to the success of the organization.

Appraisals can also make your job as a manager easier, because they give you the opportunity and framework to encourage and develop your staff. This results in a team of people who feel valued and supported, and who know that their work makes a positive difference to the organization as a whole. As a manager, you can then spend less time and energy on pushing and controlling your team, and more time on the work that moves things forward and is more satisfying.

In Week 4 we will look at how you can use appraisals to enhance the way your organization works and how they can encourage your staff to continually develop. It will give you guidance on what is important about appraisals and how they fit into the bigger picture of continuous improvement of performance. By the end of the final chapter, we hope that you will see how appraisals can make a positive difference to you as a manager, your staff as individuals, and the organization as a whole.

Setting the context: why appraise?

SUNDAY

MONDAY

TUESDAY

WEDNESDAY

THURSDAY

FRIDAY

SATURDAY

In this chapter, we will explore why it is important to set appraisals within the bigger context of the development of the whole organization, and consider the purpose and principles of appraisals. If appraisals are treated as an isolated piece of paperwork that comes round once a year and is stored in the filing cabinet until next year, or is sent to the HR department and never referred to again, then it becomes a waste of time and energy.

If, on the other hand, appraisals are seen as an important part of the overall success of the organization, then they take on a different meaning and become a vital part of everyone's role. If you are a director of the organization, you will want to ensure that everyone is working towards the same goals, and appraisals can help with this. If you are a manager of a team, you will want your part of the organization to be recognized for contributing to the whole and your team to give of their best, and appraisals can help. And as a team member, you will want to be valued for your work, and appraisals will provide a summary of that. Let's explore the importance of appraisals in the bigger context.

The context

If we don't know what can be gained from effective appraisal then we have no reason to view it as a positive and useful activity.

Often it turns into a yearly 'chat' with the individual where neither side is sure what will come out of it.

As manager, you know that you're supposed to sound positive, no matter what. Yet most of those we will be appraising are neither 'stars' nor awful at what they do. What can you say when someone just does their job well? And what do you say when someone is not doing well and you are supposed to sound positive?

It is hard to give direction to the appraisal without a clear purpose, and the manager can feel solely responsible for trying to 'make it work'.

The individual being appraised, on the other hand, may fear that if they say the 'wrong thing', they will ruin any chances of promotion.

If you are using 360° feedback, they may also fear the effect of negative responses from others and wonder how to offset that effect.

It is important to be clear about how appraisals can contribute to organizational effectiveness, so that both sides use the opportunity well.

To achieve this clarity, we need to look at the purpose of having an appraisal system, and identify how it can benefit those involved.

The purpose of appraisal

Appraisal means many different things in different contexts. Usually, in a work context, it implies some type of formal, recorded interview with every member of staff at regular intervals, e.g. yearly, and often seems to be isolated from the rest of the everyday contact between managers and their staff.

For us to use appraisal effectively, we need to see it as part of overall performance management and development.

We all like to know how we're doing as individuals, and organizations need to know how they match up to their goals and targets.

Often this is monitored in an informal way. After all, we're all very good at noticing if something isn't going according to plan, or isn't as good as we want it to be.

However, this informal monitoring tends to ignore the genuine progress and achievement that takes place.

We tend to assume that if no one says anything is wrong, then we're probably doing reasonably well! In organizational terms, this can be translated into: if we're still making a profit, we're doing OK.

Appraisal is designed as a means of monitoring the progress and achievement of the organization, to encourage and support the continuing development of that organization in a changing world.

This not only helps the organization as a whole to continue to work towards optimum effectiveness, but also provides departments and individuals within that organization with a clear overall development plan, into which their own development plans can fit.

For example, it will make far more sense to me that I should learn to use a computerized database if it is introduced into the organization with clear explanations of how it will contribute to the increased effectiveness of the organization.

If it seems that the database has been introduced just because there was some money spare in the annual budget, I am more likely to defend the old system, and resent the time I have to spend on the change.

Appraisal is also designed to encourage and motivate employees continually to develop their skills, so that they are of ever-increasing value to their organization. We will increase this motivation if we offer positive recognition of progress and achievement, as well as support and help in developing in those areas that are seen to be weaker.

Appraisals present the opportunity to give this recognition, and to identify with someone how they could improve in areas where they are weaker.

So both the individual and the organization gain from the process.

Checklist: the purposes of appraisal

- To monitor the progress and achievement of the organization as a whole

- To encourage and support the continuing development of that organization in a changing world

- To encourage and motivate employees continually to develop their skills, so that they are of ever-increasing value to their organization

The benefits of effective appraisal

To ensure that appraisal is used well, rather than just paid lip service to, it is important that the benefits to all those involved are recognized and spelt out.

We all need to feel that the process will have a pay off for us personally. Then we will be prepared to invest some time and energy in it.

We also need to feel that it has some relevance, both short term and long term, to our professional and business development.

When we put into practice the principles and processes of appraisal effectively, then there is positive benefit and development for the appraiser, for the individual being appraised and for the organization.

It becomes a welcome and useful part of the employee's working life. It is also a vital part of the manager's role, both in offering support to his/her staff, and in maintaining the development of the organization. As managers, we need to be aware of the benefits and be able to state them to others, to make sure that appraisal is treated as something which has a valuable contribution to make to working life.

Benefits for the organization

Organizations as a whole will gain from effective appraisals:

- by having motivated employees
- by learning what skills are available which can be drawn on to enhance their overall performance
- by being able to identify, before a problem arises, how they may need to train or develop their employees to meet organizational goals
- by having their finger on the pulse of the internal set-up.

Benefits for the individual

What of the person being appraised? For the individual, appraisal provides an opportunity to:

- receive recognition and support from management as they develop in the work role

- be reminded of how they are contributing to the effectiveness of the organization overall
- voice their views and offer constructive suggestions on both their own development and that of the overall organization.

Benefits for the manager

For the manager, the appraisal is an opportunity to:

- enhance the relationship with the individual
- give the individual recognition and support in their continuing development
- enhance the individual's motivation by reminding them of the overall context of organizational goals to which they are contributing
- evaluate the effectiveness of individual contributions to the overall effectiveness of the organization
- gather information which may help to develop further ways of enhancing organizational effectiveness.

Principles of appraisal

So how do we turn the appraisal into this positive and useful tool?

Whether we are appraising on an informal or formal basis, there are guidelines to the approach to take which will make it far more likely that the appraisal has the effect we want.

The principles of appraisal provide a framework to define the approach, so that we undertake the appraisal with a clear idea of our intentions and purpose.

The overriding principle of appraising is that we encourage the person being appraised to take on more and more responsibility for his/her own development. In doing this, we need to remember that the individual will have some feeling of not being in control, at least initially.

Most times, an appraisal is imposed on us; but even if we have actively asked for it, we tend to do so because we don't feel that we can sort out any problems or a schedule for development ourselves.

We also need to remember that the individual knows more about their own achievement, progress and problems than anyone else – they experience it, as opposed to observing it!

So our intention in appraisal is to enable the individual to take more and more of an active part in identifying their own strengths and weaknesses, and in deciding what to do about them.

An appraisal is an interaction between two people

In other words, the appraisee is human too, so we need to ensure that we treat them with respect, in order to build up trust.

If they do not feel that they can trust the manager, then the contribution they make will be limited, and the usefulness of the appraisal reduced.

If we do not come across as 'human', and accepting of them, then they will be intimidated. If they feel that we may use what they say against them in some way, then they will say as little as possible about any difficulties and problems they may have. As we all know, these will then show up at the most inopportune time, and cause us bigger problems because they affect the appraisee's work.

Appraisals should have a positive intention and outcome

This requires that we set a positive tone to the whole appraisal. Positive recognition is important to all of us. We like it when someone says thank you, or remarks on something we've achieved or progressed in. We can offer this recognition in the appraisal, and thereby encourage the individual.

We also know that building on strengths is easier than putting the emphasis on correcting weaknesses.

Finally, we want to ensure that any weak areas are dealt with, so we need to offer constructive help to the individual in finding a way to improve performance. After all, being told that we were not doing well enough at something never helped us to do it better – it only made us feel worse.

Checklist: the principles of appraisal

● The individual will take more and more responsibility for their own development and we will help them to do that.

● We will establish trust and a good relationship as the basis for the appraisal.

● An appraisal has a positive intention and outcome, and we will use it to help the individual to use their strengths well and identify ways of improving their performance.

The role of the manager in appraisals

Having looked at the purpose and benefits of appraisals, we can begin to identify the first stages of how we can ensure that appraisals are useful and constructive.

It is up to us, as managers, to set the context for the appraisal and educate our staff into viewing it as useful. We also need to remind ourselves of the potential of appraisal, so that we treat it as an important part of our responsibilities and prepare for it properly.

We are responsible for setting the tone which will help our staff to treat appraisal as a useful and constructive part of their overall development. This is especially important when appraisal has not been seen in this light before.

By thinking through our own way of expressing the benefits, purpose and intention of appraisal, we will already have begun the journey towards more successful appraisal.

Summary

Appraisals are not worthwhile for the organization unless we set them in the bigger context of developing performance throughout the organization, in order to achieve organizational goals. Your staff will commit to their part in the appraisal process if they can see how it will benefit them.
To do this, we need to:

● Make sure the appraisal is seen as purposeful. This means that it is related to both the overall goals of the organization and to the contribution of the individual.

● Establish how the appraisal benefits the individual being appraised, their manager who appraises them, and the organization as a whole.

● Put the appraisal in the context of overall performance development, as a formal point of recognition of progress and achievement, and a plan for the next stage of development.

● Make it easy for the person being appraised to play their part in making it an effective, positive and useful appraisal. This includes ensuring that they understand its purpose and how it will benefit them.

● Remind ourselves of why appraisals are worth giving our time to, as managers, and what the principles are that we need to apply.

The following multiple-choice questions are a reminder of what we've covered today.

SUNDAY

MONDAY

TUESDAY

WEDNESDAY

THURSDAY

FRIDAY

SATURDAY

Fact-check (answers at the back)

1. What is the purpose of appraisals for those being appraised?
   a) To have a yearly chat with an employee ❏
   b) To tell employees what they've not done well ❏
   c) To provide data to HR ❏
   d) To encourage and motivate employees to continually develop their skills ❏

2. What is the purpose of appraisals for the organization?
   a) To monitor the progress and achievement of the organization as a whole ❏
   b) To keep records on employees ❏
   c) To weed out those who aren't being effective ❏
   d) To decide on who gets a bonus ❏

3. How do effective appraisals benefit organizations?
   a) They have up-to-date records. ❏
   b) They motivate employees. ❏
   c) Their managers are kept busy. ❏
   d) They look good to shareholders. ❏

4. How do effective appraisals benefit individuals?
   a) They receive recognition and support from their manager. ❏
   b) They get a bonus. ❏
   c) HR are pleased with them for doing it. ❏
   d) They can tick something off their list of objectives. ❏

5. How do effective appraisals benefit managers?
   a) They can tick something off their list of objectives. ❏
   b) They can get rid of employees they don't see as effective. ❏
   c) HR stop bothering them. ❏
   d) They have enhanced relationships with their employees. ❏

6. What is the main principle of appraisals?
   a) To tell people what is wrong with their performance ❏
   b) To set the next year's objectives ❏
   c) To encourage employees to take responsibility for their own development ❏
   d) To say something nice to each person ❏

7. What should be the manager's intention when conducting appraisals?
   a) To get them done as quickly as possible ❏
   b) To drive home how important the objectives for the person are ❏
   c) To find something positive to say ❏
   d) To encourage the person to take an active part ❏

8. What tone should the manager set for the appraisals?
   a) Positive and constructive ❏
   b) Friendly and informal ❏
   c) Structured and formal ❏
   d) 'Let's just get through this.' ❏

382

9. How should the manager want the person being appraised to approach the interview?
a) As being something to dread ❏
b) Ready to contribute ❏
c) Hoping they will be seen as OK ❏
d) Hoping it won't take long ❏

10. How should the manager approach the appraisal process?
a) As something to get done ❏
b) Ready to tell the person what they think of them ❏
c) As an important part of their job ❏
d) Wondering what they should say ❏

MONDAY

Formulating an effective appraisal

For an appraisal to be effective, it needs a clear framework to give it meaning, for both the manager and the employee. In this chapter, we will look at how you ensure that the appraisal is relevant to both parties, and is meaningful. It needs to relate to the organizational goals, the departmental objectives and the actual work the individual is expected to do. We will also remind ourselves that doing the job (i.e. the tasks) and doing the job *well* are different, and that we need to ensure that the appraisal references *how* the tasks are done, not just *if* they are or not.

To make an appraisal really effective, it needs also to give recognition to the individual person, so we will look at how you can bring in their personal qualities and their progress in developing personal and interpersonal skills. Finally, the appraisal needs to look to the future and be seen as developmental, indicating the areas where the person can grow further, so that they play their part in the continuous development of the organization. We will look at how that development can be identified and fed into the appraisal framework.

Framework for appraisal

If we are going to conduct effective appraisals, we need to ensure that both sides are clear about what exactly is being appraised.

Of course we all know that we appraise performance, but we so often don't know exactly what that means in practice.

So we pick up on what we have noticed. This tends to be either outstanding performance or poor performance in a particular area or activity which happened recently.

This simply leaves our employee confused about what's important: 'Was my obvious lack of interest at the last staff meeting more important than consistently meeting my sales targets?'

Alternatively, if there is nothing we have noticed, we tend to make vague and general statements which closely resemble old-style school reports: 'Your work is generally fairly good, and you continue to make progress.'

Our employee is left with no clear picture of what we mean – probably because we don't know what we mean!

Even worse, we may then go on to ask them what they think. How can they comment when they don't know what we are looking at in their performance?

We need to make explicit, for ourselves and for those we appraise, what areas of performance are being considered.

Formulating relevant appraisals

The first step in establishing what to appraise with an individual is to check what the organization as a whole is aiming towards.

Your organization's mission statement, or the company's aims and objectives will tell you this.

We need to frame what we are appraising in the larger context of what the organization has as its goals, so that it is seen as relevant, both for the organization and for the employee.

For example, suppose your company has, as part of its mission statement, 'putting customers first'. It will be important to look at how your staff deal with customers as part of their appraisal.

You may also have specific departmental goals, which are derived from the overall goals of the organization. For example, suppose your department has as one of its goals 'reduction of customer complaints'. It will be important to look at how your staff contribute to reducing customer complaints.

Answering the following questions will give us the first part of a framework for appraisal.

1 What is your organization's mission statement?
2 What areas of skill, behaviour or attitude does it imply for employees?
3 What are your department's goals?
4 What areas of skill, behaviour or attitude do they imply for employees?

These areas of performance will be relevant to your organization, because the appraisal will show how the individual is contributing to the organizational goals.

They will also make sense to the individual, by relating their individual achievements to what the organization as a whole wishes to achieve.

Formulating a meaningful appraisal

The next step in establishing what to appraise with an individual is to ensure that what is appraised relates to their job specification.

If my duties and responsibilities include the management of an administrative records system, but my manager never refers to that in my appraisal, I may begin to wonder if the appraisal has anything to do with my real job – or whether that was an important responsibility after all!

Look at your employee's original job description and specification. (If this does not exist, ask them to help you to compile a list of main duties, responsibilities and requirements.) Then answer the questions below:

5 What are the main areas of performance to be appraised, based on the job description and specification?
6 What skills, behaviours or attitudes are required to fulfil this job specification?

We now have the basis for a relevant and meaningful framework for appraisal. Your answers to questions 2, 4, 5 and 6 above will identify for you the main criteria of a competent performance in this role.

You can use information from an appraisal based on these criteria to demonstrate how that person contributes to organizational and departmental goals.

The criteria are relevant and meaningful to the person being appraised because they can be shown to be related directly to the organization's goals and to their own job specification.

A comprehensive appraisal framework

So far, we have looked at how to link the appraisal criteria to both the organizational goals and the individual's role. This ensures that the appraisal will have some relevance and meaning by making its links to the work context explicit. However, it is still easy to miss information or omit acknowledgement of an individual's progress or achievement.

More and more organizations are now acknowledging the importance of the individual's continuing personal and professional development. We live in a world where change has become the norm. We need individuals who show initiative, who are willing to learn, who are flexible.

It is therefore important that we have, within the appraisal framework, some means of identifying personal and professional achievements which are not strictly related to the narrow work context. They may, however, be evidence of an individual's developmental capacity.

For example, do you know if any of your staff:

- work as a volunteer in their community?
- run a scout group?
- are on the PTA for a local school?
- are taking an Open College course or evening class?
- are expert at climbing or orienteering?
- have recently learnt to sail, or speak a foreign language, or do karate?

These and many other out-of-work activities demonstrate that the person has talents and abilities which could well be transferred to the work context in some way.

They also demonstrate willingness to learn and to be involved – vital requisites in a changing organization.

Most organizations have some form of training and development programme for their staff. However, as managers, we do not always pick up on what courses or seminars our staff have attended, and what they may have gained as a result.

389

This is particularly true of training in so-called 'soft skills', those areas which are not directly related to specific knowledge or technical skill development.

The appraisal framework needs to pick up on any professional development that the appraisee has undertaken.

Finally, there is an area of performance appraisal which is often missed because it is hard to define. This is 'what we are like as a person to work with'. Remember the stereotype of the doctor's receptionist as a 'dragon'? And the 'ordinary' person in the office who always makes everyone feel comfortable and is liked by everyone?

There are people in organizations who fulfil their job specifications exactly, yet are uncooperative or even hostile with others. And there are those who do nothing extraordinary in their actual work role, yet help to create and maintain an excellent team atmosphere.

It is important that we notice and value how people are with others, and how that contributes to the effectiveness of the organization.

Using feedback from peers, subordinates and customers can significantly add to our awareness of how someone works with others. Encouraging the appraisee to ask others for their opinion of their behaviour and attitudes in relation to questions 2, 4 and 6 will add to the information about personal qualities. The answers to the following questions will also be helpful:

7 What activities or courses are your staff involved in, outside work?
8 What training or development have your staff undertaken, and how did it affect them?
9 What are the personal qualities required of your staff?

Looking for development

In business these days, continuous improvement is a vital theme, both organizationally and individually. An appraisal system is intended to encourage the development of the individual.

We must ensure that the appraisal framework identifies and recognizes the employee's development. After all, if I have been doing this job for years I may be competent at it, yet make no effort to take it any further.

To some extent, the questions already identified will pull this out. To ensure that we have really identified development, we need some 'markers'.

At each appraisal we need to know how the person was performing at their last appraisal (or, if it's an initial appraisal, what their starting point is).

Then we need to assess with them how they have improved on that performance.

Finally, we need to agree with them how they will continue to improve their performance.

What often happens is that we only pick up on a need to improve where performance is poor. For example, if someone is lax with their record keeping, we ask them to 'get better at it'. If their work is already competent, we tend to just make lame statements like, 'Well done, keep up the good work.' This tends to bring two unwanted results:

- The individual's work standard actually deteriorates as they 'sit back on their laurels'.
- They are less motivated because there is nothing in particular to aim for.

The alternative is to ask them to identify how they could improve their performance even more, and encourage them to continue to develop their skills to do so. You need to answer the following questions:

10 How are your staff demonstrating continuous development?
11 What areas could you look at with them for further development?
12 What support and help is available to make these developments?

Using the framework for appraisal

We can use this framework in two different ways, depending on what already exists as an appraisal system.

If you haven't already developed a formal written procedure for appraising, you can use the questions asked throughout this chapter to construct an appraisal format and recording framework.

The example below shows how these questions could be used as the basis for guiding both the appraiser and the appraisee in what to look for in an appraisal, and what to 'collect' as evidence.

Example

1 This company's mission statement implies that employees should demonstrate flexibility, a high standard of customer service and a willingness to develop their skills.
   How have you (has this employee) demonstrated this?
2 This department's goals are to reduce customer complaints and to increase the speed of delivery of service.
   How have you (has this employee) contributed to these goals?
3 Your main duties are: reception of visitors, answering telephone queries, processing of repairs procedures, maintaining the records of customer usage.
   What are your (are your employee's) examples of best practice in this, and what exactly did you do?

What do you feel you (they) could improve on in your job performance, and how could you achieve that?

4 What are you (is your employee) involved in outside work which you feel demonstrates skills/abilities/potential which are important to you and/or your organization?

5 What training and/or development activities have you (has your employee) undertaken?

How have they been useful to you, personally or professionally?

6 What personal qualities do you have (has your employee got) which you feel contribute to your (employee's) value in this organization?

Give an example (examples) of how they have been used.

7 How are you (is your employee) developing your own work performance?

8 How else would you like to develop your work performance?

Notice how this set of questions makes clear what the areas for appraisal are. It ensures that all parties to the appraisal are working to the same criteria, and that those criteria are relevant to the organization and the individuals.

You can also use this framework to help those involved in appraisal to make the process meaningful.

You may already have a recording system for appraisal which asks general questions, or has general headings.

Example

- Achievements over the last year
- Targets met
- Areas for improvement
- Agreed new targets

It may then be useful to use the questions above to help both parties prepare for the appraisal by using them as guidelines for what to discuss, in order to identify what to record in the different sections.

Summary

In this chapter, we have looked at the different elements of an effective appraisal framework. This will enable both you and the employee to appraise the achievement, progress and potential of that person to play their part fully in the organization. By linking the framework to organizational objectives, departmental objectives, the individual's role and the qualities of that individual, you create something that is really meaningful.

There is work required to create a really careful and meaningful appraisal framework. It takes a while to clarify the links between an individual's job and the organizational and departmental objectives, and to clarify what really matters about how they do their work. However, this is a one-off task, and thereafter only requires occasional adjustment as the organization and the role develop.

The rewards for doing this preparatory work are that both you and the employee have clear criteria and expectations about their role, and can have genuinely useful conversations about what they do well and how they can develop further. By investing time in producing an appraisal framework, you will be making the rest of your preparation much easier, and will be able to conduct worthwhile appraisal interviews.

The following multiple-choice questions are a reminder of what we've covered today.

SUNDAY
MONDAY
TUESDAY
WEDNESDAY
THURSDAY
FRIDAY
SATURDAY

Fact-check (answers at the back)

1. What do we appraise in someone's performance?
a) How they are progressing against objectives ❏
b) What we remember of their performance ❏
c) What they have failed to do ❏
d) Anything we can think of ❏

2. How do we link appraisals to the overall organizational development?
a) We don't. ❏
b) We link objectives to organizational goals. ❏
c) We just use the functions people do. ❏
d) We give a bonus if the organization is doing well. ❏

3. How does the appraisal reflect the person's job?
a) Of course it is about their job. ❏
b) By talking about how they do their job ❏
c) By relating objectives to what their job requires of them ❏
d) We hope they tell us what they have been doing. ❏

4. Why should we include personal qualities in the appraisal framework?
a) We don't need to – it's not on the form. ❏
b) They are important in how the person goes about their tasks. ❏
c) It might make someone feel better if we tell them they are a nice person. ❏
d) To have something to talk about ❏

5. Why is it useful to find out about a person's activities outside work?
a) It's a nice thing to do. ❏
b) It fills up the time. ❏
c) They matter to them. ❏
d) They may indicate possible areas for developing the person in work. ❏

6. How do you ensure continuous development through the appraisal?
a) By looking for areas where they would benefit from developing further ❏
b) By identifying if there is anything they are no good at ❏
c) By asking them if they want to do any courses ❏
d) You only do this with really bright sparks. ❏

7. What do you record in an appraisal?
a) Whatever the form requires ❏
b) Achievements and areas for development, with action plans ❏
c) As little as possible ❏
d) Everything that is said ❏

8. How do you produce an appraisal framework?
a) We make a recording form. ❏
b) We don't have to do anything – that's HR's job. ❏
c) We collate information on the process and what will be appraised. ❏
d) We don't need a framework – it is in our head. ❏

9. How do you use the framework for appraisal?
a) To guide us and the person being appraised in our preparation ❏
b) To satisfy HR requirements ❏
c) To prove we've done it ❏
d) To record the appraisal ❏

10. Who is the framework for appraisal for?
a) It is for the HR department. ❏
b) It is for us and those who are being appraised. ❏
c) It is just for show. ❏
d) Our bosses like us to have them. ❏

TUESDAY

The appraiser's role, I: setting the framework

In this chapter, we will begin to look at exactly what your role should be as an appraiser if you want to appraise effectively. We will look at the different elements of general preparation, which will help to make the appraisal itself work well.

Most employees are unclear about what is expected of them in appraisals, so if you brief the employee to be appraised properly, you make it easier for them to play their part. This briefing consists firstly of explaining clearly what the purpose of the appraisal is, for both them and you, and what the principles of the appraisal process are, so that they know why and how they are being appraised. You also need to clarify and agree the actual procedure for the appraisal, and brief them on the preparation they need to do, so that they come to the appraisal ready to play their part.

Finally, you need to do your own preparation specific to the appraisee, collecting evidence of their progress over the year, and looking at what they might usefully develop further, from your point of view. Let's look at what will help you to do this.

Clarifying the basis for appraisal

It is not enough to sort out for yourself what the purpose of appraisal is, and what criteria you will use.

We have all been in the situation where the other person thought it was obvious why something was important, but we didn't grasp it at all. In that situation, we just feel frustrated and confused.

So don't take it for granted that the person being appraised will see appraisals as valuable, or that they will understand the framework of criteria you are using. The basic rule is: *explain and make explicit*.

This will make your life easier because it will ensure that you are both 'singing from the same hymn sheet'. It will also enable the person being appraised to come prepared with relevant information, examples and ideas. So how do you start?

First of all, you need to spell out the purpose of the appraisal, as in the example below.

Example

'Appraisals are intended to monitor your (the employee's) performance at work in a constructive way. They provide an opportunity to:

● review what you have been doing and how you have been doing it
● discuss any issues you have which you think may be slowing down your progress, and find ways of dealing with them.

They give you (the employee) the opportunity to:

- give evidence of your achievements and progress, and receive recognition and support for these
- be reminded of how you are contributing to the effectiveness of the whole organization
- voice your views and offer constructive suggestions on both your own development and that of the organization.

Finally, in the appraisal, we can agree together what goals for development you are going to set yourself for the next appraisal and how they can be achieved.'

You could adapt this to your own style, and perhaps even produce it as a written document to give to the individual as reinforcement after you have read it out and checked it through with them.

Next, you need to emphasize the principles of the appraisal and the way in which it will be handled. Remember that most people have a negative experience of performance reviews. From schooldays onwards, when someone 'in authority' comments on our work, it is generally to judge and criticize.

So you need to state clearly and explicitly that an appraisal:

- is a two-way process
- is intended to be useful and constructive
- will recognize positively what the person has achieved
- will help to identify how that person can develop further.

You should also point out clearly that their involvement and contributions are vital to the success of the appraisal.

Third, you need to make explicit what is being appraised and why. The guidelines in the previous chapter will help you and them to understand this.

Finally, they need to be clear that feedback from others is for them to use as part of their evidence on their performance, and that this information will help both of you to identify achievements as well as areas for development. Its purpose is to enhance the information available, not to criticize.

It will take a little time to make sure that these foundations for a successful appraisal are understood and agreed with the person being appraised. This time is well spent, as it is fulfilling a part of your role as appraiser. You are giving the individual the information they need to take an active and constructive part in the appraisal process. By empowering them in this way, you are laying the groundwork to make the appraisal itself more focused, purposeful and productive.

Agreeing procedures and responsibilities for appraisal

Having clarified the general principles we will be working to in appraisal, we now need to make clear the procedures for appraisal.

1 Setting a time for the appraisal interview

To reinforce the statement that appraisals are important and useful, we need to demonstrate that we take them seriously by the way we set them up.

a The interviews are given a definite time slot in the diary

Most appraisal interviews are held at six-monthly or yearly intervals. They therefore have a lot of ground to cover, and require about 2 hours to be useful. This time needs to be clearly allocated.

b The time fixed for the appraisal interview is given priority in the diaries of both parties

It is no good saying that your employee must keep this date and time clear if you then cancel because you have an urgent report to write!

As managers, we must set the example of treating appraisals as an important part of our business by keeping to the set time unless we are really forced to change it. Appraisal interviews cannot just be 'fitted in' if they are to be taken seriously.

It may be worth setting aside a set period in the week or month just for appraisal interviews, so that they become a fixture in your calendar.

c We need to fix the time well enough in advance to give our employees time to prepare properly for the interview

We want our employees to come to the interview well prepared. That means that they need time to review their own performance, and think about their evidence and examples.

If we only give them a day's notice, we are implying that their own review is not that important – assuming they are busy in their job role.

Sometimes, the dates for appraisals are set months in advance. In this case, it is useful to remind your employee a couple of weeks before the date, so that they remember to do their preparation – and likewise yourself.

2 Agreeing what preparation the appraisee needs to do

There are several approaches we can take to support the person being appraised in their preparation. It is not enough to give them time and prior warning. They also need some guidelines as to what you mean by preparation.

It can be useful to ask them to make notes, and to offer them a recording sheet which prompts useful evidence and ideas. If you use a recording sheet, it is important that you make clear to them that it is for their benefit and use, not for your records.

Otherwise, a preparation checklist can be useful, leaving them to make notes in their own way.

Before you ask them to record anything, it is important to restate what exactly you want from them. You may choose to use your own version of the following:

Purpose of record

1 To gather evidence to present at appraisal:
  a of own achievements on targets agreed last time
  b of own progress on targets agreed last time
  c of own achievement and progress on other steps towards the goal(s)
2 To remind yourself of any problems you encountered, why you think the problems occurred, and any solutions to the problems which you thought of and/or applied
3 To remind yourself of areas:
  a in which you would benefit from more training
  b in which you would benefit from further practice
  c you would like to pursue further
  d on which you would like to concentrate
4 To remind yourself of anything which felt really good – where you felt pleased with your own learning, or where you felt that the methods used to help you learn were particularly effective
5 To note anything else you might want to say at appraisal
    This is your personal record of your progress towards your goals. It is an *aide-memoire* to help you to contribute as effectively as possible towards your own appraisal.

Without the above reminder, you may well forget what you wanted to say, particularly if your appraiser is more confident than you in the process.

But *you* know more than anyone else about your own progress – so don't miss the chance to use that information.

If you would like to give them a recording sheet to use, something like the following can be useful:

Record for appraisee

Tasks done (to remind you of what you've been working on)

Training/teaching received (to remind you of what you've been offered help in, by whom, and how useful it was)

Steps towards goals achieved since last appraised

Steps towards goals made progress in (refer to your copy of the last appraisal record to identify relevant areas)

Areas where problems arose (suggest solutions as well if possible)

Areas you would like to work on next (may be for any of the reasons listed in purpose of recording)

Other comments (anything you would like to say about your progress generally)

Extra suggestions for preparation which you can make are:

● That they bring with them supporting evidence, e.g. the first set of minutes they've ever written, a letter from a customer they found difficult to deal with, the end-of-module comments from their college tutor.

This will give you the opportunity to give specific acknowledgement on things in which they have done well.

It will also mean that you can discuss specifically with them areas they are finding difficult.

● That they ask for feedback on their performance from others – colleagues, other managers, customers, trainers.

Often we don't know what others think of our performance, and their viewpoint can be very useful information.

Do stress that this is for *their* information, and it is up to them to use it constructively.

This may seem like an awful lot to get across to someone, 'just for an appraisal'.

It is worth noticing that:

- It is only on the first occasion that it takes a long time – after that, you just need to remind them.
- Most people will respond very positively to such clear guidelines, and will take on responsibility for preparing thereafter because they see how useful it is to them.
- You are empowering the person being appraised to take responsibility for making the appraisal useful and focused.
- The act of preparing is in itself a development exercise. It is teaching the individual to review their own performance, to learn from that, and to identify how they could improve.
- The preparation will help the individual to be realistic about the appraisal. They will come to the interview confident of their own ability and progress and/or aware of their need to improve and in what areas.

Explaining and actioning your preparation

If, as managers, we go through the preparatory work with the person being appraised, we have made our own preparation for the actual appraisal interview much easier. However, some preparation still remains to be done.

a Read through the previous appraisal record

This will remind us of the targets we agreed with the individual and the areas in which they had progressed at their last review.

b Gather information from other sources

There may be obvious points we need to follow up on: Did they complete that training programme? How did that project go?

It is useful and constructive to find out factual information before the interview.

If you have not asked the appraisee to get feedback from others, you may wish to consult with their peers, subordinates and customers.

Be careful how you ask about their performance, to elicit clear and specific information.

Examples of useful questions:

- Jack wanted to develop his skills in ... In what ways do you think he is progressing? Are there any ways in which you think his development could be increased?
- Can you give me any examples where Jill has shown good progress while doing ... ? Can you give me any areas where you think she could progress more quickly by approaching it a different way?
- If I ask you to summarize Jack's progress over the last month in relation to his goals, what would you say?

TIP

It is important to remind people of what the criteria for development are: Jack may be pleasant to work with, but may not have improved his carpentry skills at all.

c Consider your own view of their performance and collect your own evidence

You can use the same checklist as they use, and can also make brief notes throughout the year of things you notice, so that the information is already there. This helps us to consider the whole period, rather than just focusing on something that happened last week.

d Clarify for yourself what results you want from this appraisal

This will remind you to:

- apply the principles of appraisal
- refer to the business goals and refresh your awareness of them
- refer to their job specification
- focus your attention on learning and development rather than faults.

It is important that you tell the person being appraised that you are doing this preparation.

They will then know that you are taking the appraisal seriously. They will also know that you will have a great deal of information on them to hand, which will encourage them to make more effort to gather relevant information also.

Finally, it is important to timetable sufficient space for you to do this preparation. You can use the same device you used for the person being appraised to prompt yourself into allocating specific time for information gathering.

Explaining how the interview will proceed

We all tend to get rather nervous about 'interviews', however well we know and get on with the interviewer. It is made easier if we know beforehand the structure of the interview and the approach to be used. We will discuss this in detail in later chapters.

You need to clarify your approach and the structure you will use, and then ensure that you explain this to the person being appraised beforehand.

To a large extent, this is implicit in all the explanations you have given them so far. It is, however, still worth making explicit, so that you are sure that they really do understand how the interview will be run.

Summary

We have explored how you can use your own thinking-through of the purpose and principles of appraisal to explain them to those you will appraise, so that they are also clear about why and how appraisals will be conducted. We have also explored ways of helping them to fulfil their part in the appraisal effectively, so that it really is a two-way process, by giving them useful guidelines and by clarifying with them the preparation they need to do.

Finally, we have also looked at what you need to do specifically for each person you appraise, so that you are well informed and well prepared for the interview.

Although all this may seem time-consuming, it is important to recognize that:

● It makes a considerable difference to the effectiveness of the appraisal itself, enabling both you and the person being appraised to be ready to use the opportunity well.
● Much of it is a one-off activity. Once you have prepared the briefing on the purpose and principles of appraisal, and the procedures and responsibilities, these can be used with all your employees and will only need the briefest of reviews, to check they are still valid, in following years.

The following multiple-choice questions are a reminder of what we've covered today.

Fact-check (answers at the back)

1. Why do we need to explain to the person being appraised what appraisals are all about?
   a) Because we cannot take it for granted that they understand their importance and relevance. ❏
   b) We only need to if they haven't been appraised before. ❏
   c) Because the forms are complicated. ❏
   d) Because it's part of the process. ❏

2. How do you start to explain about appraisals?
   a) By showing them the forms ❏
   b) By giving them the guidance document ❏
   c) By talking about the purpose of appraisals ❏
   d) By telling them they have to do them ❏

3. Why do we emphasize the principles of appraisal?
   a) Because it's part of the process ❏
   b) Because they make explicit the constructive nature of appraisals ❏
   c) Because then they will know what to do ❏
   d) Because principles matter ❏

4. What procedures do we need to explain to the person being appraised?
   a) The timing of appraisals and their priority in the diary ❏
   b) What HR needs from the appraisal ❏
   c) That we fit in appraisals when we're not too busy ❏
   d) That we'll complete the forms ❏

5. How do we help the person being appraised to prepare?
   a) We give them a recording form. ❏
   b) We tell them to collect evidence for themselves. ❏
   c) We just tell them to be prepared. ❏
   d) We give them information about what to collect as their evidence. ❏

6. Why is it important to take the time to go through all the information with people?
   a) It only matters if they haven't done one before. ❏
   b) It empowers them to make the best use of their appraisal. ❏
   c) They might not get it right otherwise. ❏
   d) It means they can't complain that they haven't been informed. ❏

7. What other preparation do you need to do for yourself?

a) Recall the mistakes they've made. ❏

b) Think of something nice to say. ❏

c) Collect your own information on their performance. ❏

d) Get out last year's appraisal record. ❏

8. What do you do to ensure that you approach your preparation in the right way?

a) I remind myself of the purpose and principles of appraisal. ❏

b) I read last year's appraisal record. ❏

c) I cushion the negative with a positive. ❏

d) I give it a bit of time. ❏

9. When do you do your preparation?

a) Just before the appraisal ❏

b) When I can fit it in ❏

c) In advance, with time allocated in my diary ❏

d) When I see the appraisal interview slot in my diary ❏

10. Why do we spend time on all this preparation?

a) HR thinks it's important. ❏

b) It makes the appraisal itself much more valuable and useful. ❏

c) Because we're supposed to. ❏

d) I wish I knew! ❏

WEDNESDAY

The appraiser's role, II: attitudes and approaches

We have looked at the practical preparation that you need to do as an appraiser, but that is not the only preparation needed for the appraisal to be effective. Just as important is the way you prepare yourself and think through your attitude and approach to the appraisal interview. How we are with the person being appraised affects how they play their part in the appraisal.

In this chapter, we will consider how you can prepare yourself to approach the interview constructively and sympathetically, making sure that you set yourself up usefully and set the right tone in the interview. We will also look at how you can establish trust between yourself and your employee in the interview, so that they feel more comfortable.

Finally, we will consider the important behaviours you need to adopt, so that the appraisal interview really works, including gathering as much information as possible from the employee, listening with proper attention to what they have to say, encouraging them to take more responsibility for their own development, and coming to genuine agreement about the conclusions drawn in the interview. This way you will have a genuinely useful two-way conversation.

Being ready

We often find that we come into another meeting carrying with us the pressures of previous and following activities. Although we intend to give the meeting our full attention, the fact is that our minds are elsewhere.

It only takes a few minutes to set your 'baggage' aside, relax, and focus on the meeting you are about to go into. This will help you to pay full attention in the way in which the person being appraised deserves.

We also need to realize that, as appraiser, you can feel as tense and nervous about the interview as the person being appraised. You want it to go well, and be useful, but you may be new to the role, or you may be unsure about your credibility as an appraiser.

If this is the case, remember the following:

- This is not a test for either side, it's a joint venture, with both of you wanting it to be useful.
- The person being appraised will be more nervous than you; concentrate on making them feel alright and you will automatically ease down yourself.
- Take a few deep breaths before you start, and consciously relax muscular tension; if you can physically relax, you will be more able to perform well.

- If you admit to being a bit nervous about it to the person being appraised, they will think more of you, not less; it makes them feel less 'unique' in being nervous, it establishes something in common, and it means that they will understand if you want to rephrase a question or correct some statement that you feel isn't quite 'in the right spirit'.

Do glance at your preparation notes just to remind yourself of your focus.

> ## Checklist: being ready
> - Take a few minutes to separate yourself from previous activities and ones which you have to do afterwards.
> - Take a couple of deep breaths and relax.
> - Glance at your preparation notes.

Establishing trust

We need to ensure that the person being appraised feels safe and relaxed, in order to get the best out of the appraisal interview.

The preparation we have done with them will have established some of the trusting relationship we need in order to make the appraisal interview useful. However, we still need to make sure they feel that we are 'on their side'. The actual interview often brings out more anxiety and more formality on both sides.

We establish trust in a variety of ways:

- Make the environment comfortable and relaxed; also ensure that the interview takes place somewhere where you cannot be overheard and will not be interrupted.
- Greet them by name, in a friendly manner (the first impression always has an impact).
- Make a little 'small talk' before you start straight into the interview; it reminds you that you are both ordinary human beings, not just appraiser and appraisee.

- Remind the appraisee of the purpose of the appraisal interview, and the structure; this sets the tone and reminds you both that you are working together to achieve a useful end result.
- State explicitly that anything said or discussed within the interview is just between the two of you; if anything is raised which requires discussion with a third party, then you need to agree with them how that will be done.
- Check that your body language matches what you are saying; we all know instinctively when someone is only saying what we want to hear.

Remember that these ways of establishing trust are only the starting point. You need to follow them through in practice, so that the person being appraised knows that they are genuine.

This means:

- Don't allow interruptions.
- Greet that person in a friendly manner at times other than the appraisal interview.
- Take a few minutes to chat to them in the workplace as well.
- Make sure the whole interview fulfils its purpose.
- Maintain confidentiality.
- Remember to keep yourself open and positive.

We none of us trust someone who turns their demonstration of trustworthiness off and on with us. We are suspicious of them if they suddenly become positive and supportive in a particular situation, and don't believe that it is genuine.

TIP *Establishing trust is a continuous process, not just a set of behaviours to be 'switched on' for appraisal.*

Finding out

An important part of what you need to do as appraiser is to gather useful information from the appraisee. Once you have established some trust, they are more likely to give you genuine information, rather than saying what they think you want to hear.

For an appraisal to be useful, you need to be very clear about the appraisee's view of things, what makes *them* feel they've achieved or progressed, where *they* think they need help or improvement. All too often we impose our own view. Although the other person may go along with us, it rarely results in the effect we want because it's not quite the same as their view, so they are less committed to it.

> *'To be complimented for excellent completion of my administrative tasks may be nice, but why wasn't my representation at the regional meeting noticed?'*

> *'To have suggested that a counselling skills course may be useful is accurate, but right now I'd prefer to improve my computing skills.'*

417

We have asked the appraisee to prepare by bringing examples of their own. It is vital that we give value to that preparation, and use it as the starting point for the appraisal.

We need first to find out what they have prepared. Simple questions are required here:

'What do you think are your achievements?'

Then we need to ensure that we have really understood what their example means to them. Our normal task would be to ask why that is an achievement. This is less useful than the following questions:

'In what way do you see that as an achievement?'

'What specifically makes you feel that is an achievement?'

We then have both the example and the opinion of the individual. We can now give appropriate recognition.

Notice that at first an individual may only give one or two examples, and we may need to prompt them for more. Questions such as:

'What else do you think of as an achievement?'

'How else have you progressed?'

will tempt them into giving more examples.

In the same vein, we can find out what they think their obstacles to progress are.

'What do you think is stopping you progressing?'

'And what else?'

Finally, we want to find out what they think would enable them to progress and develop. We may have our own ideas, but theirs need to be explored first. We all prefer to implement our own solutions. So we need to ask questions like:

'How would you change this?'

'What do you think would help you to overcome this?'

'What would help you to develop this?'

Notice the common themes of these questions. They all start with 'what' or 'how' and they all ask the person to express their own view – 'what do you think ...'.

There may be information which you have which suggests something different from what they say.

- You may have something else which you consider to be improvement or progress; you can now add that to their own list, so it is a bonus not a replacement.
- You may have other areas of concern; you need to explain how they are a concern, how they relate to business or personal targets, and again ask the interviewee for their opinion and their ideas of how to deal with it.
- You may have different proposals for development or next targets; you can now suggest yours, as additional possibilities – however, what is finally agreed will be from the choice of their ideas and yours, not exclusively yours.

It is often the case that the appraisee covers all the ground you have thought of, and sometimes more. If they are allowed to tell you, rather than you tell them, they are far more likely to act on it.

You are the reinforcer, recognizer, supporter and helper, rather than the dictator.

Listening

In order to find out someone's viewpoint effectively, we need to listen with full attention. This means that we listen, not just to what they say but also to how they say it.

- Do they sound confident or doubting?
- Are they hesitating or in full throttle?
- Does their body language match what they are saying?

Listening with full attention means listening with our ears, our eyes, our hearts and our intuition. And when you notice something which doesn't quite fit, ask about it. Possible questions might be:

'You seem unsure/pleased/worried/certain about that. What makes you that way?'

'How does that affect you?'

We can often save ourselves a lot of time and energy by listening with full attention. It helps us to spot quickly what is important in the communication.

Moreover, being a good listener is a quality which others really appreciate, and it helps to enhance the relationship.

Empowering

We want the person being appraised to take on more and more responsibility for their own development. For this to happen, they need to feel empowered to do so.

Empowerment has three main components:

1 reinforcing and encouraging the taking on of responsibility
2 giving clear and useful information
3 valuing the person's own thoughts, opinions and suggestions.

Much of what we have described so far has this effect:

- giving them a clear purpose and framework for the appraisal
- asking them to prepare clear guidelines
- taking their preparation and examples first, before offering your own.

All the time, we need to bear in mind that we want them to decide for themselves, rather than imposing decisions on them. So you need to give them a lot of encouragement in the first place.

Statements that start with the following are useful:

'I think it's excellent that you ...'
'I like the way you ...'
'I'm pleased that you ...'
'I'm impressed that you ...'

We often think these things, even say them to other people, but don't remember to say them to the person concerned!

However, don't make such remarks unless they are genuine, otherwise the person may feel that you are trying to con them.

If you do feel that you have to impose a decision, make it clear why. By giving explicit information, you reduce the disempowering effect. Also notice that often, if you give them the information you have, they will make the decision for you anyway.

Example

'I have just had my budget for external training cut, so I will not be able to fund all the programmes my staff might want, and will have to find alternative methods for development. How else could we tackle this area of development which you are asking for?'

Finally, you may find that you don't fully agree with the individual's view of progress, priorities, etc.

Distinguish between your own preferences and those in the best interests of the business.

We often encourage people to agree with our personal view, as if it is factually better. We may think it is, but we need to remember that people do things they have chosen for themselves more wholeheartedly.

Wherever possible, let the person choose their own priorities. They may then be more open to your suggestions next time.

Negotiating and agreeing

There are often areas of the appraisal where there is some difference of opinion. Your role is to find a way of coming to an agreement, rather than standing your ground.

When we encounter this situation with friends, we usually handle it well: we may give some ground, and in return they give some, until we find something which suits us both and takes us both towards the result we want.

Use the same approach in an appraisal interview.

It is guaranteed that you both want the individual to perform to their optimum potential. The difference may be in how you think that will be achieved.

Anything which is a step towards that is useful, so, be flexible in your negotiating and accept the possibility of alternatives. Unless the person can genuinely agree to the targets, you will not get the results you want.

Summary

In this chapter, we have looked at the approach you need to take in order for an appraisal interview to be useful, and the importance of this personal preparation. We have emphasized the fact that you set the tone for the interview, and that your attitude and approach will make all the difference to how it goes. None of this is rocket science, just good sense if we want any interaction to go well.

We often forget that how we behave has a significant effect on the way the other person responds to us, because we are busy getting on with the task in hand.

This form of preparation is not time-consuming – it only takes a few minutes to sort yourself out before you enter the interaction. Above all, remember that this is another human being in front of you, with their own particular mix of strengths and weaknesses, and that, more than anything, they want to feel valued for what they do well, and supported in developing themselves.

And, if you are unsure of what to say or how to react, just think how you would prefer to be treated if you were sitting in their chair – that is usually a useful guide.

The following multiple-choice questions are a reminder of what we've covered today.

Fact-check (answers at the back)

1. How do you make sure you are ready to pay attention before the appraisal interview?
   a) I tell myself I need to pay attention. ❏
   b) I try and time it for first thing in the morning or last thing in the day. ❏
   c) I take a few minutes to relax and set my baggage aside. ❏
   d) I always pay attention. ❏

2. What do you do if you feel a bit nervous before the appraisal interview?
   a) I won't feel nervous. ❏
   b) I remember this is not a test for either side and take a deep breath. ❏
   c) I hide it from the person being appraised. ❏
   d) I dismiss it as irrelevant. ❏

3. Why do we need to establish trust in the interview?
   a) The trust will already be there. ❏
   b) To draw out the truth from them ❏
   c) Because they're bound to be nervous ❏
   d) To ensure the person being appraised feels safe and relaxed ❏

4. How can we establish trust at the beginning of the interview?
   a) Tell them they can trust us. ❏
   b) Say something nice to them. ❏
   c) Give them something to drink. ❏
   d) Greet them by name in a friendly manner and state confidentiality. ❏

5. What makes establishing trust in the interview easier?
   a) Being equally friendly and open during the year ❏
   b) If I know them well ❏
   c) If they've worked for me for a long time ❏
   d) Not sitting behind my desk ❏

6. How do we find out what they think they have achieved?
   a) By asking them if they agree with our opinion ❏
   b) By asking them open questions which prompt them to give their evidence ❏
   c) We both already know what they've achieved. ❏
   d) By asking them what they've done ❏

7. How do we give our opinion of their progress and performance?
a) We tell them what we think. ❏
b) We read out our assessment of them. ❏
c) By reinforcing their points and adding our own ❏
d) By our attitude to their evidence ❏

8. What do we need to listen to during the appraisal interview?
a) Not just what they say, but how they say it ❏
b) What they think they've done ❏
c) Their comments on our assessment of them ❏
d) Their opinion ❏

9. How do we empower them during the appraisal interview?
a) By telling them they are empowered ❏
b) Appraisal interviews aren't where empowerment happens. ❏
c) We let them have their say. ❏
d) By encouraging them to decide for themselves what will work best for them ❏

10. How do we set targets for them in the appraisal interview?
a) We tell them their targets. ❏
b) By negotiating with them and finding genuine agreement ❏
c) By referring to their job description ❏
d) By picking up on what they've failed in ❏

THURSDAY

The interview, I: reviewing achievement

Having prepared both the appraisee and yourself, it is now time to conduct the actual appraisal interview. In this chapter, we will begin to explore how you structure the appraisal interview, so that you have useful results.

Firstly, we will look at how you agree an overall agenda for the interview, so you are both clear about what you are doing. We also suggest that you agree the outcomes of the interview, so you are both clear about what you are trying to achieve.

Then we will explore how you can conduct the review part of the appraisal. In this, we look at how to use previous targets as the focus for review, and how to review when there are no previous targets, in an initial appraisal. We will look at how you ensure that your employee feels that they have been recognized and valued for progress and achievement, as this is the main purpose of the review stage. Then we look at how you handle a lack of progress and/or achievement in a constructive way.

Agreeing overall agenda and outcomes

In a formal business meeting, we usually have an agenda. We often forget to set an agenda for other meetings.

It helps to have something which gives a framework to the appraisal interview, and also links in to the amount of time available for it. This will enable you both to keep on track and stay focused.

Appraisal Agenda

9.30	Review of previous appraisal and agreed action therein
9.45	Discussion of general progress and achievements
10.00	Identification and discussion of organizational issues
10.15	Identification of areas for further development or support
10.35	Coffee break
10.50	Agreement of an action plan
11.15	Recording of agreed outcomes and new targets
	Confirmation of date for next appraisal

Equipped with a plan of this kind, having greeted the person being appraised, we can start by agreeing the agenda with them.

It is also well worth explicitly agreeing with them the outcomes you both want from the interview. These might be such things as:

● that both feel it has been a constructive meeting
● that recognition has been given to achievement and progress
● that realistic targets have been agreed, with appropriate action to be undertaken on both sides.

Agreeing achievement and progress

The first stage of any appraisal is the recognition of achievement and progress.

Referring to targets

We have two ways of focusing on this area, depending on whether this is a first or repeated appraisal. In the latter case, we start by referring to targets set in the previous appraisal.

We might ask:

'What progress do you feel you have made against the targets agreed last time?'

'What examples/evidence can you mention to support this?'

We can then broaden the base beyond these targets to ask:

'In what other areas do you think you have progressed?'

'What else do you feel you have achieved?'

It is then appropriate to give due recognition for their examples, and add any further examples you have collected.

It can be helpful to ask a further question, to get some sense of their priorities:

'Which of these are you most proud of/pleased with?'

As they give you this information, remember to:

- ensure that you have understood fully their example/evidence
- give value/recognition to their examples/evidence
- add to their list where you can, or certainly endorse it from your own information gathering
- encourage them to link achievements and progress to both business and personal objectives.

In this part of the process, you will need to begin to record the examples. However, beware: we often get so caught up in writing notes, that we don't give the appraisee our full attention.

It may be useful to have some scrap paper, and say to the person being appraised that you are just going to jot down a key word or phrase to remind you both of the achievement and progress covered.

Then, when you have covered all the areas of achievement and progress, use your notes to review them, and agree what should be written on the appraisal record. Completing it there and then, and showing it to the interviewee, also helps to build trust. A by-product is that it saves time afterwards.

Initial appraisal

On an initial appraisal, there are no previous targets to review. What is more, the interview often takes place soon after someone has started in their job, and they may feel that they have no significant achievement or progress to report.

We need to remember that this appraisal will set the tone for subsequent ones.

So, make sure you:

- go through the same preparatory process with the person
- ask them to produce their evidence, but give them the freedom to bring evidence from previous employment or other life experience as well

- do start with achievements and progress as the first area to focus on, and give recognition
- add in the achievement of getting the job and settling in.

What if someone doesn't feel they have progressed or achieved anything?

Do try to find some areas of progress. Sometimes people have very high expectations of themselves, and we can help them to recognize steps taken towards what they want to achieve, which they have dismissed as 'not enough'.

What if you don't think someone has progressed or achieved anything?

Again, do try to find something which can genuinely be seen as progress, as in the case above.

Are you expecting too much? As much as we can, we want to recognize achievement and progress, however small it may be. We then have something to build on for the next targets.

We all know how awful it feels to have failed utterly. That is not a good point from which to start looking at how to improve. At the very least, everyone can learn something from a failure; it's the first step forward.

Only as a last resort are we going to agree with someone that they have achieved nothing and made no progress. And if that happens, we need to question ourselves as well. How could we let that happen and have done nothing about it until now?

Dealing constructively with lack of achievement

Having established some recognition for progress and achievement, we now need to deal with the second area of focus: where someone hasn't achieved or progressed.

Referring to targets

Again, we start by reviewing the targets set at the last appraisal, to discover if there are any which have not been met.

We need to be careful with our questions about a lack of achievement. It is very easy to make someone defensive, despite our best intentions. They will already feel disappointed themselves, so we need to be constructive with them, to help them find ways of overcoming it.

Useful questions might be:

- What targets have you not achieved?
- What have you achieved towards those targets?
- What stopped you from achieving them?
- What would help you to achieve them now?

Having listened carefully to the responses, we can:

- endorse any progress towards targets, however small
- add further suggestions for what might help.

Often, people will blame the organization, or other people. They feel they have become a 'victim of circumstance'.

There is usually some degree of truth in this, and it is important to take account of it. You may be able to help make a difference, say by agreeing to a change of priorities in the job description and telling their supervisor. Or you may agree with them that the recent increased workload made the target unrealistic.

However, it is important to help them to identify some means of taking hold of the situation for themselves, so that they feel empowered rather than victimized.

Maybe they could talk directly to the colleague who is constantly interrupting them with queries. Maybe they could reorganize their workload themselves to give some regular time to a particular target area.

The question to ask, if they are feeling powerless to change the situation, is:

'And what can you do to help yourself to achieve this?'

Remember the result you want from this appraisal interview: a member of staff who feels valued for what they have achieved, capable of continuing to improve, and motivated to work on their own continuing development.

We want to reinforce their own ability to make a difference, not their failure to do so.

We may need to work with them for a while in the area of constructive ways of dealing with a lack of achievement.

Most of us are knocked back by failure, and become either defensive or helpless. We need to help our staff to feel safe in admitting to a failure, and positive about looking at alternatives.

It can be useful to remind someone that, as a small child trying to walk, they didn't say 'It's not fair', or give up, if they fell on their

bottoms. They just got up and tried again, often in a different way, with more support from the furniture, until they could walk easily. The same principle applies to any personal development.

Different approaches you might use

1 If their intended achievement or target was a large 'chunk'

An example might be: 'I want to revise all of my admin procedures, but I've only started on one or two.'

Help them to break the target down into more realistic steps which they can achieve. Separate out the different parts which need revision, or stages of revision.

2 If their intended achievement target was too vaguely expressed.

An example might be: 'I want to improve my relations with other staff, but it's not really working.'

Help them to make it more specific: with whom and in what way, and how will they know when they have?

3 If they are lacking the confidence to get started

An example might be: 'I want to express my opinions at staff meetings, but I feel nervous of looking stupid.'

Talk through with them what kinds of things they might want to express an opinion about, such as items on a staff meeting agenda. Ask them what they would like to say and how, so they have 'rehearsed' it. Offer them your support and encouragement to do it at the next meeting.

4 If they have a specific difficulty

An example might be: 'I want to learn word processing, and I started the evening class, but then missed four sessions because of illness in the family and I can't catch up.'

Explore with them possible ways past the difficulty, and look at alternatives with them. In this instance options might include extra lessons, a different learning route, such as Open Learning, help from a colleague, etc.

Our intention is always to help them learn and move on from a lack of achievement or progress. As we continue to deal with the individual's feeling of failure in this constructive way, they will:

● be more honest about talking about their lack of achievement
● begin to be more constructive themselves in finding ways to have another go.

Going beyond targets

So far, we have focused on lack of achievement or progress against targets. There may, however, be other areas where someone feels that their achievement or progress has been blocked. It is important to open up the discussion on these, because they are likely to be significant to the individual. You may use the question:

'Is there any other area in which you feel you have not progressed as you would have liked?'

We can then use the same approach as for those areas identified against targets.

What if you think there are other areas where there is a lack of achievement or progress?

If the appraisee has identified relatively few, then it may be useful to add in a couple. Make sure in each case that you explain very clearly in what way you consider there to be a lack of progress, and be careful not to expect too much of the individual.

It is important to weigh up how important your identified areas are to the business. We want to maintain, wherever possible, an emphasis on the positive and constructive.

Could these areas be used as part of the appraisee's general development plan, rather than used to highlight a lack of progress?

What if someone thinks they have no areas where there is a lack of achievement or progress?

We want to set the tone of continuous improvement, so we can delight in the lack of gaps and, at the same time, look for areas for development, which is much more positive. We might ask:

'In which areas of your work would you like to develop further? How?'

Initial appraisal

Obviously, in an initial appraisal, there can be no lack of progress or achievement.

We can therefore go straight to the positive tone of development, as set out above. This reminds both manager and newcomer that part of the purpose of appraisal will always be to encourage continuous improvement.

Recording the interview

While discussing this part of the appraisal, it is again important to make brief notes of areas raised and possible action to take.

These can be summarized and recorded, with the agreement of the person being appraised.

Summary

We have been looking at how you start the appraisal interview, to set the right tone, and then how you conduct the first part of the appraisal interview, the review stage, emphasizing the positive and constructive. It is vital that the person being appraised feels valued and supported, and that you encourage them to play their part fully.

It reminds us that the appraisal interview is dependent on the preparation by both parties that we have suggested. It also demonstrates that the appraisal interview is just a summary point for the previous year, in the review stage, and is much easier to do if you have kept regular contact with the person, to check on their progress during the year. It is an opportunity to give recognition to what people have done and how they have done it. It is the link point between the previous year and what progress, achievement and development can happen in the next year.

When reviewing, above all, remember to set a positive and constructive tone. This genuinely gives the person the sense that you want them to do well and recognize the value of what they have done, as well as being ready to support their development.

The following multiple-choice questions are a reminder of what we've covered today.

Fact-check (answers at the back)

1. What is an appraisal agenda?
   a) A timetabled structure for the interview ❏
   b) My plan for the appraisal ❏
   c) A day of appraisals in my diary ❏
   d) We don't need an agenda for appraisals. ❏

2. How do you set the outcomes for the appraisal interview?
   a) By deciding on them beforehand ❏
   b) The outcome is just a completed appraisal record. ❏
   c) By agreeing them at the beginning with the person being appraised ❏
   d) By asking the person being appraised what they want out of it ❏

3. How do you use previous targets or objectives?
   a) To remind me what I asked them to do ❏
   b) To establish what progress the person has made ❏
   c) To check what they've not achieved ❏
   d) To fill in the first part of the appraisal record ❏

4. How do you verify their progress?
   a) By questioning them hard on what they say ❏
   b) By asking them for evidence ❏
   c) By taking their word for it ❏
   d) By checking if I have the same thing on my list ❏

5. What do you need to be aware of when taking notes?
   a) That I need to fill in all the boxes on the appraisal record ❏
   b) That I make sure I get everything written down ❏
   c) That I don't want to have to rewrite it because it's untidy ❏
   d) That I might not pay proper attention to the person being appraised ❏

6. If it is an initial appraisal, how do you review?
   a) I can't do any review until they've been with me for a year. ❏
   b) I ask them how it's going. ❏
   c) By asking them to use previous employment examples ❏
   d) I make something up. ❏

7. What do you do if someone thinks they have not made any progress?
   a) Work with them to find something constructive. ❏
   b) Tell them they need to improve. ❏
   c) Try and make them feel OK about it. ❏
   d) In some jobs, I just don't – there's nothing to progress in. ❏

8. What do you do if they have not achieved their targets?
a) Tell them it's not good enough. ❏
b) Find out what stopped them from achieving them. ❏
c) Set the same targets for next year. ❏
d) Try not to draw attention to it. ❏

9. How do you help them to deal with a feeling of failure?
a) Tell them it happens – live with it. ❏
b) Use that feeling to make them try harder. ❏
c) Feel sorry for them. ❏
d) Help them to see how they could progress from that to development. ❏

10. How do you encourage someone who has achieved all they set out to do to find areas for development?
a) There's no need to. ❏
b) By asking them what they would like to take further ❏
c) By finding something hard for them to do next ❏
d) By telling them what I think they could do that would be development ❏

FRIDAY

The interview, II: looking ahead

Once we have conducted the review part of the appraisal interview, it is time to look ahead and plan for the next year's development and expected achievements. In this chapter, we will begin by exploring a little more what continuous improvement or development really means, and what we need to do to emphasize its importance.

We will then look at how you set goals and targets, so that they are clearly relevant, actionable and achievable. We look particularly at how you relate them to the review part, and how you encourage the person being appraised to actively contribute. We also look at how you can help them to put their targets and goals into an action plan, prioritizing and organizing them, so they know where to start.

Finally, we look at how you round off the interview in a way that confirms the content you have covered, appreciates the other person's contribution to its success, and reasserts the approach used throughout.

Continuous improvement and development

Let us pick up this theme from yesterday, and expand on it a little.

All too often an appraisal seems to say either: 'You've done alright, keep going,' or 'You're not good enough, do better.'

Successful appraisals say: 'You've got this far. Now where are you going?' They emphasize development rather than picking up on remedial needs.

When we look at ways of encouraging continuous improvement, we can take it through three stages:

1 improvements which will make it easier for the person concerned to perform well in their job – *job related*
2 improvements which will enable the person to contribute even more effectively to business objectives – *company related*
3 improvements which will develop the person's potential – *person related*.

In the first stage, we are encouraging the individual to look at ways of achieving their peak performance in the specific job which they have.

In the second stage, we are encouraging the individual to develop and demonstrate their potential for wider application. This may also help us to identify potential for promotion or new job roles.

In the third stage, we are encouraging the individual to 'round out' and develop their personal qualities. This, of course, will also benefit them and the company in their work roles.

With these three possible areas for development, no one can say, 'There's nowhere further for me to go.' None of us have finished our development in any of the three, and between them they open up a wide range of possible needs and wants in development.

We want all our staff to be constantly looking for what else and what more they can develop in themselves. This leads not just to successful appraisals, but also to successful organizations.

Setting goals and targets

To encourage this process of continuous improvement, we need to ensure that the person being appraised sets themselves appropriate goals and targets.

These emerge naturally from the previous sections of the appraisal interview on achievement and progress, areas of difficulty, and desired developments.

It is helpful to structure the formulating of the goals and targets, so that they are usable.

What are goals and targets?

A goal is the end result that a person wants to achieve. Examples are:

- a further qualification in their subject area
- no work backlog
- more effective staff meetings.

The problem with most goals is that they are fairly large, and often not very clearly defined.

It is important to clarify how you will know if you have achieved the goal, so that you can clarify what exactly it means.

Questions to help you do this might be:

'What evidence will you have that you have achieved your goal?'

'How will you know when you have achieved your goal?'

'What exactly will demonstrate that you have achieved your goal?'

After answering one of these questions, our previous examples of goals would be much clearer:

'I want to improve my skills in my work by taking a further qualification.'

'I want to improve my time management, so that I clear my work to deadline or before. I also want to tackle my present backlog until it is cleared.'

'I want my staff meetings to be shorter and to be fully attended.'

'I want my staff to act on decisions made at the meetings.'

A simple way of getting these fuller statements of goals is to ask people to express them in this format:

'I want to improve ... The result(s) will be ...'

Targets are the steps along the way to achieving a goal. Examples are:

- I will enrol in the college course.
- I will timetable my work for the week.
- I will ask my staff what they think would improve the effectiveness of our staff meetings.

Targets need to be kept to a realistic size, so that they are achievable. They also help us to break down the achievement of a goal into small chunks, and to identify exactly what is required of us to achieve that goal. They are the actions we need to take.

To clarify the targets, we might ask:

'What do you need to do to achieve that goal?'

'How will you work towards that goal?'

'What is the first/next step you need to take to achieve that goal?'

It is important to make the targets specific and, where possible, date their completion.

So our examples might become:

'I will enrol in the college course at Smith College by 6th September.'

'I will plan out next week's work in my diary, with blocks of time for different activities.'

'I will put together a simple questionnaire on different aspects of staff meetings to use with my staff by next Friday.'

Now we have something concrete to do, rather than an intention. And we can produce a simple formula to help ourselves and others to set targets:

'I will do ... by ... in this way ...'

Enabling others to set goals and targets

In the appraisal interview, setting goals and targets is the stage where we begin to pin down the wide-ranging review of past achievements and progress and newly identified areas for development. We want to turn this broad spectrum into a useful and manageable plan for the future.

We have, by this stage, notes on all the areas which have been covered so far by the interview. These notes comprise most of the 'menu' for possible goals and targets. First, they cover all the areas which are seen as important; the individual is far more likely to commit to further development in these areas. Secondly, they cover areas that the interviewee hasn't mentioned, but which we have already noted as important.

The only part of the menu not yet identified is anything which relates to changed or changing business or personal objectives.

For example, if the individual is about to move into a newly formed staff team with different responsibilities, this may throw up some different areas for development, which require goals and targets.

We can usually put all these elements into three areas of goals and targets to consider:

1 those based on a desire for development in areas of progress and achievement

2 those based on need for development in areas where there is a lack of progress or achievement
3 those based on a desire or need for development to accommodate coming changes.

If you have been thorough in the review so far, you may well find that there are a lot of items which could potentially be the subjects of goals and targets.

It is vital that we find a way of narrowing these down to an achievable level. Better to set a limited number of goals and targets, and encourage people to go beyond them, than to cover every area and leave them with so much to achieve that they give up.

How do we do this?

1 Sort out the possible goal with the person

Ideally, there would be between three and six goals.

Encourage them to choose their own. If you need to insist on a goal which they are not choosing, then negotiate with them.

For example, if someone is resisting becoming computer literate, and it is important for business objectives that they do take this on, then you may suggest that they take this as one goal, but also agree to their preferred goal of being more active in meetings.

Notice that sometimes the goals will still be the same as at the last appraisal. Someone may be working towards a large goal over quite a long period of time.

2 Set up targets within each goal area

Using the formula described above, we can help the individual to sort out their targets, which will be the steps towards the goal.

Again, we need to ensure that these targets are realistically sized chunks, which will help them to notice progress as well as achievement.

If they have not achieved a previous target, beware of setting exactly the same target again. We need to find out what stopped them, and if possible think of an alternative target. We don't want people simply to repeat a failure.

Action planning

Now we know what the person is wanting to work on during the period before the next appraisal, we need to help them to organize and prioritize those actions, to produce an action plan.

This is a vital part of the motivation of the person. Without it, it is easy to:

- be overwhelmed by the amount you have committed to, and put things off until the last minute
- avoid the areas you have less interest in or motivation towards
- get so involved in one area of development that you go beyond your goals in that, but neglect the other areas.

How do we action plan?

There are several possible strategies, but the most effective will have the following features:

- The action plan is clear and simple.
- The action points will each have a deadline against them which spreads them across the period.
- In each time period there will be some action points which are easy and pleasing to achieve.
- Major action points will be evenly distributed across the time periods.

To achieve this sorting, it can be useful to use a simple matrix, to begin to classify the action points.

	MUST	
+		−
	Must Want to	Needn't Want to
WANT		
	Must Don't want to	Don't need to Don't want to
−		

TIP *If any point falls into the bottom right-hand box, then it is questionable whether it is a real target!*

It is important to involve the person being appraised fully in the identification of categories for the action points.

From this, it is easy to put together an action plan which satisfies the effectiveness factors. The person themselves will usually do this part well on their own, if given the guidelines.

An example for a two-month period would be:

(M + W = Must + Want to, M = Must, W = Want to)

By the end of April

Find out about programmes on counselling available

(M + W)

Produce a new format for monthly reports (M)

Read and pass on the professional magazines which are in my pending tray (W)

Reorganize the way I file things in my trays (W)

By the end of May

Meet with the training manager to sort out which counselling programme I can attend (M + W)

Introduce the new monthly report format to my staff with an example (M)

Clear three non-urgent items from my filing trays each week (W)

Check and renew the notice board (M + W)

The individual now has their action plan divided into manageable chunks. Targets are split into monthly targets, and each month contains a good mix of the simple and the complex, the important and the interesting.

Action plan for the appraiser

There may be items where you need to take some action. It is useful to note these down, and again put dates against them
An example could be:

By the end of April

Inform the training manager of your support for the appraisee taking a counselling programme

'BYE, NOW!
DON'T FORGET!

Finishing the interview

It is important to remember to finish off the appraisal interview in a way which leaves you both feeling that it has been constructive and useful. The following points give you a framework for a satisfying conclusion:

- Briefly summarize the process and reiterate your recognition of what has been achieved by the person, plus your support for their next targets.
- Refer back to what you agreed you wanted as outcomes for the interview, and check that they have been met, on both sides.
- Give the person a final opportunity to add in anything else they may want to say.
- Ensure that you give a reminder in closing that you are both real people, not just appraiser and person being appraised – a simple reference, such as 'It's lunchtime now and I realize I'm hungry' or 'Look at that, it's pouring down out there!' is enough to bring back that fundamental reality.
- Thank the individual for their preparation, participation and constructiveness, and wish them well with their targets. Remind them that if they get stuck with any of their targets, you are there to help if you can.
- Agree with the person how and when they will be given their copy of the appraisal record, and the date and time of the next appraisal, if appropriate.

Summary

We have been looking at how we use the appraisal interview to set up the continuous improvement of the individual for the next year. It is this pattern of reviewing achievements and progress, followed by setting objectives for development over the next year, that lays the foundations for the ethos of continuous improvement. When you play your part in positively supporting and encouraging your staff, they will see this as a benefit to them, as well as to the organization.

It is important that their objectives are clearly relevant and constructive, building on what they have previously achieved. This means that they need to be job related, company related and person related. The thing to remember is that the person being appraised will know better than you do what would help them to perform even better, so your role is primarily to ensure that their action plan is achievable and realistic.

The following multiple-choice questions are a reminder of what we've covered today.

SUNDAY
MONDAY
TUESDAY
WEDNESDAY
THURSDAY
FRIDAY
SATURDAY

Fact-check (answers at the back)

1. What do successful appraisals emphasize?
   a) How the person can develop even more ❏
   b) What the person needs to improve on ❏
   c) That the person achieved their goals ❏
   d) Something positive ❏

2. Why do we look for job-related development?
   a) Because that's what they're here to do – their job ❏
   b) Because they don't do their job well enough ❏
   c) To make it easier for the person to perform well in their job ❏
   d) It's what the appraisal is all about. ❏

3. Why do we look for person-related development?
   a) To find something for them to develop in ❏
   b) Because it makes them feel good ❏
   c) c) We don't have to – it's about their job. ❏
   d) To develop the person's potential ❏

4. What is a goal for development?
   a) Getting better at something they're not good at ❏
   b) The person performing how I want them to perform ❏
   c) Achieving a job-related task ❏
   d) The end result the person wants to achieve ❏

5. What are targets or milestones for development?
   a) The same as goals ❏
   b) Steps along the way to achieving goals ❏
   c) Things we hope they may achieve ❏
   d) The less important things ❏

6. How do we help the person being appraised to set their goals?
   a) By telling them what we've come up with for them ❏
   b) By talking about what they haven't progressed in ❏
   c) By noting down areas for potential development as we go through the first part of the interview ❏
   d) We do it for them. ❏

7. How do we help the person being appraised to sort out targets for each goal?
   a) By asking them to describe the steps they will take ❏
   b) By telling them the steps they will need to take ❏
   c) By telling them to sort them out afterwards ❏
   d) By giving them a list to choose from ❏

8. Why do we help the person being appraised to create an action plan?
   a) Because it's a section on the recording form ❏
   b) Because we want them to get some things done ❏
   c) Because that's our job ❏
   d) Because we want them to be clear about how to go about their development ❏

9. What is important about the action plan?
a) It will take a year. ❏
b) It is achievable. ❏
c) It is simple. ❏
d) It summarizes the appraisal interview. ❏

10. How do you round off the interview?
a) By signing the record of the appraisal ❏
b) By saying that you'll see them next year ❏
c) By summarizing and thanking them for their part in it ❏
d) By saying it's finished ❏

SATURDAY

Completing the appraisal: after the interview

When we have finished the appraisal interview, we still have a few things to do to complete the appraisal of the person. In this chapter, we will look at how you review the appraisal interview, to ensure that you continually develop your skills in conducting such interviews. Then we will give guidelines on how to follow up on actions you need to take, to make sure you fulfil your agreement with the person being appraised.

We talk about how you ensure that the right support systems are in place to help the appraisee move on their own development, including the support of other managers, other staff and possibly a mentor. Finally, we remind you that appraisals are not a one-off activity, but are part of an ongoing appraisal throughout the year, and look at how to ensure that the person's development is encouraged and supported through to their next appraisal.

HOW'D I DO?

Review of appraisal

First we need to review the appraisal interview, to confirm for ourselves where it worked well and to identify how it could be improved.

This is most simply achieved by answering for ourselves some review questions. Examples would be:

- To what extent did we achieve the results/outcomes I wanted?
- What contributed to the success of the interview?
- What would have made it easier/even better?
- In what ways was the process of the interview effective?
- How else might I have made it even more effective?
- What are the key points I have learnt from this interview to help me to improve the next one?

By reviewing each appraisal interview in this way, we are practising what we are preaching to those being appraised: continuous improvement.

We are learning from the experience of conducting appraisals, so that we can fine-tune the overall guidelines to elicit the most effective results for us and for the interviewee. This continual fine-tuning is what produces excellence in conducting appraisals. It only takes a few minutes to conduct this review, and the results are well worth it.

Actions follow-up

In the course of the appraisal interview, you may have identified certain actions which you have agreed to take. It is important to follow up on these as soon as possible after the appraisal, while they are fresh in your mind and have some priority for you. It is all too easy to be 'overtaken by events' once you have finished the interview, and to forget to take the actions.

So we need to:

- action as much as possible immediately
- record in our diaries when we will action the rest.

If nothing else, we need to make sure that the appraisal record is complete, that the person being appraised has a copy, and that our copy is properly filed.

Both the review and the actions follow-up require that you set aside an extra 15 to 30 minutes at the end of an appraisal interview, in order to complete the process.

Support systems

So far we have dealt specifically with setting up an appraisal framework, and establishing a process for successful appraisal interviews.

However, if the approach is to be fully effective it needs to be put into the everyday work context of the individual. If we want someone to take responsibility for their own development, and to commit to targets which will enable that development, we must ensure that the relevant support systems are in place.

1 Other managers

In many organizations, staff may well be dealing with more than just their own line manager. It is important that others who may play a part in their development process are informed of the intention, goals and targets in that development.

These other people need to be enrolled into supporting the developments, so that the individual who has been appraised is not blocked by a lack of awareness on their part. This could be undertaken by the individual themselves, but your supporting advocacy will also be important.

Examples might be telling the training manager that you have agreed to a particular type of training programme for this individual; or asking the manager of another department to encourage this person to speak out in the working party which he/she leads.

2 Other staff

Sometimes the action steps we have agreed with someone will have some effect on others in the department or organization.

Again, we need to ensure that we give our direct endorsement and support in effecting any changes necessary, so that the person appraised knows that our support goes beyond fine words at the interview and into practical backing.

3 Organizational systems and procedures

There is no point in agreeing with someone that they can work on adapting their recording system if the overall organizational system will not allow for a deviation from the standard.

Similarly, there is no point in agreeing with someone that they can put forward a proposal for a new discussion group if there is no clear organizational procedure for doing so.

We need to ensure that organizational systems and procedures are flexible enough to accommodate any development plans the individual has.

We also need to ensure that those systems and procedures are known to the individual. Just because we know how they work, we shouldn't assume everyone else does.

Ongoing appraisal

There is one area of continuing support which we haven't covered yet.

However motivated the person may be when they leave the appraisal interview, they now have to maintain that motivation in the midst of the pressures of everyday work and routine.

For an appraisal to be truly successful, they will need some form of 'moral support' to keep them going for their targets. It is not enough for any of us to receive a one-off boost, however positive and useful it may be. It may be six months, or even a year before the next boost, so how can we maintain the person's motivation between times? Two things can be especially effective.

1 We need to offer some continuing thread between one appraisal interview and the next

The way in which we do this may range from a formal arrangement through to something much more unstructured. What matters is that we demonstrate a continuing interest in and support of that individual.

Appraisal means according value, as a continuous process. People are not objects which don't usually change and can therefore be appraised just the once. People change and develop and therefore deserve continuous reassessment. What is more, the continuous reappraisal encourages and motivates them to continue to change and develop.

This may sound onerous, but you don't need to follow through by increasing the number of in-depth appraisal interviews. It is simply a matter of noticing and giving recognition to some elements of that person's development, and we can do that in a sentence in passing: 'I notice that you're enrolled on that programme – good for you!'

We also need to ensure that they know we are available to offer help if they are feeling stuck, and the offer of this help at the interview stage needs to be followed through in practice.

If someone says to you, 'I need a word with you. I'm still not getting anywhere in meetings', then you need either to give them time there and then, or to arrange a definite time to see them and talk about it. Then they will know that the offer of support and help was genuine.

Some managers may prefer to structure this support by putting in review times in between appraisals. This formalizes the opportunity to recognize progress and to offer help on areas of difficulty.

2 We may need to identify some form of mentor

We may, as managers, be too busy to be the reference point for all our staff in their continuing development. Rather than feel guilty because we can't offer the level of support and encouragement we would like, we can identify, with the individual concerned, someone who could fulfil that role for them.

When this is done formally, we call this person a mentor. However, it can also be set up informally. We simply identify with the individual a person whom they feel would be appropriate and useful in encouraging them to sustain their development. It may be another manager, a supervisor, a member of personnel department or a colleague.

We then talk with that person about taking on that support role with the individual.

Most people choose well when consulted, and most people are pleased to have been chosen.

Conducting successful appraisals

We have now covered all the factors which can make a difference to the effectiveness of your appraisals.

When we go through all the different aspects of a successful appraisal, it can look like a daunting task!

So where do we start on improving our appraisals?

We can use the same principles and model for our own improvement as we do for enabling others to develop. Ask yourself, 'When I look at the full appraisal process:

- which parts do I already do well?'
- which parts do I really want to develop?'
- which parts would it be most useful to develop?'

From the answers to the second and third of these questions, establish goals and targets, and start to action them.

Remember that some of the recommendations in this guide may require some investment of time in the first place, but will save you time in the long run.

Remember that appraisals are successful when you have a clear intention in mind: to enable this individual to aim for and achieve their optimum.

Remember, above all, that you are dealing with a human being just like you. How would you like to be appraised? It's the simplest guide of all!

Summary

In this final chapter, we have explored all the different aspects of completing the appraisal process in ways that will ensure that your appraisals successfully lead to the development of your staff.

We have emphasized the importance of ongoing support for the appraisee, so that the appraisal interview is not an isolated event. This is how you create the ethos of continuous development in the organization, so that it becomes the norm to see appraisals as a valuable part of an ongoing process of developing your people.

There is clear evidence that successful appraisal processes lead to higher retention, better morale and good overall performance. We hope that you are now able to use your appraisals to achieve these results.

The following multiple-choice questions are a reminder of what we've covered today.

SUNDAY   MONDAY   TUESDAY   WEDNESDAY   THURSDAY   FRIDAY   SATURDAY

Fact-check

1. Why do we review the appraisal interview?
   a) Because it was a bit stilted ❏
   b) Because it's the first one we've done ❏
   c) To sign off that part of the task ❏
   d) To check what went well and what could be improved ❏

2. How do we use our review of the appraisal?
   a) To continually refine how we conduct appraisal interviews ❏
   b) To revise the record of the interview ❏
   c) To fill in our records of what we've done ❏
   d) We don't really. ❏

3. What do we need to immediately follow up after the appraisal interview?
   a) When the next one will be with this person ❏
   b) Any actions we have agreed to take ❏
   c) Getting the record of the interview to HR ❏
   d) Other jobs we have to do ❏

4. Why do we need to take actions we have agreed?
   a) We said we would. ❏
   b) HR will check if we have. ❏
   c) To get them off our 'To Do' list ❏
   d) To show that we are genuinely supporting their ongoing development ❏

5. How can other managers support your person in their development?
   a) It's my job, not theirs. ❏
   b) By monitoring their actions for me ❏
   c) By knowing what they want to achieve and encouraging them ❏
   d) By giving them things to do ❏

6. How do we keep people motivated in their ongoing development?
   a) By having some form of ongoing monitoring of their progress ❏
   b) By telling them we will check how they're doing ❏
   c) By picking them up on it if we notice they're not doing something they said they would ❏
   d) That's up to them. ❏

7. What is important about the ongoing monitoring of their development?
   a) That mistakes or failures are picked up on ❏
   b) That it is positive and supportive ❏
   c) That it happens in some way or other ❏
   d) That the person knows they are being monitored ❏

8. What role could a mentor play?
a) Teaching the individual something they need for their development ❏
b) We don't use mentors in our organization. ❏
c) Giving the ongoing support the individual needs ❏
d) Keeping an eye on the individual ❏

9. How do we choose a mentor for someone?
a) We talk about it and ask them who would suit them. ❏
b) We identify who should do it. ❏
c) We pick someone who isn't too busy. ❏
d) We use whoever is available. ❏

10. When are appraisals finished?
a) When all the records have gone to HR ❏
b) When I've finished the interview ❏
c) When we're back to business as usual ❏
d) Never – it is a continuous process. ❏

Surviving in tough times

1 Value your team

Value your colleagues *as a team*, with yourself as one person in that group. Consider not only the day-to-day minutiae of your colleagues' jobs but also their broader roles within the team – look back at Belbin's nine team roles (Week 1, **Tuesday**). Be genuine in listening to, and motivating, your colleagues.

2 Encourage good teamwork

You are the team leader. It is your responsibility to get the best out of your colleagues. Communicate a strong and inspiring vision for your team (see Week 1, **Tuesday**). Where is the team going? What is its core purpose? In uncertain economic times morale can be low, so draw attention to success whenever you can. Lead by example in your dealings with team members. Be fair and treat all your colleagues equally, even though you may like some more than others.

3 Be clear about your goals

Your team vision needs to be expressed in practical steps. Really know your objectives and express them clearly. All goals should be SMART – specific, measurable, agreed, realistic, timed (see Week 1, **Monday**) – but this is all the more true in difficult times. An uncertain economic environment is unforgiving of vagueness at all levels of a business enterprise. Make your team count.

4 Manage your systems efficiently

Take a step back and objectively consider your managerial systems, e.g. for setting and managing budgets (see Week 1,

Wednesday]. Now may not be the time to install a new IT system, but you can probably find more efficient ways of working in some areas. What procedures can you streamline?

Work at making your team undertake tasks more effectively – this should free up more of your own time for problem solving and making decisions, which should be your priorities.

5 Make informed decisions

Concentrate on solving problems creatively, knowing that mistakes will cost money. Stay informed of what is happening in your wider organization and in the industry as a whole. If your boss's aims and challenges are changing, this will obviously impact on you and your team. Consider your management style (see Week 1, **Saturday**) and whether this needs to change if members of your team are facing difficult circumstances.

6 Improve communications

When things get tough and colleagues become stressed, you need to be even more certain that you are getting your message across well. Keep lines of communication open to avoid misunderstandings. If you are able to have regular one-to-one meetings with your team, so much the better. Keep focused both on the medium and long term by continuing to plan ahead, and on the short term by working on your listening skills (Week 1, **Thursday**) and keeping on top of your email inbox. Be open, honest and consistent in your dealings and others will do the same for you.

7 Delegate

As a manager, you need to focus on the big issues. Working yourself into the ground is not going to solve anything, and is just as likely to be counterproductive. As discussed (Week 1, **Tuesday**) delegate: to colleagues who are 'nearly ready', whole tasks wherever possible, having completed thorough planning. Supervise the delegated task, and offer yourself for problem solving, but do let it go. Remember to express your appreciation of your colleague(s) when the task is completed.

8 Plan better meetings

If you ever find yourself in a meeting thinking, 'What is the point of this?' (or suspect this in others), it's time to make some changes. Effort put into preparation and follow-up will be well rewarded. Look back at the notes on chairing a meeting (Week 1, **Thursday**) and ensure that you lead the way by participating fully yourself. Consider the possibility of having fewer meetings.

9 Improve your project management

Think ahead when managing a project. Don't assume that everyone is clear about their responsibilities – make sure they are. If necessary, produce a scope of work (see Week 1, **Friday**), particularly for outside suppliers. Work out – and keep to – your aims, outputs, costs and schedules. As manager, your monitoring systems are key to spotting looming problems; your aim should then be to deal with these firmly and speedily. Above all, learn from experience.

10 Take steps to manage yourself

If you have not already done so, work out the hourly rate which you personally cost your company (see Week 1, Friday). You may not be able to create an economy-busting strategy for your employer, but you can – and should – aim to save them money by being more efficient with your time. Organize yourself. Plan ahead. Compose emails thoughtfully. Get things – even small things – right first time, knowing that going back over them later is inefficient and costly. Remember to be positive about what you have achieved as well as looking to everything that still needs to be completed.

11 Demonstrate that you are indispensable

If cuts in staffing are taking place in a business, senior managers will be reluctant to make redundant those people managers who have demonstrated their value to the company or organization. While it is true that no one is indispensable, if you have shown exceptional commitment by going beyond your duties on a number of occasions, the likelihood is that management will do what they can to retain your services in times of cut-backs because of your value to the business.

12 Be your own PR (public relations)

You may be an excellent people manager and extremely valuable to the organization, but if senior management are unaware of your successes they are unlikely to consider you for retention if times are tough. In order to secure your continued employment and possibly obtain advancement, it is vital that you let those in positions of authority and influence know what you are achieving and your value to the business. Wide communication about your own and your team's successes and business improvement ideas can help in this respect. Engaging in informal discussions in the coffee bar or after meetings is a subtle way of getting the message across that you are highly committed to the future of the business.

13 Be aware of organizational politics

Organizational politics are difficult to avoid. It is a sad fact of life that in the majority of organizations many people are more concerned about playing organizational politics in order to pursue their own career advancement than the welfare of those for whom they are responsible and the performance of the business. Survival in tough times means being aware of organizational politics and the behaviours of the key actors, and playing a part in the politics to ensure you are not overlooked or being subjected to reputational damage as during difficult times the worst of human behaviours can emerge.

14 Demonstrate flexibility and adaptability

Those employees who have demonstrated a great deal of flexibility and adaptability in carrying out their jobs are more likely to be retained during company restructuring or downsizing exercises. In both these situations, job roles are likely to be changed so if you have shown rigidity in your tasks and a reluctance to do things differently, senior management would be less inclined to find you a position in a newly formed or restructured business.

15 Save or make money for the company

All organizations are having to reduce costs and increase profits in order to survive. If you can show that you have saved money through reducing wastage, cutting down on travel expenses, using staff resources efficiently and streamlining processes, you are more likely to survive in the organization during difficult times. It would also be to your advantage if you could come up with some worthy new service delivery or new product ideas that have the potential to increase the business's profits.

16 Monitor trends and act upon them

There are so many business failures as a result of not keeping up with and adapting to economic, social and environmental trends. We operate today in a global economy and within a fast, unpredictable environment. The survival of businesses is dependent on keeping up with economic, social and environmental changes, in particular those that affect a business's customers or clients. These changes also present opportunities for innovation or diversification. Although, strictly, this is the role of more senior managers and directors, people managers who can contribute to internal discussions around the future of the business by presenting a wider, strategic perspective are going to be looked upon favourably in terms of retention and/or promotion.

17 Keep your CV updated

It is too easy to neglect keeping your CV updated. We are all busy people and while in employment do not always see the need to maintain our CVs. However, if your CV or career summary is not regularly updated you will soon forget some significant achievements that could impress a future employer. In tough times, it is worth reviewing your CV monthly and comparing it with job advertisements to identify knowledge and skill areas for development, and to act upon these.

18 Develop and widen your transferable skills

It is worthwhile monitoring the job market to see what opportunities are available and the types of knowledge, skills and experience companies and other organizations are seeking. This information should be used to develop your transferable people management skills in a way that will be attractive to a number of organizations in a variety of sectors. The principles of people management and the tasks involved in successfully managing people are the same regardless of the type of business. However, it is vital that you have a number of examples of the sort of experience and skills deployment future employers are likely to be seeking. It is your responsibility to seek out this experience and develop the skills demanded by future potential employers.

19 Never stop learning

Current and future employers welcome people managers who are shown to be keen on their own personal development. In people management you never stop learning. Every situation and the people involved are different and require a different way of managing. A focus on your own continual professional development, particularly through reflection and mentoring, while keeping up with wider professional developments is beneficial for you, your team and your organization. It also helps you stand out as exceptionally committed in tough times.

20 Network and maintain good relationships

Generally, people choose to do business and work with people they like and respect. Business-related relationships within and outside the organization are therefore important. These relationships need to be maintained and developed as there is no way of knowing when you may need the help and support of a business colleague, especially during difficult times. Always be pleasant and helpful to people you interact with in a work context and where possible do favours. In all probability this will be repaid to you in tougher times. Networking continually within and outside the organization is vital if you are to survive as a successful people manager in difficult and challenging times. If you are not always in view, people will forget you or be under the impression that you are content in a secure job.

21 Help your team overcome the extra stress

When the business conditions become difficult, we can all become more anxious and worried. This can lead to tension, friction and conflict within your team, leaving them in the 'storming' phase. You must rally and inspire your team to help keep them positively aligned and not to allow them to waste any of their valuable time and energy.

22 Work harder than normal to retain your top performers

In difficult economic times your team will have to work harder than usual to achieve its goals and you will need your top performers more than ever. Other organizations may try to headhunt them for exactly the same reasons that you want to keep them: high-performing staff can really help any team through tough times.

23 Do not hold on to poor performers for too long

In tough times you really need the entire team to rise to the challenge and to all perform better. Keeping poorly performing or underperforming members in your team is not ideal. They cost money and their roles would be better filled with someone with more potential to succeed in difficult economic conditions.

24 Communicate openly and honestly

There may be gossip and rumours circulating among your team about topics such as potential downsizing, lay-offs, declining client orders or your company having cash-flow problems. In troubled economic times there may be some truth to these rumours and it is your role as the team leader to be as open as you are able (and allowed to be by your company). Too much negative gossip can be demoralizing and demotivating and will sap the energy of your team at precisely the time that they need to work harder.

25 Keep your team totally aligned and focused on its goals

In tough times, your team might become depressed and lose sight of its goals and growth plans. You must work very hard to motivate, inspire and lift your team to keep the members on track. You may also have to change the targets and goals if the business environment continues to slow down and deteriorate.

26 Look after yourself more than usual

As a team's manager you will face additional stress as you try to help your team steer through troubled times. You may find yourself having to deal with more change and uncertainty and may work longer hours than normal. When possible, step back, take a break and pause to make sure that you are doing the right things with your limited time and energy. Do not overwork and burn yourself out.

27 Spend more time with your team and show empathy

Improve your emotional intelligence and show your team that you care by spending extra time with its members, sitting down and listening to their concerns and troubles. Understand that your team members cannot work well if they are full of concerns and uncertainty. As an empathic manager, you can let them share with you what is troubling them.

28 Work with your team to think out of the box more

Encourage your team to help you solve the new challenges that you may be facing, especially since you may be expected to achieve more with fewer resources (both finances and headcount). You might be surprised by the creative and innovative ideas that your staff come up with if you encourage them to do so.

29 Try harder to motivate your team and to maintain team spirit

Your team members might become quite depressed and despondent in the face of tough times, where all the news and gossip might seem to be negative and depressing. It can get worse for your team if they fear for their jobs. Make time for some motivational and uplifting activities; even if there is less money available, you can still do things with your team.

30 Be more patient and understanding with your team

This may be your team's first experience of a difficult economic environment. They may have no idea how to react to requests to cut costs, to client orders being cancelled etc. You may be in a hurry to implement some changes and new ideas, but you must give your team enough time to understand and to accept the changes that you ask of them.

31 Do appraisals and reviews!

The appraisals or reviews give you the opportunity to fully engage your staff and to encourage them to play an active part in helping the organization through tough times. They are a powerful way to keep a positive spirit going in your area, and to identify what will help to make you even more effective.

32 Take time to set an appraisal framework

If you have clearly linked individual appraisal objectives to the objectives of the business, you can ensure that everyone is playing their part in helping the organization to be successful. In tough times, the organization may need to adapt its objectives. Make sure you adapt individual objectives to match.

33 Emphasize the purpose and importance of appraisals

Make clear to your staff that valuing, encouraging and developing them is a priority for you in tough times. It takes nothing from the bottom line, but does mean that they want to play their part in helping the organization to survive. You can invest in them by helping them to see how their contribution can help the organization overall.

34 Add a question to the guidelines for preparation

As well as the normal guidelines for appraisees, ask them to consider how they could help the organization to be more efficient, more effective, find more business in tough times. Doing this can often produce some useful ideas and, at a minimum, it will remind them that they all play a part, directly or indirectly, in helping the organization to survive tough times.

35 Use preparation time constructively

It is always important to prepare yourself properly for appraisals, and in tough times, you can use some of that time to think through what more you want your area to contribute to the success of the organization. It may be being more effective internally, or more joined up with other parts of the business in some way. Then you can use that to guide development choices.

36 Value their achievements and progress

This is a vital part of any appraisal, but in tough times you can pay particular attention to those aspects of their achievement and progress which actively help the organization. This will help to make them aware of how their role contributes to the success of the organization, and how they might be able to develop it further.

37 Ask what is holding them back

It is more important than ever in tough times to encourage your staff to identify what holds them back from giving of their best. Often, small things can make a big difference to how effectively they do their work. If action is taken when people voice their blocks to effectiveness, they up their game and contribute more. Remember, you may not think it's a significant issue, but they do.

38 Invest whatever you can in developing talent

It's always tempting to put any development on hold during tough times – it's an easy budget to cut. Yet when business is not so busy, it is the ideal time to ensure that your staff will be up to speed and motivated when the business comes back in. Finding even small amounts of budget and giving people the opportunity to develop their skills will pay off in the long term.

39 Find innovative ways of developing them further

The continuing development of skills and talent is vital if an organization is to succeed in tough times. Rather than stopping all training and development because of budget cuts, find other ways of offering development, using internal resources such as other experienced members of staff, or work shadowing.

40 Be honest and open to possibilities

It is harmful to pretend that it's all OK when the organization is going through tough times. Use appraisals and reviews with individuals to acknowledge the tough times and to actively engage them in thinking of ways to make it through and to improve the situation. You may have your view of what's needed, but they will also have some excellent ideas if they feel you will take notice of them.

Answers

Week 1: Introducing Management

Sunday: 1c; 2d; 3b; 4b; 5a; 6c; 7d; 8a; 9c; 10d.
Monday: 1d; 2c; 3b; 4b; 5a; 6c; 7b; 8b; 9b; 10d.
Tuesday: 1c; 2b; 3a; 4d; 5b; 6b; 7c; 8a; 9d; 10c.
Wednesday: 1c; 2d; 3c; 4b; 5a; 6d; 7c; 8b; 9a; 10b.
Thursday: 1b; 2b; 3c; 4c; 5d; 6c; 7b; 8a; 9d; 10b.
Friday: 1d; 2b; 3c; 4c; 5b; 6a; 7d; 8a; 9a; 10c.
Saturday: 1c; 2a; 3d; 4a; 5d, 6b; 7c; 8b; 9d; 10c.

Week 2: Successful People Management

Sunday: 1c; 2d; 3a; 4a; 5c; 6c; 7d; 8d; 9c; 10d.
Monday: 1c; 2c; 3a; 4 Specific, Measurable, Attainable, Relevant, Time-bound; 5b; 6d; 7c; 8d; 9d; 10c.
Tuesday: 1d; 2c; 3c; 4a; 5a; 6c; 7c; 8d; 9b; 10d.
Wednesday: 1d; 2c; 3c; 4b; 5c; 6b; 7b; 8a; 9b; 10c.
Thursday: 1c; 2b; 3b; 4a; 5c; 6 Political, Economic, Social, Technological; 7c; 8d; 9b; 10c.
Friday: 1d; 2c; 3d; 4a; 5b; 6b; 7d; 8d; 9c; 10a.
Saturday: 1c; 2d; 3d; 4a; 5b; 6c.

Week 3: Managing Teams

Sunday: 1b; 2d; 3c; 4a; 5b; 6b; 7c; 8d; 9d; 10a.
Monday: 1b; 2a; 3d; 4d; 5b; 6d; 7a; 8c; 9d; 10b.
Tuesday: 1d; 2c; 3d; 4b; 5b; 6a; 7d; 8b; 9a; 10b.
Wednesday: 1b; 2d; 3d; 4d; 5b; 6c; 7d; 8d; 9d; 10a.
Thursday: 1b; 2d; 3d; 4d; 5d; 6a; 7b; 8d; 9d; 10d.
Friday: 1b; 2d; 3b; 4d; 5c; 6b; 7a; 8d; 9a; 10d.
Saturday: 1b; 2a; 3c; 4b; 5d; 6d.

Week 4: Successful Appraisals

Sunday: 1d; 2a; 3b; 4a; 5d; 6c; 7d; 8a; 9b; 10c.
Monday: 1a; 2b; 3c; 4b; 5d; 6a; 7b; 8c; 9a; 10b.
Tuesday: 1a; 2c; 3b; 4a; 5d; 6b; 7c; 8a; 9c; 10b.
Wednesday: 1c; 2b; 3d; 4d; 5a; 6b; 7c; 8a; 9d; 10b.
Thursday: 1a; 2c; 3b; 4b; 5d; 6c; 7a; 8b; 9d; 10c.
Friday: 1a; 2c; 3d; 4d; 5b; 6c; 7a; 8d; 9b; 10c.
Saturday: 1d; 2a; 3b; 4d; 5c; 6a; 7b; 8c; 9a; 10c.

Notes